CONTENTS

LIST OF TABLES AND CHARTS

TABLES

CHARTS

ACKNOWLEDGMENTS

I want to thank all my students who have made teaching a lifetime of satisfaction and who have taught me a great deal over the years.

I want to thank the staff members of the Art Department, Miami University, for their interest and support in this writing.

I want to thank Dean Charles L. Spohn of the School of Fine Arts and the administration of Miami University for a zero-teaching load grant for one semester, which gave me more time for writing, and for some financial aid for illustrations.

I want to thank those who provided illustrations: Craig Roland, art teacher at the American School Foundation of Monterrey, who provided photographs of his students, and my former junior and senior high school students who provided me with art work. I also want to thank those who typed the final manuscript.

And, of course, this writing would not have been possible without the discovery of my work by Lawrence H. McGill and the assistance given me by Lois Patton, Kerry Kern, Esther Persson, and the staff of Teachers College Press for which I am very appreciative. This writing has allowed me to record the results of more than forty years' experience in art education.

Grateful acknowledgment is made for permission to use quotations from the following sources:

"Adolescent Suicide: A Problem for Teachers," by D. F. Smith, *Phi Delta Kappan*, vol. 57 (1976), 539–542.

"Androgyny vs. the Light Little Lives of Fluffy Women and Chesty Men," by S. L. Bem, *Psychology Today*. Copyright © 1975 by Ziff-Davis Publishing Company.

Art Education in the Junior High School, edited by John A. Michael, National Art Education Association, copyright © 1964.

The Basis of Criticism in the Arts, by S. C. Pepper, Harvard University Press, copyright © 1946 by the President and Fellows of Harvard College; © 1973 by S. C. Pepper. Used by permission of the publishers.

Creative and Mental Growth, Third Edition, by Viktor Lowenfeld, Macmillan Publishing Co., Inc., © 1957. Reprinted by permission of Macmillan Publishing Co., Inc.

Drawing on the Right Side of the Brain, by Betty Edwards, Houghton Mifflin Company, copyright © 1979 by Betty Edwards. Reprinted by permission of Houghton Mifflin Company.

"The Effects of Training for Enthusiasm on the Enthusiasm Displayed by Preservice Elementary Teachers," doctoral dissertation by Mary L. Collins, Syracuse University, 1976.

"Eight Keys to Creativity," by L. Cassels, *Nation's Business* (R), February, 1959. Copyright 1959 by *Nation's Business* (R), Chamber of Commerce of the United States. Adapted by permission.

"An Open Letter to an Educator," by Judith Ott Belle.

Public Relations for Art Education, National Art Education Association, 1973.

Taxonomy of Educational Objectives: The Classification of Educational Goals: Handbook I: Cognitive Domain, by Benjamin S. Bloom et al., Longman, Inc., copyright © 1956 by Longman, Inc. Reprinted by permission of Longman, Inc., New York.

Taxonomy of Educational Objectives: The Classification of Educational Goals: Handbook II: Affective Domain, by David R. Krathwohl et al., Longman, Inc., copright © 1964 by Longman, Inc. Reprinted by permission of Longman, Inc., New York.

The Vanishing Adolescent, by Edgar Z. Friedenberg, Beacon Press, copyright © 1959, 1964 by Edgar Z. Friedenberg. Reprinted by permission of Beacon Press.

"Wilson-Stuckhardt Art Attitude Scale" by Christine Wilson Sanders and Michael H. Stuckhardt.

INTRODUCTION

This writing is about teaching/learning in visual art for adolescents at the secondary level—junior and senior high school. It is assumed that the reader has an art background, especially in the fine arts: drawing, painting, design, sculpture, crafts, and art history. Such a background should include a knowledge of art/design elements and principles, various art procedures, and art processes. This writing builds upon the above art expertise as concepts are developed for working with adolescents in the school art room.

After teaching art for many years at all levels, I have found the secondary level to be the least understood. Perhaps this is a result of—or is reflected by—the meager amount of research and writing which has been done in this area. Art teachers in the field seem to approach the teaching of art at the junior and senior high school either from an emphasis on creative child art or an emphasis on professional adult art. Neither approach is appropriate. It is my hope that this writing may offer alternatives that are valid for the adolescent, for that confusing time between the art of the child and the art of the professional adult artist.

In any consideration of art education for adolescents at the secondary level, two aspects are of paramount importance. First of all, teaching of art, as the teaching of any other subject area, is a profession. A professional art teacher, primarily, is one who diagnoses each student/class and teaching situation and prescribes a method, medium, reading, viewing of art work, and art process that will meet the needs of the students, bringing about learning and development so that students know how to think for themselves, make up their own minds, and are able to express themselves. This prohibits a stereotypical approach, teaching in the same manner in every art class. Secondly, it is assumed that the individual, as a human being, is of primary importance regardless of subject matter being taught. This means that art experiences are used to develop the abilities needed for a fulfilled life; it means satisfying the needs of the adolescent. Some of those needs are aesthetic; some are creative; some are perceptual and sensuous; some are intellectual; some are emotional; some are social; some are cultural; and some are physical (coordination and skill oriented). Too frequently it is felt by educators and also by the general public that adolescents have *no* aesthetic needs. This can be noted by the few secondary students enrolled in art classes and by the lack of an art requirement in the curricula of most secondary schools. This writer believes that adolescents, as with all human beings, have many aesthetic needs. For example, all adolescents need to reckon with their visual and physical environment (both man-made and natural), which is composed of the art elements of line, shape, texture, space, and color. Art education develops one's ability to deal with these visual and aesthetic qualities of images and objects—to understand, respond to, talk about, and create with them. Understanding the man-made world is to understand one's culture and heritage, to be educated and in control of one's life. In addition, all adolescents are consumers of man–made objects and need aesthetic criteria for making choices. All adolescents need to develop sensitivity and awareness concerning visual symbols that communicate, from TV advertisements to the clothes we wear. All adolescents need many means of expressing their ideas, feelings, and perceptions—the arts being the only means of making these visible. All adolescents need to appreciate the aesthetic qualities of the natural environment for all of life depends upon our sensitivity, concern, and love for our planet. The aesthetic needs of adolescents are more fully developed in chapters 2 and 3.

Art education, as we perceive it today, means (1) a concern for students— their needs, values, personal/social considerations, intellect, emotional stability, perceptual and aesthetic sensitivity, talent, skills, creativity, and attitude; (2) a concern for the field of art—media, processes, methods, artists, art in society (culture), art goals and purposes, art history and criticism; (3) and a concern for teaching—objectives, curricula, theory/philosophy, methodology, evaluation, school organization, the community, and environment. Superior teaching demands a total commitment with knowledge, enthusiasm, and sensitivity relative to all of the above.

Over the years, many approaches to art education have been developed. Some believe art education to involve the making of art products, that is, drawings, paintings, sculptures, constructions, and so forth for the vocational/avocational purpose of developing skill and training as an artist. Others use the making of art as a means for the adolescent to learn and develop in many areas, for example, creative, perceptual, aesthetic, and intellectual. Others believe art activities are primarily for developing creative problem-solving ability and/or for self-expression and release (therapy). Still others place emphasis upon applying aesthetic considerations to the environment and social/cultural concerns. Recently, great importance has been placed upon knowing about and responding to art, artists, and art history in addition to talking/writing about art as a critic. Another recent concern is that of relating visual art to the other arts and subject fields—arts education. For some students and for particular teaching situations, aspects of all of the above considerations, which are developed throughout this writing, particularly in the last chapter, may be valid. It is my belief that *art education is a multifaceted area that is historically based* and all aspects of the field may be appropriate and important for particular students. *The needs of adolescents as emerging adult members of our society are paramount and determine what the art teacher does in the classroom, the field of art being integrated with these needs in developing a viable art program.* Therefore, understanding the characteristics of adolescents, as developed in chapter 3, is absolutely mandatory for art teachers in order to carry out a successful secondary art program. Such a program generally involves much studio art activity. This is to be expected since state certification requirements are primarily in the area of studio art. Art teachers, then, have a greater understanding of studio and feel they can meet the needs of adolescents via studio art activities better than by any other means. In addition, adolescents tend to expect, desire, and usually need expressive studio activities in the art class to balance the cognitive academic subjects so typical of most high schools in the United States. These two factors tend to bring about a preponderance of studio work in secondary art classes. The art teacher must be aware that studio art activities should be used as springboards to learning about the many conceptual and cognitive aspects of art and to developing to a higher level all of the adolescent's abilities that are involved in art class.

It is hoped that the reader will consider the material presented herein as a framework or outline on which to build such a viable secondary school art program. Although some may consider this writing as skeletal, an effort is made to provide enough information/inspiration to get one involved as a teacher. Teaching is, indeed, a closure experience wherein your own enthusiasm and creativeness, your education in art and in professional education, your work as an artist and critic, plus the students in your classes and all that they bring to the situation make up the components of the ideal art education which we all seek. With the myriad of art-teaching situations around the nation, no one approach, curriculum, or method can be presented that would be appropriate and right for every art class or individual. "Right," herein, is relative. However, we do need guidelines that provide flexibility in developing a secondary art program.

Secondary school art education involves both teaching and learning. In the past, emphasis was placed upon teaching and the teacher. Methodology, curriculum, and evaluation were developed with great emphasis on the role of the teacher. Currently, emphasis is placed upon learning and the learner. Student competency developed through specific objectives to be assessed through measurement is the order of the day in many sectors. (See chapter 7.) In this approach, teaching, learning, and learners are perceived as being equally important and are equally stressed. Without the teacher, there is little learning and without students, there can be no teaching of secondary school art.

In addition, it should be pointed out that learning (nurture) and growth and development (nature) are believed to make up one's education. Herein, learning means knowing and assimilating aspects of the field of art; development refers to bringing out and expanding students' capabilities.

The hope of the field of art education is that all art teachers will become professional in carrying out the tasks of art education. Such professionalism means that after analyzing a particular teaching/learning situation, decisions and prescriptions must be made by the teacher. Many options are presented here for art teachers to draw upon. Although a bias may come through at times, every teaching option presented is probably valid for some place, and neither the beginning nor the experienced teacher should shy away from trying any suggested options that he or she feels is appropriate for a particular teaching situation. Sometimes the seemingly most incongruous solutions work best.

Given a background in art education, the key to successful teaching is believing in yourself and in what you are doing, as well as believing in and understanding the adolescents with whom you are working. Student respect and enthusiasm emanate from the teacher's integrity and a belief in what you do as a teacher. Characteristics of good teachers are developed in chapter 5.

Not only must secondary art teachers develop viable school art curricula, as discussed in chapter 4, but they also need to relate those to the community at large.

Secondary art programs must have school and community support or they may be deleted from the school offerings. Public relations, therefore, has become a new responsibility and must be noted in any consideration of the role of an art teacher. (See chapter 1.)

In this writing, the reader will find many classifications and symbolic diagrams in the form of tables and charts. These have been devised for a better understanding of the concepts presented. Although these various categories may suggest a rigid structure that attempts to put students, as well as the teacher, into particular cubbyholes with accompanying labels, this definitely is not the purpose of the writer. Few things or individuals are classic examples of anything and few fit perfectly into any classification. Everything in life tends to be a little of this but also a little of that. However, without a structure, there is chaos. A structure merely provides a framework or a configuration for better comprehension of the total situation. Knowing and being able to identify certain attributes help the teacher understand and evaluate various aspects of the art teaching/learning process and should permit a more immediate analysis and penetration, the basis of decision making in the classroom. Realizing that each educational circumstance is unique, I firmly believe that a means of evaluating, understanding, and sizing up an art teaching/learning situation is necessary. It is my hope that this writing will provide art teachers with those means which are needed at the secondary level, resulting in greater sensitivity to adolescents, more profound decisions by the art teacher, and an ever higher level of learning and development by the student.

For more than forty years, the ideas of many persons in the field have had a profound influence upon me as I have studied and taught hundreds of students at all levels. This writing, then, should be considered as historically based upon valid concepts and practices derived from many outstanding art educators of the past and the present. References necessarily are from many sources and time periods. It is my belief that all education should be based upon meaningful work of the past as it relates to the problems at hand. Stephen M. Dobbs (1982) notes that "a sensitivity to the specific incremental changes and evolution in a field of knowledge is crucial to a mature understanding of its character. It is analogous to comprehending architecture: knowledge of the structure must start with its foundations, basic organizing principles, and so forth." The professional diversity and richness of our field is seen when one considers it historically and certainly we can learn from those who have preceded us, from an understanding of the problems they found and resolved. We should be aware of our inheritance from the field and of those to whom we are indebted—aspects more fully developed in chapter 7.

And finally, all the considerations of art education at the secondary level are for naught if the art teacher cannot manage, control, and work harmoniously with adolescents in the classroom. This aspect is seldom considered in books of this type but is presented in chapter 6 in order to assist those who have difficulty in relating to students of this stage.

REFERENCE

Dobbs, S. M. Remembering Our Roots. *Art Education,* 1982, *35* (6), 4.

CHAPTER 1

WHAT WE BELIEVE
Point of View

We believe art activities are important learning experiences for all adolescents. In order to provide significant and creative art activities, teachers trained in the visual arts (possessing art knowledges, sensitivities, attitudes, and skills) are needed. Just as physicians must know the human body and drugs, secondary art teachers must understand adolescents, the field of art, and the meaning of art experiences at this level, as well as having knowledges and abilities necessary for teaching. Whereas physicians prescribe certain drugs and diets for curing specific ailments, art teachers prescribe certain media and art experiences for satisfying the learning and developmental needs of students. Both medicine and teaching are considered to be professions, in part because decisions by the practitioner are based upon much learning and experience in the field. An art teacher should also be characterized by a creative imagination and a value system (philosophy) concerning art.

Art teachers must be well prepared because so much is expected of them. In many schools they have been called "miracle workers." As an art teacher you will be expected to work successfully in art classes with all students including the most talented and the most serious discipline-problem and handicapped students. You may be expected to select the curtains for the stage of the school auditorium; to produce art on your own time; to cooperate with other teachers in integrating art with other subjects; to be in charge of the school yearbook; to design the commencement program covers; to hold all-school art exhibits; to draw caricatures at the school carnival; to help write a meaningful art curriculum; and to make a presentation at a school board meeting. Such is the case because art teachers, themselves, are usually looked upon as being creative, artistic, gifted, and talented, as well as being well organized. Fortunately, most art teachers are!

THE IMPORTANCE OF TEACHING

Teaching is one of the noblest and rewarding of professions for two reasons: the teacher is helping pass on to the next generation our cultural heritage; and the teacher is helping young people develop their abilities and unfold into knowl-edgeable, sensitive, and aware adults. Thus, teaching involves both nurture (ex-trinsic aspects of which the content of a field, such as art, is to be learned by the student) and nature (intrinsic qualities and abilities which are to be developed by the student). Such learning and development on the part of the student bring great satisfaction and pleasure. What a tremendous feeling it is to learn to stand up without falling on one's new skates and then to be able to skate around the rink, to turn, to skate backward. These are exciting accomplishments, the likes of which occur in every aspect of life including the arts. The adolescent who says, "I never really knew how to draw and to see before I had you as a teacher," or "I didn't know what art was all about before this class," is telling you what a great influence you have been on his life. And, as a teacher, it gives you a great feeling, knowing that you have been responsible for enriching another's life.

Although learning does not always come easily for all students, those who have difficulties simply add challenge and excitement to the teaching situation. When the teacher is able to get students to understand some concept, such as negative space, which they were not able to comprehend before, it is indeed a wonderful experience.

Learning in the arts at the secondary level is especially rewarding because so little learning in this area has usually taken place, art experiences being either absent or trivial, or given a meager place in elementary curricula. To discover and develop art abilities in an art-deprived adolescent is to discover the riches of life itself. For example, as a result of having high school students model for figure

This black-and-white wash of a still life was painted by a sophomore high school student who "found" herself in the art class and continued her art education at the university level, becoming a professional artist.

drawing, I found one young man who seemed to take poses in a most sensitive and dramatic way, becoming very involved. I remarked about his special ability and encouraged him to try out for the next school play. Within two years, this young man became "the" actor of the school, appearing in all the plays and being acclaimed by his peers. As a result, he became confident, poised, and much more interested and involved in all subject areas, but especially in the arts. Students with learning and communication problems in the verbally oriented academic subjects, and students considered as behavior problems, will often "find" themselves in the visual, expressive, and creative world of the arts. To be the teacher who helps such students make this discovery is truly a fulfilling experience. Art teachers at every grade level can help students find themselves, but it is during the adolescent period that such a discovery becomes most meaningful to the student. At this time, careers, values, and adult goals and behaviors are becoming very important. And decisions made in the art class may affect the rest of the student's life.

It is apparent, therefore, that teachers are important, for without them nothing will happen in the classroom. Art students left on their own generally repeat past art work which was originally made under the supervision of an art teacher. However, the repeated work is usually of a much lower expressive and aesthetic quality than the original work (Brittain, 1968). Teachers are the leaders of learning in a classroom, the stimulators—the spark plugs—who get students to want to learn and who direct learning to an ever higher level. Yes, art teachers are vital and have a most important role to play in the learning process.

THE IMPORTANCE OF THE ARTS/VISUAL ARTS

The arts are vital to our culture; therefore, we believe all individuals in our society should have some participatory experiences in the arts. The arts vivify and extend human experience, make us sensitive and aware of who we are and what we believe, mirroring ourselves and our society—even though somewhat painfully at times. A work of art presents thoughts, feelings, and perceptions for our contemplation. The arts deal with the uniqueness of each individual and the glorification of one's being and creative imagination. Without the arts there would be no architecture— no great buildings—no music, no dance, no theater, no creative films, no fashion, no painting or sculpture, no landscaping, no harmonious ordering of the environment, no beauty. One cannot imagine life without the arts. Surely the arts are as important in our daily lives as the sciences and humanities. Unfortunately, the arts are frequently looked upon as the "finishing touches" of life which many feel they can live without. Unknowingly to these naïve people, the arts penetrate to the core of every human activity where there is a concern for how things look, for harmonious order and organization. Many people make aesthetic decisions without ever realizing that any relationship to the arts is involved. To plant a tree in one place rather than another; to listen to one musical composition rather than another; to hang a picture in one place rather than in another; to select an object of one color instead of another; to wear one garment instead of another; to attend a particular event to see the color and movement of the participants rather than another—all because of appearance and feeling—have to do with making aesthetic choices. As arts teachers, we must make people aware that such choices involve aesthetic criteria and that better decisions can be made if one has had experiences in the arts.

Now let us consider the visual arts. Few are aware of the important part the visual arts play in our daily lives from the design of advertisements, containers, fabrics, cars, furniture, houses, streets and parks, and public and commercial buildings to the very clothes we wear and the utensils with which we eat. The visual arts contribute greatly and are essential for an enriched life.

Visual Arts as a Means of Communication

Susanne Langer states that "a basic need of man is the need of symbolization. The symbol-making function is one of man's primary activities, like eating, looking, or moving about. It is a fundamental process of his mind, and goes on all the time" (1951, p. 41). We use symbols to organize our experience in order to understand and/or communicate it. As language, math, and science provide ways of symbolically communicating and representing one's understanding of things, so the visual arts provide other ways. In our society, great emphasis is placed upon verbal communication (written and oral) generated from our verbal-linear-analytical intelligence. However, we need also to think in terms of images since the visual symbols of art have been a most valid form of communication down through the ages. Some argue that the brain only stores images in its memory bank. Art has been used to speak of the animals in the forest, the changing moods in nature, the greatness of kings, queens, and gods, as well as to relate the everyday life of ordinary people. Long before the development of alphabets, drawings were used as communication. Even today, much of contemporary advertising is based upon a rapid form of conveying visual messages. The language of art is evident in packaging, posters, television advertisements, and in every other aspect of commerce. Art as communication is an integral aspect of our daily lives.

Picasso's painting, *Guernica*, Michelangelo's Sistine Chapel murals, and the prints of Goya would certainly lose much of their grandeur and power if they could only be talked about and not seen. So, we see that visual language, coming from our visual-aesthetic-creative intelligence, does exist and frequently offers the most effective means for relating our interpretation and expression concerning that which we have experienced. Our dress and our homes visually communicate to such an extent that we can identify and predict behavior. We learn that certain clothes are designed for sports wear and certain others are designed for more serious and formal occasions. Herein our visual language becomes culturally oriented. In a civilization with no symbolic communication system for identifying status and roles through dress, architecture, and artifacts of jewelry, ceramics, or fabrics, there would be a major breakdown in information about who does what (McFee, 1962). The visual symbols developed by artists/designers help us to grasp unique information that cannot be transmitted through other modes of communication.

Visual art works permit us to go beyond verbal language since many of our senses and abilities are involved in producing and experiencing a work of art. Individuals possess both verbal and visual abilities and should be given the opportunity to develop both creatively. Certainly we do not want to take away from anyone an important avenue of communication or expression. Visual and nonverbal communication provide a balance in our verbally oriented culture.

Visual Arts as a Means of Expression

We need to use visual symbols in order to express our feelings. As we go through life, we have emotional responses that result from our associations with people, events, and things. Art experiences deal directly with the subjective and intuitive and can bring about an awareness of these references, as well as a refinement of them. To feel what we know and to know what we feel is a vital aspect of emotional stability. One way to eliminate emotional illiteracy is to use art for activating and expressing emotions (Moholy-Nagy, 1947). Art experiences result in emotional release, stability, peace of mind, and help in the discovery of one's own worth and identity in our fast-moving society. This is especially important during adolescence when tensions, irritations, and frustrations build and need to be released. Art experiences permit such a release and the expression of aggression

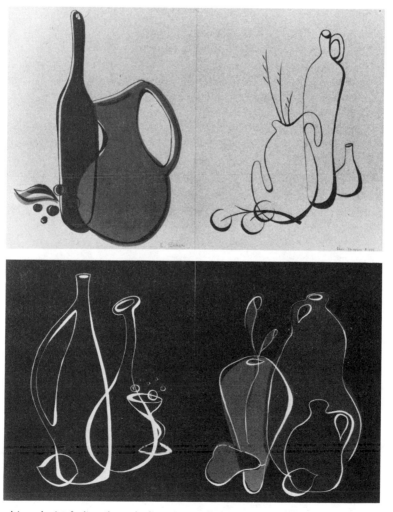

Bottles and jars depict feeling through distortion and exaggeration in these studies of flowing lines and flat areas.

in a socially acceptable and positive manner. When individuals express themselves in art, they put themselves into their creations—they project their ideas, feelings and perceptions into the art piece. They "see themselves" somewhat mirrored in their own expression. As a result of facing themselves in their art work, they begin to see themselves more objectively. A student may draw or paint about his hatred for a peer, a parent, or a teacher resulting in a very expressive portrait. The art work, a portrait in this case, permits the student to deal positively with strong, negative, inner feelings. When one's feelings are expressed in a painting or other art work, one can see one's feelings "out there." Students begin to know how they perceive the world through their own art expression and, therefore, can deal more objectively and effectively with their feelings. It is important, at times, to "let off steam," to get our thoughts and feelings out where we can handle them. In this respect, art experiences become therapeutic and bring about emotional stability and mental health. It should be noted that, at times, everyone has such a need to express frustrations and deep-seated feelings.

Visual Arts as a Means of Perceptual Sensitivity

We only know the world we live in through our senses—through seeing, hearing, touching, tasting, smelling, and moving. Art experiences force a sensitivity and an awareness because one must be concerned with the uniqueness of the particular to create or appreciate art. To draw an object means to study the object in detail, to observe it under many differing conditions and to see the art elements of line, shape, color, and texture, as well as pattern, rhythm, balance, order, and variation. Many students have told me how they have looked at the door of their home for years but never really saw it until they were asked to draw it. Art expression brings a keenness of total sensory awareness because the hand cannot guide the pencil to make lines and shapes that the person does not perceive. The deep satisfaction engendered by creating with art media motivates one toward a more intense use of the senses, which may be called the development of perceptual literacy.

Note the details of this car observed by a student who developed a perceptual sensitivity concerning line, shape, and pattern.

Visual Arts as a Means of Aesthetic Awareness

Art experiences involving line, shape, texture, and color develop an aesthetic awareness which is the basis for making choices not only in matters of painting, drawing, sculpture, and the crafts, but also choices as consumers and selectors of various objects and commodities used in our daily lives. From where else does one derive criteria for choosing material objects: our clothes, cars, houses, appliances, and the like? Art class is the only place in the school curriculum wherein an understanding and awareness of good design is consciously and seriously developed. Basic art experiences involve order, organization, and design qualities (balance, consistency, composition, rhythm, unity, variety, and subordination) and, as such, develop aesthetic sensitivity, taste, and the culture of our nation. Our homes, our cities, even our selves look as they do because of someone's choice involving buildings, streets, parks, cars, clothing, and the multitude of objects we use in our daily lives. Such an aesthetic awareness requires a great many art experiences over a period of years. If the taste of the nation is low, it is because we have not been willing to allow enough time and enough quality art experiences in the school curriculum for this development. It is crucial that the school accept this responsibility since most parents do not provide quality art experiences at home.

Visual Arts as a Means of Knowing and Understanding

Knowledge of art, past and present, develops our insights and understanding of man (McLuhan and Fiore, 1967). Concepts and emotions are presented to the participator (creator or observer) in an art experience that might otherwise have been missed. Art helps one to grasp unique information that cannot be transmitted through other modes of communication (Lansing, 1971). It helps one to understand the visual particularities of life. Art experiences force a person to pay attention to these ideas, feelings, and perceptions and in so doing one develops such insights— one knows and understands. Our frame of reference is extended. We know more about ourselves, the world we live in, and the field of art.

For example, if a person draws a baseball player, a player swinging the bat and hitting the ball, there are many aspects of this situation that must be taken into account. Will the figure fit on the drawing paper? What medium would be most appropriate? How does the player stand? Is he leaning over? How does one lean? Where are the feet? Where are the arms? Where is the player looking? How do the hands hold the bat? Is the player wearing a uniform? What are the parts of a baseball uniform? How do they look? How does the light condition affect the player? How does the player feel when the ball is hit? What happens to the facial expression, the muscles? What is going on around the player that may contribute to the idea and feeling expressed? In looking at the art work of someone else, similar detailed questions may be asked, the artist's expression giving us his insight into the situation. As you can see from this example, art expression serves as a vehicle for expressing one's ideas, feelings, and perceptions and requires an identification with whatever we draw, paint, sculpt, or construct. It helps us understand not only ourselves but other people and how they view the world.

Similarly, to know and understand the art of the past is enriching and broadening. The history and sensitivity of the human race are conveyed through the visual arts. For many cultures, it is only through the artifacts that we are able to piece together what life was really like at that particular time. Even in a culture that had developed an alphabet and writing, the remaining artifacts add much to our understanding of the past. To view the portrait sculpture of the Crusaders in Winchester Cathedral, to see the great spire of Salisbury can only bring an expression of awe and wonder of life in medieval times. Words simply cannot convey the spirit held in these art objects, which are keys to our knowledge and understanding of these peoples of an earlier era. Such experiences with art objects of the past elicit compassion, challenge the mind, and stimulate the imagination. A study of art history confronts us with the peoples of times past and with an endless number of styles, symbols, concepts, perceptions, and feelings. Surely the most significant visual expression of the past, our cultural heritage, should at least be recognized by all adolescents.

Visual Arts as a Means of Creativity

A work of art is characterized by the individuality and uniqueness of the artist, qualities that are projected into the work itself. This thread of human inventiveness and creativity runs through the history of art whereby each artist pushes beyond that which has been done before, discovering original and imaginative symbols, shapes, forms, colors, ideas, perceptions, and feelings, as well as solving new problems or finding answers to old problems. Every work of art must have some spark of this creativity, this discovery and imagination in it. Therefore, all people who work at making art must develop and also bring forth unique creative personality attributes which are projected into their work (Burgart, 1961).

All persons possess creativity as they possess intelligence and other human abilities; some persons possess more, some less. No one knows, however, what the potential of an individual really is—or what the key may be that will unlock this potential. We must never accept abilities that are now functioning as being the final level of achievement for an individual. Some of us are very creative early in life while others are "late bloomers."

Many of the activities of life involve intuitive/creative thinking, making educated guesses, and "hunches" such as the choice of one's vocation, one's home, one's clothes, or one's spouse. Such decisions need self-confidence, a willingness to make mistakes, and a valuing of the unconventional—all aspects of creativity. Psychologist Jerome Bruner (1960) believes that we need training for such experiences somewhere in the school curriculum. Every time an individual creates a work of art, a painting for example, many intuitive/creative decisions are made: the placement of the objects/shapes in the picture; the size of the objects/shapes; the style of painting; the colors of the objects/shapes. For every stroke of the brush, the artist makes an educated guess and feels confident that the brush stroke will be appropriate and go with the other strokes in the painting. Bruner argues that so much of life involves personal intuitive decisions which are unique to each of us that we should have training in this area of intuitive/creative/divergent thinking.

E. Paul Torrance (1980) insists that more emphasis should be given to the development of creative intelligence in the 1980s, the thrust of society being toward increased diversity rather than a standardization of life. He notes it is possible to facilitate the learning of subject matter through creative learning activities. He believes that creative intelligence can be used in studying future problems, practicing important academic skills, as well as enlarging, enriching, and making more meaningful images of the future.

Many times the results of our creative thinking go far beyond ourselves and touch the lives of others as in the case of Edison, Kettering, Bell, the Wright brothers, and all the other great inventors of our time. Surely there would be little progress without those who have brought their creative genius to bear upon the industrial and technological world. This is also true for every other aspect of life— in government, in business, in agriculture, and, of course, in education and the arts. Without such creative genius going beyond what we have known before, there would be no progress.

Researchers have shown that art experiences are ideal for cultivating, exercising, and stimulating the imagination and for developing creative thinking (Educational Policies Commission, 1968). The secondary art student may be creative in his *first* effort in working with clay, paints, or three-dimensional media. Unlike other fields, no great background and knowledge are needed before one can do creative work with art media.

Visual Arts as a Means of Skill Development

Although no great skill is initially needed to be creative with art media, the thrill and satisfaction of success in producing creative work stimulates the desire to develop skill and craftsmanship at an increasingly higher level. Motor development and physical coordination are concomitant developments in the studio-art process. As we become more involved with our art work, the more sensitive we become and feel the need to control carefully the brush, the pencil, the pen, or the chisel. In so doing, we develop the small muscles involved in eye/hand coordination, and craftsmanship improves.

Visual Arts as a Means of Balance in Life and Education

Art has been universally valued in the life of most civilizations. It is an important aspect of man's culture. People everywhere have found joy and meaning in it, perhaps to offset the utilitarian, the mundane of existence.

Since education prepares people to live, art is important in education. Herein we see that art is used to transmit this cultural aspect of the heritage of mankind and it is the duty of schools to impart that cultural heritage. An education that does not include art instruction is deficient, because it does not teach a valid aspect of the culture.

In addition to transmitting our cultural heritage, it is important that all persons participate in art experiences to develop the human processes needed for a satisfying life in our contemporary world and to balance the development of abilities of the right side and left side of the brain. (See chapter 5.) These human processes are thinking, feeling, perceiving, and expressing/communicating. In our Western, fragmented way of life, which has resulted from our industrialized and technological society wherein we all tend to work on a part of a much larger whole, art can bring us fulfillment and satisfaction, as well as sharing in the whole of a meaningful experience wherein all these processes are involved. Many times the totality of experience is not seen in our world of work. In art we experience the procedure from the beginning idea to the conclusion and, we hope, successful end product.

No school curriculum is complete without art, not only for what such experiences can do for transmitting our cultural heritage, for an enriched personal development, and as a preparation for a vocation involving art, but also for leisure time activity. In looking to the future, when computers, robots, and other technologies take over what we now consider as work,

> what does become important? If war and boredom are avoided—and this is a big if—then a resulting society without work might be made up of individuals who concern themselves with each other, with themselves, and with whatever expressive endeavors might meet their taste. Science might be appreciated in the future society for the excitement that comes with exploration, discovery, and invention rather than for its usefulness. In such circumstances, art would be vitally important, for it would be the kind of thing which people would be doing, for themselves and for each other. In a sense, it is through this kind of psychological, emotional, creative, expressive, and intellectual exchange that "usefulness" in such a future society will be felt (Educational Policies Commission, 1968, p. 6).

RELATING THE SECONDARY ART PROGRAM TO THE SCHOOL AND LARGER COMMUNITY

Unlike English, mathematics, and the social and natural sciences, few school systems require art(s) to be studied after the sixth or seventh grade, implying that visual art and other arts are not important in adolescent and adult life—even for leisure. Many people still believe that art is a frill; and when moneys for education are in short supply, art classes are frequently the first to be deleted. The public, generally speaking, does not value art very highly in the school program. This point of view is probably a result of the writings of an Englishman, Herbert Spencer, who between 1854 and 1859 proposed a hierarchy of values for developing the school curriculum and which appears to have permeated the value system of many Americans.

Spencer (1911), in logically analyzing what knowledge is of most worth in his first essay on education, proposed the following activities/subjects in order of their importance for the good life:

1. Activities related to staying well and the preservation of life: physiology and hygiene. One must first have good health.
2. Vocational activities: math, chemistry, physics, and biology. One must then have knowledges and skills for earning a living.
3. Domestic activities related to family life: physiology, psychology, and ethics. After assuring good health and a job, one then should establish a home and family.
4. Social and political activities related to citizenship: history, economics, politics. One now should become interested in community and government affairs—be a good citizen.
5. Leisure activities related to the gratification of taste and feelings: music, art, literature.

Spencer argues that as the arts "occupy the leisure of life, so should they occupy the leisure part of education" (p. 32). He was aiming at an educational organization in which a *few* would no longer be trained for a life of elegant leisure as had been the practice in the education of the aristocracy in the seventeenth and eighteenth centuries but a life in which *everybody* would receive an education that included some of the elements of all areas. Spencer's work had a profound influence on Americans, including his contemporary, Charles W. Eliot, president of Harvard University. Even today, for many people, an analysis of the above hierarchy will result in an acceptance of Spencer's ordering. In fact, in a recent statement, the president of the National Art Education Association (Feldman, 1982) argues that school art is important because it is a type of work which relates, of course, to vocational concerns. He also notes that art is a visual language and deals with values—which relates somewhat to Spencer's concern for citizenship.

It behooves us as art educators to counter Spencer's hierarchy, to point out the undue emphasis on academic subjects and linear thought. We must be prepared to justify the arts, and more specifically visual art, as being valid and basic in comtemporary life and culture and a necessary inclusion in the curriculum of every secondary student. Here it should be pointed out that Spencer *did not omit the arts* from the curriculum, he merely put the arts last, after everything else in life. If art programs are to flourish in the schools of America, it is our responsibility, as art teachers, to exert much more leadership in demonstrating to the public what art/art education is all about and what art teachers are trying to do, especially noting the purposes, benefits, and rewards of an art program for every student at the secondary level.

Art teachers must continually relate the art program—goals, curricula, content, and achievements—to the school community and to the public in order to maintain art teaching positions and to recruit students for secondary art classes. This is simply making people aware of the benefits of art. By building a positive reputation for the school art program the art teacher can attract students within the school. The single most important means of recruitment is an excellent art program. If students are interested, learning, and developing in the art classes, they will enthusiastically relate this to peers and parents. It is easy to "sell" your art program if you, the teacher, are creatively involved and enthusiastic about it yourself. "The most powerful influence on public opinion is consistent, superior performance" in the art room (Baker, 1979, p. 21).

In addition to students, the art teacher also consciously needs to relate the art program to three important groups that control the finances and programs of most schools: school board members, school administrators, and influential parents and other members of the community at large. Suggestions by the National Art Education Association (1973) for relating the art program to these individuals are summarized here.

DISPLAYS OF ART WORK.   Maintain an art exhibit at the board of education's office building. Use captions that explain the values of art, the nature of the exhibit, and your objectives. Statements from the student artists also add interest.

Display art work in the superintendent's and principal's office (with permission). Make the office walls a little gallery. When putting up the display, talk with the administrator about the students who did the work and the learning and development that took place. Take the time to explain your goals and objectives—and achievements. For instance, point out examples of art work that show how students' lives have been improved by the development of a greater confidence, expressiveness, and sensitivity. Point out that schools with a heavy emphasis on

Photo courtesy of Craig Roland

Student art exhibits are an excellent means of interpreting a secondary art program to the community. Statements of objectives and contributions of art experiences to life should be displayed along with art work.

the arts have fewer discipline problems and lower vandalism costs. Students involved in self-expression lose much of their anger and hostility because they have a constructive outlet (Houston, 1981). Note that the arts can enhance student learning by reinforcing basic skills and providing opportunities for alternative learning. After the display is in place, take photos of the art work with school board members and administrators and submit these photos with appropriate captions to the local newspapers.

Arrange for art displays at music, drama, and sports events in the school and in shopping centers and other places where many people gather in the community. Personally invite school board members, administrators, and influential leaders of the community and escort them through the exhibit explaining about the art work and the school art program. Such art displays give parents a reason to be proud of the school and develop student morale and school spirit at a low financial outlay.

SOCIAL ART EVENTS.   Initiate an art(s) parent night or an art(s) fair at your school and let the junior and senior high school art students teach their parents to create art. Pass out brochures discussing the value of art. Take photos for the local newspapers and other media.

Invite school board members and administrators to the art room; explain what students are doing and why. Encourage students to talk about art and their work with the visitors.

Hold openings for art exhibits and displays at which time the values of art may be explained to those present.

SPEAKING ABOUT ART.   Request permission to speak about the importance of secondary school art experiences and the art program at school board meetings and parent group meetings. At this time, case studies may be presented involving various adolescents' art work so that the value and significance of art experiences in the lives of students and the impact of art experiences upon students can be seen.

Volunteer to speak at local nonart organizations and invite nonart community leaders to speak on the values of art at parent meetings, in-service meetings, workshops, and school assemblies. Invite these leaders to write a brief statement on the arts for the school newspaper.

WRITING ABOUT ART.   Use the media to inform the community about art social events, the school art curriculum, art exhibits, art honors, and art conferences. Keep the community informed concerning your own professional activities, as well as the school art program.

News articles should be written about some aspect of the art program that is special and interesting to you. Be concise but explain what, where, why, and who. This basic information should be given in the first or second paragraph. Details can follow. Articles should be typed double-spaced, with your name, address, and phone number in the upper left corner in case the editor needs to call you. Include a headline since it gives the idea of the story content. Get advance stories in well ahead of time, usually ten days before the event. Photographs add a great deal of interest to the article. Photos should be at least 5" x 7"; close-ups are preferable. Always note the full names and titles of persons on the back of the photo.

Send copies of articles that promote art to school board members, administrators, and influential people in the community. Follow up with phone calls or notes asking for their opinion of the articles. Share professional art education publications with school board members, administrators, and others.

Prepare a brochure conveying the importance of art education. Statements by influential people in the school and the larger community can be quoted. Include photographs of students working on their art. These brochures may be distributed at school functions or whenever there is a gathering in the community. The National Art Education Association and several state art education associations have brochures that are available for a small fee.

COMMUNITY ART RESOURCES.   Make school board members, administrators, and the public aware of things of aesthetic value, as well as of local artists, in the community: paintings and sculpture (private and public collections), architecture and its antecedents, and fountains in the parks. Local artists may be invited to exhibit their work at the school. Art classes can emphasize aesthetic community assets by producing paintings of important buildings and sculptures. These student art works can then be displayed in prominent places in the community.

Whatever is done in regard to educating others concerning the value of school art, always be positive, assume that others are for the arts. When possible, involve "nonart people" in the art program but make them feel they are really "art people."

Professionally, we need to reach out to leaders in other fields. Influential persons in government, business, industry, and religion may not know why art should be a part of education. Although classroom art teachers may have little opportunity to relate the values of school art to these leaders in other fields, they can support the professional associations such as the National Art Education Association and the Alliance for Arts Education that do have such public relations programs. Many states have art education associations with standing committees that are continually involved in public relations and advocacy programs for school art.

The most influential behavior for an art teacher is to live what you believe, be what you are promoting. Being a role model will make others believe in your sincerity and, therefore, they will respect your beliefs and integrity. Your own art values are reflected in the enthusiasm or lack of it in your everyday actions.

A PHILOSOPHY CONCERNING ART

It is important for art teachers to have an understanding of various philosophic approaches toward art, because your belief and value system have a direct bearing not only upon how you create art but also upon how you teach art. There are basically three approaches to producing and viewing art. Most art teachers believe that certain aspects of all of them are important and develop their own philosophy so as to involve aspects of all three, probably emphasizing one more than the others. However, in teaching, the various needs of students may dictate a greater emphasis upon one approach more than upon another at particular times in a student's learning and development.

Art as an Instrument

Art may be perceived as being a means, an instrument, toward an end. Herein, art and art experiences become catalytic agents for helping the student achieve some goal other than that of making art or learning about art. Art experiences in this regard may be used to develop certain personality and behavioral attributes such as building confidence, promoting creativity, engendering responsibility, bringing about skill and coordination, and developing perceptual sensitivity and aesthetic awareness. The art teacher who uses only this approach is concerned more with the individual and his development than with learning about art or with the making of art products. A teacher who uses art as an instrument is generally student-centered.

Art as a Means of Expression

Art may be regarded only as a means of expressing one's feelings, ideas, and perceptions with emphasis upon any one of the three. However, individuals subscribing to this approach generally are concerned with presenting their feelings *about* their thoughts and visual stimuli. Herein, artists are expressing and interpreting, giving the viewer their viewpoints—communicating via the art work. Artists embracing this approach necessarily have to be moved and stimulated by the subject, object, or situation so as to have a definite and committed feeling about it before expressing via art work. The teacher who uses art as a means of expression, therefore, is concerned with stimulating students so that students do have something they want to express—something they want to say—about the subject being painted, sculpted, drawn, or constructed.

Art for Art's Sake

Art is perceived as being a legitimate and important area of human experience and study for its own sake by persons embracing an "art for art's sake" point of view. Herein, we learn the formal aspects of art: what it is, what it means, including the history of art and the components of art (that is, the elements and design/compositional principles). Not only must one know the content aspects as noted above, but one must also be able to perform as an artist; be able to use all the knowledge and experience one has gained to produce, write, and talk about art (that is, art criticism). Famous artists of the present and past are to be respected, if not revered, and their work is to be remembered, if not loved! The art teacher who uses only this approach is generally concerned with the production of quality art work regardless of the student's background, confidence, coordination, and ability. Although these attributes may be necessary for the making of quality art products, they are, for the most part, ignored by the teacher. A standard is maintained that is based upon the art work of the past—professional artists and/or former students' work. The teacher who uses this art for art's sake approach is only concerned with knowledge of art and the quality of the art work produced by the students.

DIFFERENTIATING BETWEEN CREATIVE
AND NONCREATIVE LEARNING BEHAVIOR

It is important for the teacher to differentiate in the art experience between creative and noncreative (imitative) behavior. These differences should be conveyed to students, resulting in a greater understanding and less confusion. At times both creative and noncreative behaviors are valid but students must understand when each is appropriate in the art experience. For the most part, whenever we make original and imaginative art work (such as a painting of a city of the future), we are concerned with creative behavior; whenever we follow directions to carry out various procedures (such as the steps in the making of a block print) and develop various skills in the use of art media (such as how to hold the pen or knife), we are concerned with imitative and noncreative behavior.

Now let us compare these two modes of learning in more detail. Creative learning involves working from what we know and perceive at the present time, and going into the unknown. We are discovering the future. It's like driving without a road map. This is an unnerving situation and beginning students may become anxious and self-doubting. It takes much courage (May, 1980). But as we experience a creative approach to working in art over a period of time we generally will feel satisfaction and involvement that make it all worthwhile. In contrast, in noncreative learning, we are mastering a body of knowledge, learning only about known aspects of the world. The goals are clear cut and we know rather precisely where we are going. Because this noncreative type of learning is characteristic of most academic school subjects with which students have had experience, students are not threatened by the learning situation. The information is laid out before them and all they have to do is memorize, know the information, and apply it to achieve the desired ends. Burkhart (1960, p. 9) called noncreative learning "academic learning" be-

TABLE 1
Creative Versus Noncreative Behavior

CREATIVE	NONCREATIVE
Work from knowledge to the unknown	Master a body of knowledge
No model to follow	Model/example to follow
No right or wrong answers	Right answers
Open-ended response	Fixed response
Trial-and-error, discovery methods	Imitation, memorization methods
Tolerance for frustration, ambiguity	No tolerance for frustration, desire security

cause it is so characteristic of most subjects as taught in the typical school curriculum. (See Table 1.)

There is no model to follow in creative learning. There can be no example. The individual must come up with his own unique response whereas in noncreative learning, an example or model is provided which the student can easily imitate for a successful experience.

There are no right and wrong answers in creative learning. Solutions can not be predetermined. Creative learning involves a completely open-ended situation versus a fixed, known answer situation in noncreative learning when the response is judged to be either right or wrong.

The method in creative learning is one that is characterized by trial and error, discovery, and experimentation. For one who feels secure with models, right and wrong answers, the creative learning process at first will probably appear to be ambiguous, frustrating, and frightening. The method of noncreative learning involves imitation, memorization, and repetition as in a drill.

An example of creative learning in the art room is making a painting of a storm in the mountains. Here we can only rely upon our past experiences having to do with mountains and storms. We can recall certain concepts we hold about the wind, rain, lightning, and clouds associated with storms, as well as the trees, rocks, and snow associated with mountains. We also recall our feelings—perhaps the danger of high winds, flooded mountain streams, and of lightning striking trees and causing a forest fire. In addition, we recall our perceptions of the moving clouds, the wetness of the rain, the dark shadows of the forests, the reflection of lightning on the wet rocks. These concepts, feelings, and perceptions are based upon our past experiences with storms and mountains—of these we are aware. This is where we start. Creative people will take these known aspects and manipulate, abstract, arrange, and rearrange them into new relationships so as to communicate and express personal experience concerning storms and mountains. This results in a creative statement which is in contrast to a noncreative impersonal copy of a photograph or a painting by someone else.

In addition, there is a creative interaction with the medium as one works on the painting. Each brush stroke changes the Gestalt and must be reacted to as the painting develops. If a stroke is not placed appropriately or is of a color intensity that is inconsistent with the others, there must be some action to make these harmonious and to express that which is felt. It is in this respect that creativity and aesthetic sensitivity become combined.

To promote creative learning, the teacher must develop a permissive atmosphere so that the student feels free to express new and unusual ideas—to let go, without fear of the unknown; without concern about what others may think; where problems, rather than solutions, are sought; where there is no concern about wasting time or materials; where there is no fear of failure, and where there is no concern with usefulness and practicality. Any aspects which tend to be evaluative should be considered only after the creative experience has taken place. Individuals involved in creative learning must feel confident, and be process oriented rather than product oriented. They must have the ability to fantasize, to become sensory alert, to become lost in the process, to be imaginative, patient, and courageous in their pursuit and to be willing to feel frustrated at times. The art teacher should realize that it is not easy for students to develop these attributes, which usually are not called for in noncreative academic situations. However, if students are made aware of the differences between creative and noncreative learning, they should feel a certain security in knowing what is expected of them in either situation. It is when teachers themselves are ambiguous concerning the learning situation that students become confused for they do not know what is expected of them—what role they are to play. Teachers must make students aware of creative learning and noncreative or imitative learning experiences. Both are valid at particular times in the art room.

Now let us consider the attributes of creativity that differentiate creative persons from less creative persons as defined by two researchers in the field, Viktor Lowenfeld and W. Lambert Brittain (Cassels, 1959). Most writing in the area of creativity tended, in this country, to be philosophical until the 1950s, when much empirical research took place. This research is still valid and remains an important cornerstone in art education.

If teachers are to develop creative ability in their students via their students' art work, then, indeed, we must know the attributes we want to develop of this multifaceted phenomenon. Most researchers have found eight attributes of creativity. Although these can be identified individually to the extent that various tests for each criterion have been formulated, these attributes tend to function in concert in creative behavior. These eight criteria permit the teacher to analyze this phenomenon of creativity and to develop an understanding of each attribute rather than dealing with creativity in a somewhat nebulous global manner. Knowing the

Creativity can be developed through art experiences wherein students are placed in a situation that demands an imaginative solution. In this example, areas of watercolor were painted on a page, with a narrow white space around each color. Students were then instructed to find objects in these shapes and draw them in detail with pen and ink.

various aspects of creativity permits the art teacher to develop specific and meaningful goals and objectives. One of these eight attributes is no more important than another; however, the teacher may find that one student needs experiences concerning one attribute more than another and, therefore, may assign different criteria priorities for each student in the teaching/learning process. The eight criteria are discussed in the following sections.

Sensitivity

A creative person is very much aware of all aspects of a situation. This includes social, perceptual, and aesthetic considerations. It means being aware of the needs of people, sensing (seeing, touching, hearing, smelling) the environment, and realizing aesthetic/creative problems that exist therein. The individual develops a heightened awareness of anything that is unusual, odd, or promising in the person, material, or situation at hand. This, in reality, is sensitivity to one's self, to life. It means sensitivity to small differences in the particular. The opposite of sensitivity is generalization. Sensitivity to problems is necessary for creativity to take place. The more aware we are of details, the more sensitive we become. The sensitive individual walks into a room and recognizes problems in the design and décor whereas an insensitive person walks into the room and is not aware of any problems, accepting the room as it is.

Fluency

A creative person has the ability to think rapidly and imaginatively, quickly relating one thing to another in a given situation. Ideas occur in rapid succession, one after the other, following any stimulus. In every art experience, especially in the beginning, thoughts flow concerning the idea, object, and/or feeling being expressed. As the individual thinks of an object to be painted, related objects come to mind and these are integrated into the composition. Likewise, when colors, shapes, and forms are considered, each suggests another and another, producing a creative flow.

Flexibility

A creative person has the ability to adjust when confronted with new developments and changed situations whether these are external or are from within. As one paints, he must make a continual adjustment to whatever is happening on the canvas. If a brush stroke is too brilliant or raw in color, the artist must either change it or adjust the colors around it for a consistent and harmonious expression. Often accidents occur in carrying out an art activity. Flexible people take advantage of such situations whereas less creative people tend to be distressed by such developments. For very creative persons, a painting that starts with a particular subject may end up being entirely different not only in subject but also in color and style.

Originality

Originality, the attribute most people think of concerning creativity, has to do with the uncommonness of an individual's response to a given stimulus. Uniqueness, unconventional and unusual, the only one of its kind in a class, characterizes the response. The opposite of originality is conventionality and regimentation wherein all perform in the same way. A good exercise to develop originality is to draw a line on the drawing paper and ask the student to complete the picture. The line may become the edge of a table, the horizon, a roof line, or anything else according to the imaginative ability of the student.

Analysis

A creative person has the ability to deduce details from a whole, to abstract, to analyze, to penetrate a subject. Herein, we start with the whole and break it down into its component parts ending with details. Whenever we observe we do this—going from the whole to its parts. One should never be satisfied with just a spontaneous impression of the whole for this may leave us with a superficial meaning, with a shallow generalization. When we look at a tree, we see the general shape but as we analyze it, we see the limbs, leaves, bark, and all the idiosyncracies therein.

Synthesis

A creative person has the ability to bring several elements into a new and meaningful whole. It is the reverse of the analytical process previously described. Synthesis happens in every art work since we combine lines, shapes, and bits of color (brush strokes) into a new whole—a painting, a print, a sculpture, or a construction. Analysis and synthesis tend to happen simultaneously in most art experiences. We see the whole; we see the parts; and we relate them together into a unified expression.

Redefinition

A creative person has the ability to redefine lines, shapes, colors, and textures, to shift the function of objects, and use them in new ways. Herein, the individual is using old familiar things for new purposes. Buttons may be transformed into the eyes of a clown in a circus collage; a piece of poodle–cloth may become the body of a woolly sheep; a stroke of vermilion in a painting may become the brick chimney of a house. In every realistic painting, lines, shapes, textures, and colors are re-defined to become aspects of the objects we see in the picture. Paintings are actually made of lines and areas of color—paint and canvas—not the houses, trees, people, rivers, and mountains that we read into them.

Consistent Organization

A creative person has the ability to organize all aspects in such a manner that all the parts are related harmoniously with no superfluous parts—saying the most with the least. A work of art is so well organized that one part cannot be exchanged for another. It is so consistent that the single parts are where one feels they ought to be. If any part were changed, the situation/art work would appear to be un-balanced. The greater the work of art, the more consistent it is. Some works become classics, appearing to be very consistent to generation after generation.

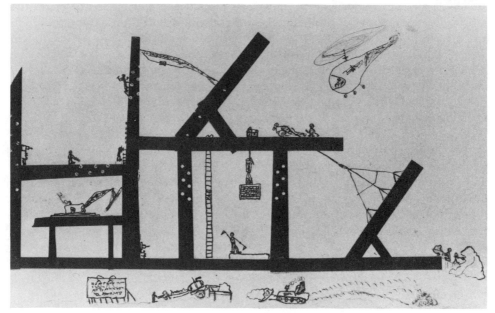

Black strips of construction paper are redefined as girders and steel beams in this expression inspired by the building of an addition to the school (junior high level).

BRIDGING THE GAP BETWEEN CHILD ART AND ADULT ART

Whereas all children draw and paint with great gusto and enthusiasm—unless they have been interfered with by the imposition of adult standards—most persons after childhood tend to feel a lack of confidence when asked to perform in these areas. Many adolescents look on their art work as childish, naïve, and lacking in finesse. Something seems to happen between childhood and adulthood that makes many individuals in our society shy away from the visual arts, as borne out by the fact that only about ten percent of all secondary students enroll in art classes. Obviously, this is a critical time concerning visual art expression.

Enrollment in art classes at the secondary level, indeed, is low for two reasons. First, around the age of eight or nine, an awareness emerges of visual and spatial qualities such as distance, the effect of light on objects, shadows, atmospheric qualities, texture, and movement and is probably the result of an increased differentiation of the right brain at this time (Samples, 1976). The ability to express these visual and spatial aspects in a drawing or painting is idiosyncratic and differs from one individual to another, but all persons develop some ability in the area of visual perception. Although this development generally begins to be reflected in children's art work around the age of eight to ten, for most individuals it does not appear with intensity until adolescence, when students have a very intense desire for representation according to nature. When this desire for perceptual reality is accompanied by the psychological changes that occur as a result of the physiological changes brought about by puberty, an awareness comes about on the part of the individual who now consciously and critically looks at his art work as an adult. This is in marked contrast to the unaware manner that children view their art work (Michael, 1965). Adolescents feel they cannot do art and will avoid this area if the art work does not come up to their expectations, which are usually realistic, if not photographic.

Secondly, we must consider the attitude of society toward the arts. The Puritan work ethic and the influence of value systems, which relegate the arts to leisure time and to the last item to be considered in life, have made their mark on the minds of Americans, being handed down from one generation to another (Spencer, 1911). Therefore, the art teacher can generally expect adolescents to find little or no support for their attempts at making art from the adult world unless certain outstanding abilities are evident in their work. For the most part, the general public values skill and realistic/naturalistic work. Adolescents showing marked abilities in these areas may expect to receive commendation from many art-naïve adults.

The problem, then, appears to be one of getting adolescents to become aware of qualities in their work in which they can take pride. Ideally, this should be done before puberty when preadolescents are not fully aware and do not look at their work with the critical eyes of adults. At this time we can get students to explain how they achieved certain aesthetic/creative/perceptual qualities in their own work, as well as in that of others. A similar approach may be used after puberty when adolescents are critically aware. However, then it is more difficult because students may already have a negative attitude toward art, especially their own art work. But it is still possible for the persevering teacher to build confidence in students by pointing out specific aesthetic/creative/perceptual qualities in their art work. For example, the teacher may note how the student has achieved distance in a picture by having the trees and people larger in the foreground than those in the background; the expressive quality of the sky by using a subtle blending and flow of watercolors; the unity in a painting by having balanced the colors—all of which the student probably is not aware. One word of caution when using this procedure: the teacher must always be truthful and point out only aspects that are felt to be of quality. Closure experiences may also be used by the teacher to get students to create art work of expressive, creative, and aesthetic quality wherein various aspects of achievement can then be pointed out. This method is more fully developed in chapter 5.

In addition, the art teacher should make the preadolescent, as well as the adolescent, art student aware of the world of adult art, noting the uniqueness and individuality of the work of various artists down through the ages. A collection of reproductions or slides showing a great diversity of styles, schools, and individual artists should be permanently maintained in the art room for use in working with students who have lost confidence in themselves and their own art. A persuasive teacher can also convince students of their uniqueness by pointing out how a particular quality, seen in adult art work, is reflected in their own work, thereby developing confidence and acceptance of their own art expression.

REFERENCES

Baker, D. W. Program planning and the public. *Art Education*, 1979, *32* (5), 19–21.
Brittain, W. L. An exploratory investigation of early adolescent expression in art. *Studies in Art Education*, 1968, *9* (2), 8–9.
Bruner, J. S. *The Process of Education*. Cambridge: Harvard University Press, 1960.

Burgart, H. J. Art in higher education: The relationship of art experience to personality, general creativity, and aesthetic performance. (Doctoral dissertation, The Pennsylvania State University, 1961.) *Dissertation Abstracts*, 1962, *22*, 2285–2286 (University Microfilms No. 61–6776).

Burkhart, R. C. *Progress in Creative Learning: Secondary Art*. Mt. Pleasant, Michigan: The Central Michigan University Press, 1960.

Cassels, L. Eight keys to creativity. *Nation's Business*, February 1959, 6–9.

Educational Policies Commission. The role of the fine arts in education. *Art Education*, 1968, *21* (7), 3–7.

Feldman, E. B. Art in the mainstream: A statement of value and commitment. *Art Education*, 1982, *35* (5), 6.

Houston, P. D. Stalking the school administrator: Advocating the arts. *Art Education*, 1981, *32* (5), 18–19.

Langer, S. *Philosophy in a New Key*. New York: Mentor, 1951.

Lansing, K. Art education today: Its nature and its needs. *Art Education*, 1971, *24* (2), 30–32.

May, R. *The Courage to Create*. New York: Bantam, 1980.

McFee, J. K. Implications for change in art education. *Western Arts Bulletin*, 1962, *48* (4), 16–30.

McLuhan, M., and Fiore, Q. *The Medium Is the Message*. New York: Bantam, 1967.

Michael, J. A. Art experience during early adolescence. In W. R. Hastie (ed.), *Art Education, Sixty-fourth Yearbook of the National Society for the Study of Education* (Part 2). Chicago: University of Chicago Press, 1965.

Moholy-Nagy, L. *Vision in Motion*. Chicago: Paul Theobald, 1947.

National Art Education Association. *Public Relations for Art Education*. Washington, D.C.: N.A.E.A., 1973.

Samples, B. *The Metaphoric Mind: A Celebration of Creative Consciousness*. Reading, Massachusetts: Addison-Wesley Publishing Company, 1976.

Spencer, H. *Essays on Education*. London: J. M. Dent and Sons, 1911.

Torrance, E. P. Creative intelligence and an agenda for the 80s. *Art Education*, 1980, *33* (7), 8–14.

SUPPLEMENTAL READINGS

Bassett, Richard (ed.). *Open Eye in Learning: The Role of Art in General Education*. Cambridge, Massachusetts: MIT Press, 1974. The importance of training the eyes for improving the environment as an aspect of education.

Bills, Robert E. *Education for Intelligence*. Washington, D.C.: Acropolis Books, 1982. Critical evaluation of purposes of schools with many suggestions for improvement.

Brittain, W. Lambert (ed.). *Viktor Lowenfeld Speaks on Art and Creativity*. Washington, D.C.: National Art Education Association, 1968. Creativity, art, and social values analyzed.

Chapman, Laura H. *Instant Art, Instant Culture: The Unspoken Policy for American Schools*. New York: Teachers College Press, 1982. Critical commentary on the current status of the arts in schools.

Eisner, Elliot W. (ed.). *The Arts, Human Development, and Education*. Berkeley: McCutchan Publishing, 1976. Series of lectures illuminating some social realities that shape what we do in the arts in schools.

Ghiselin, Brewster (ed.). *The Creative Process*. Berkeley: University of California Press, 1952. Thirty-eight outstanding persons from many fields reveal how they begin and complete their creative work.

Hajcak, Frank. *Expanding Creative Imagination*. West Chester, Pennsylvania: Institute for the Study and Development of Human Potential, 1981. Conditions, situations, and stimuli necessary for generating creative behaviors.

Hatfield, Thomas A. The administration as a resource: How to win friends and influence principals. *Art Teacher*, 1979, *9* (3), 10–12. Suggestions for working with principals.

Hausman, Jerome (ed.). *Arts and the Schools*. New York: McGraw-Hill, 1980. Collection of position papers in support of the arts. Basic questions answered concerning arts education.

Kaufman, Irving. *Art and Education in Contemporary Culture*. New York: Macmillan, 1966. Philosophical insight into the study/teaching of art; perceptual appreciation in preventing cultural deterioration in a technological society.

Lansing, Kenneth M. *Art, Artists, and Art Education*. New York: McGraw-Hill, 1971. An in-depth treatise exploring philosophical and practical aspects of art education.

Michael, John A. *The Lowenfeld Lectures*. University Park, Pennsylvania: Pennsylvania State University Press, 1982. Philosophical basis for creative art education.

Plummer, Gordon S. Twenty highlights in creativity research. *Art Education*, 1982, *35* (1), 30–33. Chronological review of research/writing concerning creativity.

Remer, Jane. *Changing Schools Through the Arts*. New York: McGraw-Hill, 1981. A rationale for arts in general education.

Rockefeller, D. J. *Coming to Our Senses: The Significance of the Arts for American Education*. New York: McGraw-Hill, 1977. Significant contributions by the arts to general education and life in America.

Shallcross, Doris J. *Teaching Creative Behavior*. Englewood Cliffs, New Jersey: Prentice-Hall, 1980. Updated information on creativity.

CHAPTER 2

WHAT WE ARE TRYING TO DO
Objectives/Evaluation

In the beginning, we, as art teachers, must ask ourselves, "What are we trying to do with our students?" And shortly thereafter, we need to ask, "Have we achieved that which we set out to do?" Such questions give the art teacher a sense of direction and keep the art program meaningful and consistent—and unrelated experiences and trite, busy-work exercises will not infiltrate the curriculum.

At this point, it is appropriate to consider various steps in the development of an educated person, a creative individual who is open to new ideas, perceptions, and feelings—as suggested by William G. Perry's prototype (1970). Most adolescents can be identified as being some place on a continuum from naïve and closed to sophisticated and open in their orientation to life, learning, and development. Individuals may be classified as those viewing solutions to problems as being singular and either right or wrong, answers being handed down by an authority, or as those viewing solutions to problems as being many-faceted with relevant qualifications— with many graduated steps between these two dichotomies of which the art teacher should be aware. (See Table 2, part A.) Here one notes a gradual movement toward self-determination and the acceptance of and commitment to an openness and balance in the consideration of many divergent solutions to any problematical situation. Some may even find enjoyment in discovering the problems.

In early childhood, it is necessary for adults to protect children in many ways, but particularly in relation to the environment. It is wrong to touch the hot stove, to play in the street, or to swallow mother's medicine; it is right to smell the flower, to pet the dog, or to eat the apple. These are simplistic actions which the child learns as a result of parental love and authority. In this process children also learn an orientation to life: that there are either correct or incorrect actions and answers handed down by someone who knows, by some authority. Children learn a particular way of dealing with their world. However, as the child grows older, becoming an adolescent, and later an adult, problems in life are not so simplistic, becoming more involved and complicated as authority gives way to self-determination. The

TABLE 2
Naïve—Sophisticate Continuum

Naïve Academic Convergent						Sophisticated Creative Divergent
1	2	3	4	5	6	7

A. Development of an Open, Educated Person

MODUS OPERANDI

1	2	3	4	5	6	7
Right/wrong answers perceived in society and reinforced by authority	Right/wrong answers arrived at by self solving problems	Acceptance of self-solutions without any qualifications	Acceptance of self-solutions with qualifications	Acceptance of a multiplicity of relevant divergent solutions with qualifications	Commitment to a multiplicity of relevant divergent solutions with qualifications	Balance of a multiplicity of relevant divergent solutions with qualifications

B. Development of an Open, Creative/Aesthetic Person

ARS MODUS OPERANDI

1	2	3	4	5	6	7
Correct conceptual form perceived in environment and reinforced by desire for knowledge and assurance (stereotypical/schematic)	Correct naturalistic forms (likeness)	Acceptance of deviation from likeness forms	Seeing abstraction in forms as a basis for art expression	Acceptance of personal deviations of abstraction and those of others as valid in art expression	Commitment to personal deviations of abstraction as valid in art expression	Balance of personal deviations of abstraction to preserve unity/oneness of art expression

mature, creative, and open adult becomes aware of a multiplicity of diverse solutions and a need for a balancing of a consideration of these in most situations. Decisions must be arrived at on one's own. Most educational experiences at the secondary level and beyond are planned to develop an acceptance and an ability for the adolescent to handle such a multiplicity and balance in decision making.

This *modus operandi* in life is reflected in a person's graphic art expression. (See Table 2, part B.) For example, young children (ages 4–8) try to find a correct or "right" way to draw people, houses, trees, and all the things that are meaningful in their lives. These things are depicted as symbols or schemata, which are repeated over and over again as the child believes he has found the right answers, the right way to draw a house, person, and so forth. For most children, these correct symbols come about after a period of searching and experimenting to find the "right" symbolic representation. Although there is a tendency to feel that these symbols are the same for all children, they are quite individual and personal depending upon the child's experiences and relationships with a particular object or person. As the child grows and develops, these concepts give way to visual percepts. In moving away from symbolic concepts, there is first a characterization that leads to a naturalistic emphasis on depicting distance, the effects of light, shadows, atmospheric qualities, textures and movement—a photographic emphasis. This development takes place in all children and, without art instruction, art expression usually remains at this level: from a somewhat schematic characterization to naturalism depending upon the child's perceptual/intellectual/emotional abilities.

However, with art instruction, the individual goes beyond this naturalism (seeing an object: tree, house, person per se) and learns to perceive abstraction (seeing lines, form, and color areas in all things) as the basis for art production and expression. Personal, creative deviations of the abstract are eventually accepted and the individual becomes committed to perception of the abstract as necessary for valid art expression. The need for a balance of unique, personal, expressive deviations also becomes a consideration. This combination, then, is the ultimate objective of education as seen in the art work of a creative, aesthetic individual: the development of an openness to and a balance of personal, creative deviations and a consideration of abstraction for the purpose of preserving unity and harmony in expression.

Objectives in visual art education should always be based upon the needs of students—learners/human beings—as they are distributed along this continuum. The field of art must also be considered. However, we should keep in mind that no field of study is as important as human beings and their learning and development, but it is our desire that adolescents become sensitive and aware and develop some expertise in the field of art for it is the area of visual art upon which the teacher relies in working with students. Nevertheless, needs of students should take precedence over those of the field. Herein, art/art experiences are used to help students in their learning/development move to a higher level of knowing (about themselves, art, and their culture), of feeling, of perceiving, and of personally/creatively expressing with art media. As a result, these refined sensitivities and concepts will vivify and enrich a student's entire life experience.

Evaluation should relate to the objectives with the means of evaluation being appropriate for the objectives in both studio art and art history/art appreciation. Evaluation, at best, is a subjective judgment based upon all the data that are

The sharp angles and well defined areas suggest that this student is going beyond naturalism and an awareness of the subject matter (a posing model) per se and is seeing abstractly—lines and shapes—as the basis for this portrait.

available. Such a judgment by the teacher is necessary to give insight concerning the next action to take in dealing with students to move them to a higher level of learning and development. Therefore, evaluation is a continual and crucial aspect of learning/teaching in the school art room.

STUDIO ART

Let us analyze the studio art experience as a means of education appropriate and valid for *all* persons after childhood. It is the studio experience that serves as the basis for most art programs and which the art instructor must thoroughly understand.

The Problem of the Artist

First of all, the problem of the artist, which may be thought of as underlying all studio art experience, remains somewhat constant (Michael, 1980). Art media, subject matter, symbolism, style, society, and economics may change and, on the surface, may lead us to believe that the problem has changed. But the basic problem of the artist has not changed! Every time a painter approaches a new canvas the same underlying problem is there. The approach and style may vary, but basically the problem remains the same. The problem Picasso faced as a young painter was the same problem he faced at the end of his career as a painter with years of experience. The problem the child or amateur faces in starting with a blank paper is the same as that of the professional artist.

The writer learned this lesson many years ago from study in a related art field: music. My marvelous teacher had sung at the Metropolitan Opera and had an uncanny understanding of her field. In the initial lessons she presented me with the problem of the artist in the field of music. Five years later she was still presenting me with exactly the same basic problem. But in the intervening years, I had begun to understand what the problem meant—her words began to take on new meaning as I progressed and began to feel and understand proper breathing, tonal quality, control, projection, and expression. Sometimes I felt that I could actually achieve the expression of the artist. I gradually began to realize that I was using the same approach in teaching my art classes by constantly reminding my students of the problem of the visual artist.

As teachers we must realize that, in the beginning, the problem of the artist in any of the arts may appear so complex, so foreign and overwhelming to the neophyte that it is difficult to comprehend the total meaning, the total Gestalt. Good teachers, however, do not give up but help students to understand and enjoy the challenge of the problem, a new vocabulary, revelations of the self, and the excitement of learning in a new area. Poor teachers attempt to simplify the problem by breaking it down into parts but usually lose the student's interest and understanding by trying to dissect art.

Exactly what is the problem of the artist? As art students and as teachers, we all know it innately when we do art but we need to clarify our thinking and express this verbally to our students. (See Chart 1.) Periodically, we also need to refresh ourselves by analyzing the process as we do our own art. Simply stated, *the problem*

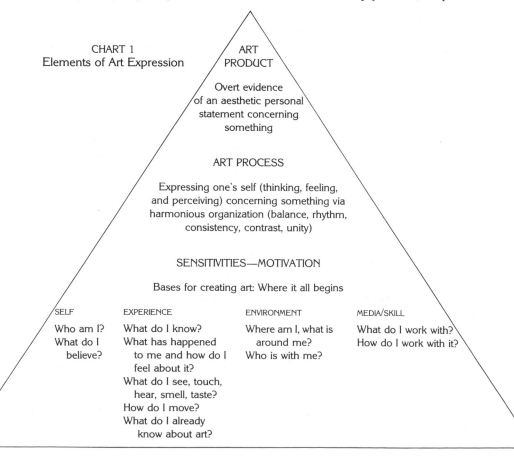

CHART 1
Elements of Art Expression

ART PRODUCT

Overt evidence of an aesthetic personal statement concerning something

ART PROCESS

Expressing one's self (thinking, feeling, and perceiving) concerning something via harmonious organization (balance, rhythm, consistency, contrast, unity)

SENSITIVITIES—MOTIVATION

Bases for creating art: Where it all begins

SELF
Who am I?
What do I believe?

EXPERIENCE
What do I know?
What has happened to me and how do I feel about it?
What do I see, touch, hear, smell, taste?
How do I move?
What do I already know about art?

ENVIRONMENT
Where am I, what is around me?
Who is with me?

MEDIA/SKILL
What do I work with?
How do I work with it?

Photo courtesy of Craig Roland

The problem the beginning student faces in starting to create art is the same as that of a professional artist: to express one's self aesthetically at the highest human level.

of the artist is to express one's self aesthetically at the highest human level. Let us analyze this statement more closely. The phrase, "to express one's self" means that the person is giving and projecting his or her point of view, interpretation, personal and individual feeling, thinking, and perceiving about something within one's experience and environment. In art, this projection is shown in visual form, an art product, created with various media. In music, it is done with sounds; in dance, with movement. This expression necessarily will be creative because each person is singular and unique (Jefferson, 1981). Clones are still science fiction so far as humans are concerned. If we do our "own thing" it will be an original and unique statement because each person is unique. "Aesthetically" has to do with sensitivity to color, shape, line, texture, form, movement, and value as these elements are ordered, arranged, composed, or simply put together so as to give a feeling of "presence," "completeness," and "unity." We have many principles that bring about a high level of ordering, such as balance, rhythm, contrast, variety, transition, opposition, consistency, and subordination. "At the highest human level" means that we use our human functions of thinking, feeling, and perceiving as best we can at any one time to express ourselves aesthetically. Here is where quality comes into the art experience. The wise teacher is always trying to extend the student to a higher and more sensitive level of achievement in each and all of these areas.

The Process of Creating Art

Having an awareness of the problem of the artist, let us now consider the process that should take place when one undergoes a studio experience in attempting to solve the problem of the artist. There appear to be five steps to the art process. Although some may not like to categorize these because several of the steps may happen simultaneously and not necessarily in a particular order, a listing does help one to understand the process and to become aware of what is happening to the student.

MOTIVATION.   First, of course, you must have something to say about whatever it is that you are doing, creating, interpreting, making, or expressing. Art is a means of communication, a visual language—what are *you* saying? Many artists have something in mind before they touch the canvas. This may be a vague idea, a suggestive sketch, or even a precise drawing. An artist may emphasize an abstract shape, tell a story, or make one aware of a mood. Some start with media, and ideas come as the medium is manipulated. These artists become stimulated through the thoughts and feelings that come to them from observing the medium in this situation. Edward Sturr (1982) suggests that secondary students, who are developing a self-consciousness, are also stimulated by conceptual concerns involving value and purpose in all aspects of art. This is made possible by the ability of

Note the feeling of destruction that is communicated in this photomontage, "And the Walls Came Tumbling Down."

adolescents to think abstractly, to judge and reflect. Art teachers, then, should challenge this intellectual potential by insisting upon reasons for all aspects of creating and observing art, as well as philosophical concerns. Sturr calls this "rational motivation," believing that knowledge and motivation are intimately connected. Certainly, it is true that intellect consciously plays a far greater role in the art experience of adolescents than that of young children.

Unfortunately, many art teachers only become concerned with developing skills in handling media and never let students do any art—never let them use the media and skills for personal expression. These art teachers tend to use art as a disciplinary means of controlling classes, afraid to let students think, feel, and perceive on their own and to express this in a creative and personal way. These teachers are "skill/product oriented," and in such classes all the products tend to look alike, being controlled by the teacher. Art becomes exercises with various media.

If students have nothing to say about a subject, they cannot use it as a basis for doing art. It behooves the teacher to place students in a situation wherein they will have ideas and feelings about what they have experienced. I have gone so far as to build a model house and burn it before my class to give students the feeling of flames and smoke consuming a burning building. The teacher with a flare for dramatics can dress in appropriate costumes (or have the students do so) and read or act out a particular scene, story, or poem. The possibilities for stimulation are endless for the creative teacher. However, most students have a bank of experiences upon which the teacher can draw.

CONFIDENCE IN ONE'S ABILITY TO EXPRESS WITH ART MEDIA.   To be emotionally open to new experiences and to possess a belief in one's self are not only prerequisites for creating art, but are important for one's mental health. The art student must feel "I can," and be willing to try to work with various art media. The wise art teacher is able to utilize *closure* experiences in art to achieve confidence for those students who are lacking in this attribute. Herein the teacher helps the student in getting started, the student completing the experience, which must end so that it will be perceived as being successful by both the student and the teacher. With the teacher pointing out specific aesthetic/perceptual/creative successes in a student's work over a period of time, the student begins to feel that he or she can do art and thus gains confidence. When students take the initiative in creating art, the teacher can be assured they are feeling secure in their ability to express themselves.

There are many ways to bring about closure experiences; however, media are frequently used for this purpose in art classes. A typical example is the wet paper approach to using water-based paint media wherein the paper is soaked with water and various colors of paint are dropped on it. As the colors run and mix together, the student sees various shapes and forms that remind him of previous experiences and serve as inspiration to continue working on the picture, finally completing the forms suggested by the mixed colors. Scribbling over the page is another closure approach. The student "finds" something in the scribbled lines and develops the suggested objects by continuing to draw and add to them. Drawing a line on a blank page and asking the student to make it into something is another form of closure. For students who lack confidence, the art teacher must be very encouraging and supportive during these initial experiences by praising students for "finding"

This painting was started by dropping watercolors on wet paper—a closure experience approach. As the colors ran, objects and ideas were brought to mind by the student, who was emotionally disturbed and hyperactive. The flowing colors and forceful lines express his desire for movement and action.

ideas as well as for continuing work on the picture. Usually many such experiences are needed to convince students that they can do art work, that they are creative. In such closure situations, it is possible to develop knowledge and many sensitivities about color, expression, composition, and other aesthetic aspects, in addition to bringing about a feeling of confidence. The development of such awareness and knowledge reinforces confidence because students are developing an art vocabulary and knowledge of the field and will find themselves verbalizing about what they had previously been afraid to do. Most students are at various levels in the area of confidence in their ability to express themselves in art. I have found students who were very free and expressive in drawing and painting but were afraid to touch clay or anything three dimensional. I have also seen teachers who were reluctant to teach various art areas. All need to develop confidence to the point where they feel free to express themselves in any media and with any subject. However, it is only natural that most of us have preferences for various subjects and media. The art teacher should honor these by stimulating students to go beyond their usual expression of a subject, taking it to a higher level. Learning must always take place.

KNOWLEDGE OF ART AND ART PROCESSES AND PROCEDURES. Not only must students have something to say and have the confidence to communicate this, but they must also know the problem of the artist—what is the artist trying to do when he makes art? What is his purpose as an artist? This is where so many art teachers fail their students, assuming that to stimulate and encourage are the only requirements of the art teacher. Not so! Students must know what artists try to do, the problem of the artist. This must be kept before students and explained on each student's level, be it kindergarten or college.

In addition, students must understand the media and the art procedure with which they are involved. Aspects of these are generally easily explained but should not be omitted since they are important considerations of the art process. Without a familiarity and understanding of the limitations and characteristics of the medium and the procedures related to it, students may become hopelessly discouraged.

As students become involved in their art work, art history and the whole field of art should be introduced so that students see themselves and their work on a continuum with that of the field. This is especially important at the secondary level when perceptual development is usually well under way. It is then that students can identify with art work based upon visual perception and can relate this, in turn, to their own art expression. Seeing relationships and similarities between their own work and that of others is, indeed, ego building and aids greatly in developing their confidence and understanding/appreciation of the field of art.

SKILL IN THE USE OF MEDIA.   Students must develop enough skill in working with a medium so that they can express their wishes. For very young children, the only skill necessary is to be able to make marks with a crayon and for the eyes to focus upon the lines created. For older students, particularly adolescents, skills with media, tools, and processes become intriguing and challenging. Unfortunately,

Here we see a student experimenting with media (watercolor and ink) and value, but keeping the subject, the dog, constant. Knowledge of media, as well as processes, are important for adolescents.

some art teachers use this desire to develop skill as an end in itself. The art curriculum then becomes a series of skillfully executed exercises with no art work being produced. Every product made with art materials is not necessarily a work of art. It may be merely an objective report, ably done but with no personal involvement, expression, or feeling. The product becomes superficial with no "soul" or expression. It is the wise art teacher who appropriately develops the skill of the students *as a means for them to create art*. Skill should always be a secondary consideration and should contribute to the expression so as to bring about a harmonious integration (skill/media/expression).

EVALUATION OF EFFORTS.   Indeed, it would be an unusual person who did not evaluate what he has done. Certainly this procedure is not unique to the art field. In my survey (1970) of more than 350 professional artists, it was found that almost nine out of ten do consciously make an aesthetic judgment of what is good and bad in their art work after the work is finished. However, only 20 percent compare it with others' work during work in progress, and only 42 percent compare it with others' after completion. In an effort to find out how they evaluate their work, the artists were asked, "How do you know when your art work is finished?" Their responses suggest many ways in which a work of art can be evaluated. These can be summarized as follows:

1. Intuition, one feels it
2. Technically complete, excellent craftsmanship
3. Requirements demanded by the artist are fulfilled; the problem is solved; idea is embodied
4. Complete expression, says all the artist wanted to say
5. Aesthetically satisfying design, visually successful; unified clarity, parts related to the whole; suitable equilibrium achieved
6. Dictation by the art piece; authoritarian sense of rightness; unique aesthetic personality, life of its own
7. Comparison with one's other work—each new piece must say something new and more
8. Deterioration of interest, no urge to continue
9. No change is possible without altering the whole; anything added would detract
10. Ideas for other work emerge; it starts to change into something else
11. Possibilities for continuing are exhausted; cannot think of anything else to do

The above may serve as a guide to the art teacher in helping students evaluate their own work via questions, comments, and suggestions.

Objectives/Evaluation

For the art teacher, the purpose of evaluation is to gain insight into the student's fulfillment of the learning objectives in order to determine what to do next (instruction versus outcomes), all for the purpose of having the student learn more, progress to a higher level of accomplishment and expression. Evaluation is, in reality, a form of research that alters what we do. For the purpose of evaluation, one must always refer back to one's objectives, which derive from the problem of the artist and the studio art process. The student and the teacher should be aware of the same objectives. These objectives, based upon the problem of the artist, have been formulated here as questions that may characterize the stance of the student learner as he produces works of art.

Communication/Expression

Does the work indicate what the student was trying to say, to communicate? Is the expressive concern(s) of the student apparent in the visual statement? Does the student understand the subject matter? The communication should be obvious concerning mood, feeling, texture, pattern, form, or whatever the student is trying to tell us. However, some artists purposely veil their statements and, when this happens, it must be taken into consideration as an aspect of the artist's purpose.

Confidence/Self-Esteem

Does the work indicate that the student was confident and unrestrained in approaching his art? This is shown in the deftness and sureness in handling the subject matter and media. Lines may be bold and forceful, precise and measured, delicate and demure, or free and flowing, but all are put down with a feeling that

This drawing, made on scratchboard, conveys an eerie mood through the subject matter and the handling of value that the student desired to communicate/express.

the artist "knew what he was doing." A lack of confidence and emotional problems generally are indicated by imitation, copy work, and stereotypes.

Perceptual Development

Does the work indicate perceptual awareness and sensitivity? Has the student been cognizant of what he has seen (lines, colors, textures, shapes, movements), touched, heard, or smelled? Some styles and approaches to art tend to emphasize one aspect of perception more than another. For very young children, visual perception is usually not shown in their expression with art media; however, cognition is. Usually, until the age of nine, the child symbolizes visual percepts, which are expressed as mentally derived schemata in drawings. However, most adolescents are well into perceptual development, which more and more takes on a refinement via correct proportions, perspective, and details, or expressive exaggeration of important parts and body feelings—autoplastic sensations. Whether the cognitive symbols of the young child, or the strong visual percepts and/or body feelings of the adolescent, or a combination of these, an awareness of the world is reflected in one's art work—in interpretation and projection.

Aesthetic Organization and Consistency

Does the work indicate aesthetic sensitivity, harmonious organization, and consistency? The basic aspect of any aesthetic consideration is order or an ordering that is complete, unified, and consistent. Such an order involves not only shapes

Photo courtesy of Craig Roland

Perceptual experiences involving touch make for greater sensitivity—to the texture of tree bark in this instance. The blindfold tends to emphasize tactile experience.

and forms, but also color, texture, and all other elements in the composition. Artists order and compose in many different ways; there is no one way. However, various types of composition tend to become more fashionable in one period than in another. For example, whereas formal balance seems to characterize the eighteenth century, informal balance appears to be looked upon with great favor today. But as long as there is an ordering that is harmonious and consistent, an aesthetic sensitivity is indicated by the artist.

Knowledge of the Field of Art

Does the work indicate a knowledge of art and art history? Knowledge of the problem of the artist, as well as various styles and periods of art are important, especially for advanced students. Usually the more knowledge students have about art and art history, the more advanced will be their aesthetic achievement in studio work, because such knowledge provides students with a philosophic base from which to reach out in their own work. For example, some may work with line, or texture, or with cubistic overtones while others may work from an expressionistic or surrealistic base, or with any other stylistic consideration.

Creativity

Does the art work indicate creativity, uniqueness, and originality? Is it a personal statement? Unusual colors, shapes, configurations, composition, and the original handling of subject matter and media are all indicative of an individual and personal statement. The art work tends to be different from that of others; it tends to "stand alone." Children are usually creative when very young, but tend to lose this attribute as they grow older. Creative art experiences counteract this trend and should be given emphasis during adolescence.

Skill/Craftsmanship

Does the art work indicate skill in handling media and processes that are appropriate for the expression? Technical excellence is indicative of physical discipline and control of media and process. However, skill and process must not overwhelm the expression, but contribute to it in such a way that technical handling becomes an integral aspect of the total statement. Media and skill must be suited to the idea expressed.

Enjoyment/Satisfaction

Does the art work indicate that the student was involved, enjoyed the experience, and probably has a good attitude toward art? Usually the depth of involvement is indicated by the candor of expression and the technical excellence of the piece. One who enjoys his work tends to relate well to the subject, media, and total Gestalt, spending the time and effort necessary for a high level of achievement. Needless to say, for the beginner this will necessarily not be at the same level of one who has been working with the medium and process for a long time. However, the beginner may still be greatly involved and enjoy the experience even though the product may be somewhat naïve.

Desire motivates the development of skill and coordination. Aesthetic/creative success encourages an even more skillful handling of media. Appropriate emotions follow any action.

The preceding eight objectives and criteria for evaluation review the many personal attributes that tend to combine cognitive, affective, and motor considerations that can be developed via the creative studio art experience in the hands of a good art teacher. These objectives have been classified in Table 3; however, no hierarchy is intended. The importance of the various behaviors under each heading will depend upon the student's needs as viewed by the art teacher. Surely, these overall objectives are important for the evaluation of all human beings: *communication/expression*; *confidence/self-esteem*; *perceptual development*; *aesthetic organization and consistency*; *knowledge of the field of art*; *creativity*; *skill/ craftsmanship*; and *enjoyment/satisfaction*. Art teachers should not shy away from a listing of purposes or rationales for including studio art experiences in school. These experiences can heighten the development of all the basic human abilities of thinking, feeling, and perceiving in addition to bringing about an integration of all experience via the aesthetic organization that occurs when one creates a piece of art work. (See Appendix 3.) Art teachers need to make others aware of these attributes (objectives) of studio art experiences while also making students in their classes aware. It is here that we have our greatest audience and can do the most good—for our students and for ourselves, and for an understanding/appreciation of art by society.

TABLE 3
Evaluation: Studio Art Experience and Art Work[1]

Using this evaluation, a profile of student achievement in studio art work in relation to eight learning objectives can be compiled. Rate the achievement for each behavior, using a scale of No, None, or Little to Yes, Very Much. Insert the rating in the blank at the right of each entry.

Objective Concerns	*No⟷Yes*

1. COMMUNICATION/EXPRESSION

Does the student have something to say, to express, something he wants to communicate in the art work? _____

Are the expressive concerns of the student evidence of a mood or feeling, and readily apparent in the art work? _____

Does the art work indicate an understanding of the subject matter? _____

Does the student freely discuss his objectives for doing the art work, in group and individual evaluations? _____

Is the student's expression sincere; is it truly representative? _____

Is the student able to communicate expressively with a variety of art media? _____

2. CONFIDENCE/SELF-ESTEEM

Is the student confident in his ability to express ideas, feelings, and perceptions with art media? _____

Is the student flexible, being able to work with many media? _____

Is the student open to changes in plans in the art room? _____

Does the student find satisfaction and pride in his own art work? _____

Does the student recognize strengths in his art work and make the most of them; does the student recognize weaknesses in his art work and do something about them? _____

Does the student show initiative toward self-directed art goals? _____

Does the student show an ability/desire for leadership in the art class? _____

Does the student relate aesthetic values to his whole life? _____

3. PERCEPTUAL DEVELOPMENT

Has the student developed sensitivity to visual qualities in the environment, such as light, color, space, proportion, distance, shadows, and volume as shown in his art work? _____

Has the student developed sensitivity to nonvisual qualities, such as auditory, tactile, kinesthetic, and body sensations as shown in his art work? _____

Does the student perceive visual and/or nonvisual qualities as sources of expression? _____

Is the student sensitive to small differences in shape, color, line, value, and texture? _____

4. AESTHETIC ORGANIZATION AND CONSISTENCY

Does the student understand relationships concerning ideas and materials: could it have been done better in another medium? _____

Is there a harmonious organization of line, form, color, value, and texture in the art work? _____

Are all the parts of the student's expression consistent and related to the whole? _____

Does the art work indicate a sensitivity and awareness of art principles, such as balance, rhythm, subordination, variety, and contrast? _____

Does the artwork tend to have a presence, a sense of "being," and a unity all its own? _____

(continued on next page)

TABLE 3 (*continued*)

Objective Concerns	No⟵⟶Yes
Is the student concerned with the organization and appearance of the visual environment, as well as his art work?	_____
Has the student progressed in ability to solve more complex aesthetic problems in his own art work?	_____
Is the student aware of the aesthetic quality of the various aspects in his everyday life?	_____

5. KNOWLEDGE OF THE FIELD OF ART

Can the student identify art processes, tools, media, as well as the problem of the artist?	_____
Can the student predict what various tools/media will do?	_____
Can the student identify/analyze pattern/structure in his art work?	_____
Can the student evaluate the method of working, media, composition, and expression of his art work in relation to the art of others—past and present?	_____
Does the student comprehend abstract concepts concerning art?	_____
Can the student identify various influences of artists and styles of working in his art work, such as Cubism, Expressionism, Symbolism, and Surrealism?	_____

6. CREATIVITY

Is the student sensitive in recognizing problems that exist in the art work at hand?	_____
Does the student generate personal and unique (verbal and visual) ideas for his art work?	_____
Does the student show independent, inventive, original, and uncommon colors, shapes, and composition in the art work at hand?	_____
Is there an interpretation of the student's feelings, perceptions, and ideas in a personal and individual manner?	_____
Can the student redefine lines, shapes, colors, forms, and various materials into new relationships, for example, a button may become an eye in a collage?	_____
Does the student investigate diversified solutions in solving aesthetic problems?	_____
Has the student developed a conscious awareness of the uniqueness of himself and others?	_____
Is the student fluent, having many ideas occurring as he works?	_____
Is the student flexible and able to adjust and find solutions as problems arise in the art work?	_____
Is the student able to penetrate and analyze, go from the whole to the parts, in the art work?	_____
Is the student able to synthesize, start with parts and build a whole from these, in his art work?	_____

7. SKILL/CRAFTSMANSHIP

Has the student developed and improved his skill in handling materials, tools, and processes?	_____
Does the student have control over the art work, being able to depict or deviate from naturalistic proportions and increase or lessen details at will?	_____
Can the student use various types of lines, shapes, and colors when he desires to do so?	_____
Does the student take care of tools and equipment, keeping them in good workable condition?	_____

Objective Concerns   No⟵⟶Yes

8. ENJOYMENT/SATISFACTION

Does the student enjoy producing art work?   _____
Does the student seek out opportunities to do art work?   _____
Does the student encourage others to get involved in art experiences?   _____
Does the student express a satisfaction with his own art experiences and art
products?   _____
Does the student desire to exhibit his art work?   _____
Does the student talk about art with others?   _____
Does the student get involved in art experiences outside the art room in
other aspects of life, such as purchasing art books and reproductions, and
listening to art programs?   _____

¹See also Appendix 2, "Outcomes of a Secondary Art Program."

ART HISTORY/ART APPRECIATION

It is an accepted point of view in the field of art education that students in art classes in addition to becoming confident, creative, expressive, and aesthetic in the use of art media and aware of aesthetic aspects of the environment should also become knowledgeable about art/art history and develop a favorable attitude and interest that we call art appreciation. Initially, every discipline has been concerned that students not only become acquainted with the content of their field but also develop an appreciation of it. However, over a period of time, for one reason or another, teachers in a given field tend to become indifferent and to disregard the student's attitude toward the area. We concentrate upon the factual content, upon knowing about the field. Krathwohl, Bloom, and Masia (1964, p. 16) found that, among educators, there is a real shift toward the cognitive that comes with time, and that the erosion of affective (attitudinal) objectives is a result of the difficulty of grading student achievements based upon affective objectives; the difficulty of instructing for affective goals; and slowness in the attainment of affective objectives.

Although most secondary art programs are based primarily upon studio art experiences, some knowledge of art works of the present and past and an appreciation of such works should be a vital aspect of the program. Only to know art processes and qualities and to be able to express one's self with media deprive the adolescent of a background necessary for a deeper and more profound approach to art and to life itself. The study of art history and the development of art appreciation, then, are other important objectives of art education.

Art history, including the art work of contemporary artists, may be defined as a study of artists, their art products, and aesthetic and other events of the past and present (cognitive aspects) that affect the work. Art appreciation may be defined as a valuing, a feeling of the importance of such work (affective aspects). It should also be noted that an appreciation of one's own art work and the tools and processes involved in studio art production are equally important. Some scholars have used other terms to denote art appreciation—such as interest, attitude, and even preference. However, art appreciation as a term is a concept of long standing in the field of art and has come to have a special meaning—referring to many aspects concerned with the valuing of art.

The Problem of Art in Our Culture

Before one considers the study of art history and the development of art appreciation in the classroom, one must look at the society and its cultural values from which our students come. Too many of us, as art teachers, assume that our students and their parents are as interested and involved in art as we are, and we cannot understand why our students do not become ecstatic when shown reproductions or slides of De Kooning, Cézanne, Rembrandt, or Chartres Cathedral. Many students appear to have been "turned off" to art history before they come to us, desiring only to paint, to weave, to make jewelry, or to throw pots.

We must remember that art is not generally accepted by many people as being a vitally important aspect of our American culture and the school curriculum. Our Puritan work ethic and the newness of our country probably are two important reasons for this attitude (Rockefeller, 1977, p. 19). Whereas the children of Milan or Salisbury or Cologne grow up in the shadow of great cathedrals built many centuries ago and filled with beautiful sculptures, stained glass windows, and paintings or mosaics, Americans grow up with the gas station on the corner, TV graphics, and the cacophony of flashy electric signs and store fronts on the commercial strip so typical of all our cities. Our houses, for the most part, either lack consistency and are not reflective of our time or become monotonous because of a mass-produced sameness. Children who grow up in older cultures know art history firsthand through seeing and living with historic monuments. When art is around it becomes a landmark and infiltrates the thoughts and feelings of people and they become protective of it. Parents' values concerning art are passed on to their children and art becomes a part of their lives. Americans grow up with a pioneer heritage of cowboys and wide open spaces that is reflected in an emphasis on nature and the great national parks of the West. Now, in our industrialized society, Americans continue to value the conquering of the environment, but the emphasis is on technology and material ends.

However, as our country matures and ages, we are becoming more and more aware of our aesthetic heritage, a fact borne out by museum attendance and public involvement in the arts (*Americans and the Arts*, 1981). Recent interest in the register of historic buildings and landmarks and the restoration of old buildings, as well as the price tags on paintings at auctions are examples of this change in attitude. Concern for the aesthetic quality of our cities, especially the core areas, is another indication of our developing sensitivity. Examples can be seen from Market Street in San Francisco to Faneuil Hall in Boston to riverfront redevelopments in Louisville, Cincinnati, New Orleans, and other river cities. Most people do not realize that we are becoming design and art conscious because no art title has been given to this movement and because it has come about so gradually. Therefore, the art teacher may find that students do not make any connection between the experiences in the art room and the new City Center Plaza in their town or the restoration of Olde Town with its brick sidewalks. This connection must be made if we are to alleviate the reluctance to accept art as a vital and contributing aspect of our lives. The secondary school level is an excellent time to build an awareness and knowledge of art history and to develop an appreciation of the importance of art in our daily lives, in our community, and in the world.

The Process of Viewing Art

The point of view or approach one holds in viewing, criticizing, and/or evaluating a work of art, one's own or that of others past or present, will determine how one values or appreciates it. The student may approach art from several philosophic bases of which the art teacher should be aware. Students must be helped in assuming an approach or in combining approaches and must be made aware of the basis of their approach so as to develop an understanding of their own value system concerning art. Now let us consider four approaches as developed by Stephen C. Pepper (1945, ch. 2–5) that characterize the process of viewing art.

Hedonistic Approach

The most frequently encountered beginning approach of many students is hedonistic in that it is based upon the immediate feelings of pleasure and/or displeasure the art object produces in the viewer: pleasures of the senses, of association, of composition, and of recognition. The amount (number), duration, and intensity of pleasure(s) become the relevant and quantitative standards. Since pleasures received from objects vary from person to person and with one's mood and physiological state, it follows that all elementary aesthetic judgments are relative. The same object may give a different amount of pleasure, or even displeasure, to another or to the same person at another time. The student using the hedonist approach sees a work of art through the sources of delight in sensation and images of form. At the highest level, a work of great aesthetic value, then, is one that affords a great deal of immediate pleasure to a highly discriminatory taste. Aesthetic value of a work of art has nothing to do with the number of people who enjoy it but with the amount of enjoyment it gives to those who are discriminating enough to enjoy it. While students, upon a first encounter with a work of art, may say, "I like it," or "I don't like it," the more they become acquainted with art objects of similar nature, the more discriminating will be their taste. For example, the more Impressionistic paintings that students observe and study, the more discriminating they will become and the more they will enjoy the works they consider as having great quality. The art teacher, following up on this approach, should provide the student with information and many examples of the particular type of art work under consideration, for example, Impressionistic paintings. The hedonist views a work of art as a physical object outside of a person. The direct objects of aesthetic value are the sensations and images stimulated by the external physical object or associated with it.

Contextualistic Approach

All the considerations of the hedonistic approach are changed in the contextualistic approach wherein appreciation depends upon the context of the activity, the vividness of the "situation" in which one views the object. Herein the person becomes a constant consideration, and every situation has a unique quality and depends upon the person's perception causing each situation to have a certain character and quality. Emphasis is placed upon the unique quality of the experience that results in the criterion: the more vivid the experience and the more extensive and rich its quality to the person, the greater its aesthetic value. Vividness is brought about by the unusual, nontraditional, intuitive, and creative aspects of the situation. Habit and convention dull experience. Any pleasure contained in the experience is purely incidental and is simply a contribution from the person involved in it. The situation itself is independent. Intensity and depth of experience become the contextualistic standard of beauty. According to John Dewey (1934), who subscribed to this approach, the highest aesthetic experience occurs when the total situation is absorbed in a vivid, fused, satisfying quality. Vividness of quality can be increased by the "discreet use of conflict" and the "spread of quality." These may be accomplished by carefully planning all details of the situation. A well planned experience of keeping students in the hall before showing them a painting that is spotlighted in a darkened room is an example of the teacher developing an intensely vivid experience involving some conflict. The contextualist's conception of a work of art is that of a succession of cumulative perceptions leading up to a total Gestalted perception that takes into account all the aspects of the physical art object, as well as other aspects, such as the location of the art work, lighting, time of day, background music, and the attitude of the viewer when the object is seen. One becomes aware of a work of art by many separate experiences with it, each experience giving a new and different aspect according to the situation each time one views the work, all of which enlarges upon one's previous total Gestalt.

Organicistic Approach

A third approach may be called organicistic, the viewing of art that stresses an internal relatedness, the organization of the piece. This approach deals with an integration within the art piece wherein everything belongs and is related to everything else; every part "fits" with all the other parts. Like the hedonists, the organicists perceive the aesthetic field to be defined by its origins among pleasures. This is explained by feeling the demand of pleasant things for other pleasant things to complete them or to enlarge upon them. This idea was put forth by Coleridge (Pepper, 1946), in what he termed "creative imagination," a process of following out and building up feeling connections of what ought to be, what should come next. A work of art, then, is judged by the degree of integration (thoroughness with which feeling connections are carried out in an aesthetic object) and the amount of material integrated (where every detail of the object calls for every other detail and no feeling demands are unfulfilled). No detail can be taken away or altered without marring or affecting the whole—the organic unity of the piece. The viewer simply follows the paths of achievement in the creation of the piece, questioning aspects or parts where inconsistencies, frustrations, or gaps occur, the ideal being when all parts of the art work function in a consistent and unified manner that is expected by the viewer. Herein, the student views the work and is pleased with the completeness of all the parts—the whole seeming to be more than the sum of the parts.

Normistic Approach

Another approach to viewing art is the normistic, which is concerned with norms, with normal perception and judgment of values, versus a perception and judgment that diverges markedly from the anticipated. The hedonist would look at the abnormal simply as a freakish or perverted taste but so far as the person feels he enjoys them, they are his values. The contextualist would regard abnormal taste as a failure to take in all the factors of a situation. The organicist would carry this a step farther, noting that the peculiar taste precluded an integration, a harmonious fitting together of the parts of the piece. Normism stresses the fact of the normal, seeks to isolate it, and to define value in terms of it. Plato and Aristotle were exponents of this view which persists in much of classical thought. An example of this approach in science would be when the norm of the species becomes a norm of value. Aesthetic value, accordingly, is the representation of a norm, such as the *ideal* (most representative) cubistic painting. This is the basis of the approach in defining beauty as imitation, not imitation or copying of a particular object but of the norm that the object represents. The artist seeks the norm, the universal through the particular. If he is working as a cubist, he must subscribe to all the ramifications of this style to produce a cubistic painting of quality. Beauty then becomes the degree in which the artist has been able to find the universal in the particular and exhibits the ideal. The more characteristic is the painting of cubism, the better it is. The work of art thus acquires a universality of value embodying universal norms. In this approach, style, craftsmanship, and culture (expression of an age) all become norms and a basis for analysis and evaluation of art works. Students subscribing to normism would evaluate works of art according to ideal norms noting the style or type of work in any evaluation; for example, "This is a good *cubistic* painting," or "This is a fine example of *French Gothic* architecture."

Eclectic Approach

In viewing art, most persons are not purists in applying the above approaches. They do not subscribe to any one approach, but develop a personal approach that combines various aspects of the four approaches. In so doing, a broader consideration is given the art that may lead to a deeper understanding and appreciation thereof. Definitions may be developed with students and may serve as a basis for valuing and viewing art/art experiences. For example, an aesthetic object is a normal perceptual integration of feelings highly pleasant and vivid in quality. An aesthetic experience is one vivid in quality, highly organized, and a source of immediate enjoyment. Ways of dealing with art history and art appreciation in the classroom are presented in chapter 4.

Objectives/Evaluation

Whereas art history deals with knowledges, concepts, and information—the cognitive—art appreciation, on the other hand, deals with feeling, attitude, and valuing—the affective. Although both knowledge and feeling may occur simultaneously, evaluation of art history and appreciation must be considered separately. As in studio art, evaluation can only take place in reference to what we, as teachers, are trying to accomplish with our students. Objectives, then, should be clearly in mind in each area.

A committee of college and university examiners (Bloom, 1956; Krathwohl, Bloom, and Masia, 1964) developed ordered classifications, called taxonomies, under which educational objectives fall. Such a hierarchy permits the teacher to see levels of achievement and to determine which objective/behavior is more advanced than another. With this information, the art teacher can plan a series of experiences for the art class that will gradually bring about a higher level of participation and learning. These taxonomies can only be applied in part to the studio experience because it involves an integration of the cognitive, affective, and motor activities. As yet no generally accepted classification has been developed for motor experiences.

Art History

Objectives/evaluation concerned with the student's knowledge of art history are similar to the objectives/evaluation of knowledge in academic subjects such as math, history, and science. The loftiest objective in the cognitive domain involves critical judgment in terms of internal and external evidence/accuracy in reporting facts, documentation, and the comparison of facts, theories, generalizations and standards concerning various individual works of art, styles, schools, countries, and periods. Herein the teacher usually uses a simple to complex approach starting with knowledge of vocabulary and classifications of art, progressing to a higher level involving judgment, art criticism, and analysis. In achieving objectives, the creative teacher will use many teaching styles and approaches. (See chapter 5.) Table 4 classifies levels of objectives and examples of corresponding student behaviors which indicate achievement of these as the student develops cognitive aspects concerning art history.

TABLE 4
Evaluation: Art History (The Cognitive Domain)

With the aid of this evaluation scale, a profile of student achievement in art history in relation to objectives in the cognitive domain can be compiled. Rate the achievement for each behavior, using a scale of No, None, or Little to Yes, Very Much. Insert the rating in the blank at the right of each entry.

Cognitive Levels (Goals)	*No⟵⟶Yes*
1. Knowledge (recall, remembering, bringing to mind the appropriate material)	
1.1 Knowledge of specifics in art history	
Does the student know terms and/or facts (dates, events, persons, places, art work) in the history of art?	_____
1.2 Knowledge of ways and means of dealing with specifics	
Does the student know conventions, trends, sequences, classification/ categories, criteria for judging, and/or methods of study in the field of art history?	_____
1.3 Knowledge of universals and abstractions in art history	
Does the student know the principles and generalizations, theories, and structures of art history?	_____
2. Comprehension (the lowest level of understanding)	
2.1 Translation	
Can the student paraphrase information concerning historical works of art in a faithful and accurate manner, giving an objective part-for-part rendering of a communication?	_____
2.2 Interpretation	
Can the student reorder, rearrange, and present a new view of the material?	_____
2.3 Extrapolation	
Can the student go beyond the given data to determine implications,	

consequences, corollaries, and/or effects based on the information at
hand?

3. Application
    Can the student apply abstractions (general ideas or methods of art
    history) in particular and concrete situations; can the student make
    predictions based upon the information at hand?

4. Analysis (breakdown of historical art works into their constituent elements so
   that the relative hierarchy of ideas is made clear and explicit)
   4.1 Analysis of elements
       Can the student identify the important elements in the historical work
       of art?
   4.2 Analysis of relationships
       Can the student make connections and see interrelationships based
       upon the given information and assumptions concerning historical
       works of art?
   4.3 Analysis of organizational principles
       Can the student recognize form, pattern, structure, and consistency in
       works of art as well as the significance of the historical period and
       place, when and where they were created, as aids in understanding
       their meaning?

5. Synthesis (putting together elements and parts in such a way as to constitute a pattern or structure not clearly there before)
   5.1 Production of a unique communication
       Can the student communicate (write or speak) using an excellent or-
       ganization of ideas, feelings, and/or experiences in his statements
       concerning historical works of art?
   5.2 Production of a plan or proposed set of operations
       Can the student develop a plan of work or operations concerning his-
       torical works of art?
   5.3 Derivation of a set of abstract relations
       Can the student formulate appropriate hypotheses, develop a set of
       abstract relations to classify or explain particular phenomena con-
       cerning historical works of art?

6. Evaluation (quantitative and qualitative judgments about the extent to which
   certain historical works of art satisfy criteria)
   6.1 Judgments in terms of internal evidence
       Can the student indicate logical fallacies in arguments based upon
       logical accuracy (documentation, proof), consistency, and other inter-
       nal criteria concerning historical works of art?
   6.2 Judgments in terms of external criteria
       Can the student evaluate the works of art of the past with reference
       to certain remembered criteria; can the student compare a work of
       art of the past with the highest known standards, especially with other
       works of recognized excellence?

Art Appreciation

The highest level of appreciation and/or positive attitude toward art/art experience is the development of a group of values that are internally consistent, a
value system or philosophic approach that tends to characterize the individual in

everything he does. This, then, is our ultimate objective—a well formulated value system concerning art. However, the teacher must start at the level of the student. The taxonomy of the affective domain permits us to identify where the student is in his development and aids us in developing appropriate goals which are challenging in present and future learning experiences. Table 5 classifies levels of objectives and examples of corresponding student behaviors as they view art work.

Attitude scales have been developed by Michael Stuckhardt (1976) and Stuckhardt and Jerry Morris (1977, 1980) which indicate a positive or negative change in a student's attitude toward art experiences. Such scales are given before art instruction and again after instruction. An improved score indicates a positive change in attitude. The Wilson-Stuckhardt Art Attitude Scale was designed especially for secondary art students. (See Appendix 1.) By using this scale and Table 5, the art teacher can obtain a good indication of the student's attitude/appreciation of art.

TABLE 5
Evaluation: Art Appreciation (The Affective Domain)

With the aid of this evaluation scale, a profile of student achievement in art appreciation in relation to objectives in the affective domain can be compiled. Rate the achievement for each behavior, using a scale of No, None, or Little to Yes, Very Much. Insert the rating in the blank at the right of each entry.

Affective Levels (Goals)	*No*←——→*Yes*
1. Receiving (attending)	
1.1 Awareness	
Is the student conscious of the existence of the art work?	
(The student is aware that a painting is in the room.)	_____
1.2 Willingness to receive	
Does the student give attention to the art work?	
(The student notes the painting in the room is of a woman.)	_____
1.3 Controlled or selected attention	
Does the student note the art work despite competing stimuli?	
(Of all the paintings in the room, the student studies only the painting of the woman.)	_____
2. Responding	
2.1 Acquiescence in responding	
Does the student make a response concerning the art work when asked?	
(If asked, the student says there is a painting of a woman in the room.)	_____
2.2 Willingness to respond	
Does the student voluntarily and from his own choice tell about the art work without being asked?	
(The student describes the painting voluntarily.)	_____
2.3 Satisfaction in response	
Does the student respond, feel satisfied, and enjoy the art work?	
(The student describes the painting and is proud of his description.)	_____
3. Valuing	
3.1 Acceptance of a value	
Does the student accept and like the art work when it is viewed but is somewhat tentative and may change?	

(The student notes that the painting is acceptable but there may be other paintings that are better.)

_____

3.2 Preference for a value

Is the student committed to the art work, seeking it out and preferring it over other works of art?

(The student prefers the painting of a woman by Picasso and looks up reproductions of Picasso's work in books.)

_____

3.3 Commitment

Does the student have a strong conviction and certainty, having no doubts at all, and even trying to convince others concerning the quality of the art work?

(The student praises Picasso and his art work and tells others they should also like Picasso.)

_____

4. Organization (internalization of many values, building a system)

4.1 Conceptualization of a value

Does the student see how a value concerning the art work relates to those he already holds?

(The student identifies aspects of Picasso's work that are preferred, such as his line quality, color, symbolism.)

_____

4.2 Organization of a value system

Does the student bring various values concerning works of art into some order that is consistent and harmonious?

(A specific type of line quality is preferred by the student whenever it is seen, not just in the work of Picasso.)

_____

5. Characterization by a value or value complex

5.1 Generalized set

Does the student possess a group of values concerning art work that gives internal consistency; does the student possess a determining tendency and orientation toward phenomena, a predisposition to act in a certain way concerning art work?

(The student is consistently sensitive to line quality in all art work, not just in the work of Picasso.)

_____

5.2 Characterization

Does the student possess a value system concerning art that tends to characterize him almost completely?

(The student internalizes particular aspects of art, such as sensitivity to line quality, which are noted in his own art work and everything that is experienced in life itself. The student consistently lives his beliefs.)

_____

Adapted from D. R. Krathwohl et al., *Taxonomy of Educational Objectives, Handbook II*, pp. 176–185. Copyright © 1956 by Longman, Inc. Reprinted by permission of Longman, Inc., New York.

COLLECTING INFORMATION FOR EVALUATION

There are many ways of collecting data that shed light upon the educational progress of students. The most obvious and tangible evidence is, of course, the art products made by the students themselves. Unfortunately, many art teachers believe student art works are the only aspects of the student's behavior that can or should be evaluated. To collect and evaluate only the art products will give a somewhat limited understanding concerning the student's learning. Over the years, psychologists who have been involved with art education have pointed out the importance of the art process—the work period—as a time for learning much about the student (Krotzsch, 1917; Buhler, 1930; Lowenfeld, 1957). Observation of the student during the art process is necessary to answer many of the questions in the evaluation charts presented in this chapter.

Other means of gathering information for evaluation purposes are self-evaluation records, rating scales, and interest inventories. (See Appendix 3 for examples of rating scales.) These are especially revealing of confidence/sensitivity and achievement in art expression and attitude toward one's self. Informational tests can be used to determine knowledge of any aspect of art that has been presented in class. Less definitive means of collecting information but very revealing are written statements, individual conferences, class discussions, anecdotal records noting specific behaviors of the student, and exhibits selected and arranged by students. A culminating program or project by the class or a group of students may also indicate the level of learning by the students, as well as their attitude toward art. Outside-of-school behaviors, such as voluntary visits to art exhibitions, purchase of art books, collecting reproductions, discussions with family and friends concerning art, and purchase of art work certainly indicate a high level of involvement with art. All these are in-life situations that demonstrate the student has internalized and assimilated the art instruction presented in class. Perhaps these in-life behaviors are the most valid indications of all that the student has learned and has a positive attitude toward art. (See Appendix 2.)

Photo courtesy of Craig Roland

Local artist, Sylvia Winslow, visits a classroom and offers suggestions to a student concerning her linocut print. Contact with local artists can be a meaningful experience for students interested in careers involving the visual arts.

SPECIAL SECONDARY OBJECTIVE CONSIDERATIONS

There are three special concerns of adolescents in the junior and senior high school period: vocational, avocational, and in-school life. These must be addressed by the art teacher at this critical period in the student's life and, therefore, become objective considerations for instruction in the art room.

Vocational

Many students at the secondary level, in thinking about the possibility of a career in some aspect of the visual arts, need information concerning art as a vocation. It is the responsibility of the art teacher to satisfy this need by making students aware of the many job opportunities in which training in the visual arts is a valuable asset. An outline of career opportunities is presented in Table 6. In addition to this information, persons from the various art fields in the community may be invited to the school to talk with students. The secondary art teacher and interested students should make every effort to visit advertising agencies, artists' studios, newspapers, department store display departments, and any other places of employment of artists, as well as schools involved with the education of artists so that intelligent advice is given and decisions can be made concerning employment and educational opportunities.

Avocational

Although some students are interested in art as a vocation, others are interested in art as a leisure time pursuit, having an avocational interest. Both are valid

TABLE 6
Career Opportunities in the Visual Arts

PROFESSIONAL ARTIST	ART EDUCATOR	
Craftsman: Ceramics	Art/crafts instructor:	
Craftsman: Fabrics	college and university	
Craftsman: Metals	Art/crafts teacher:	
Painter	children and youth	
Printmaker	Art supervisor/museum educator:	
Sculptor	local, city, state	
COMMERCIAL ARTIST	RELATED ART FIELDS	
Advertising artist	Architecture	Homemaking
Art director	Art criticism	Industrial design
Cartoonist	Art history	Interior design
Fabric designer	Art therapy	Landscape architecture
Graphic designer	Arts management	Marketing
Illustrator	City planning	Museum work
Lettering artist	Display and merchandising	Stage design
Photographer	Elementary education	Textile design
	Fashion design/costume design	

objectives. With the four-day work week a reality in many localities, people need participatory, creative, and involving activities, which the visual arts and the other arts provide (Educational Policies Commission, 1968). According to a 1980 survey conducted by the National Research Center of the Arts (*Americans and the Arts*, 1981), 46 percent of all Americans are presently involved in some art activity as an avocation, from very little to a great deal: 42 percent engage in needlework and weaving; 44 percent engage in photography; 10 percent engage in sculpturing or working with clay; and 28 percent paint or are involved in graphic arts. In all areas, participation has increased sharply since the 1975 survey. The percentages are even greater for young people under thirty. These data suggest that art experiences begun in secondary school do carry over into adult life.

In-School Life

Another concern of students in junior and senior high schools is that of using art abilities in school activities outside the art class. The art teacher should look with favor upon these activities since herein art becomes a living aspect of the students' lives. Certainly this is what art education is all about—getting people to use the visual arts as an aspect of their daily lives. The yearbook, scenery and costumes for plays, program covers and illustrations, posters and signs, art for publications, school decorations, art work for the band, and banners and booths for the school carnival are all valid art activities with which students may become involved. These are real in-life situations. Many art teachers become overwhelmed with the requests and demands for art work in these extracurricular art activities. Certainly the art teacher cannot let these demands take over the whole art curriculum, but, whenever the activities are part of the planned curricula in other subject matter areas or are a part of the on-going tradition of the school, then it behooves the art teacher to cooperate, and the art activity probably should become part of the planned art curriculum. For activities that are not part of the art class curriculum, the art teacher should be sympathetic and encourage the students involved but may want to insist that the art work *not* be done in the scheduled art class. However, we do not want to discourage students from using art in these in-school life situations.

REFERENCES

Americans and the Arts. New York: American Council for the Arts, 1981.
Bloom, B. S. (ed.). *Taxonomy of Educational Objectives, Handbook I: Cognitive Domain*. New York: Longman Company, 1956.
Buhler, K. *The Mental Development of the Child: A Summary of Modern Psychological Theory*. New York: Harcourt, Brace, 1930.
Dewey, J. *Art as Experience*. New York: Minton, Balch, 1934.
Educational Policies Commission. The role of the fine arts in education. *Art Education*, 1968, *21* (7), 3–8.
Jefferson, B. T. Teaching art from the inside out. *Art Education*, 1981, *34* (2), 30–32.
Krathwohl, D. R., Bloom, B. S., and Masia, B. B. *Taxonomy of Educational Objectives, Handbook II: Affective Domain*. New York: Longman Company, 1964.
Krotzsch, W. *Rhythmus und Form in der freien Kinderzeichnung*. Leipzig: Haase, 1917.

Lowenfeld, V. *Creative and Mental Growth* (3rd ed.). New York: Macmillan, 1957.

Michael, J. A. *A Handbook for Art Instructors and Students Based upon Concepts and Behaviors*. New York: Vantage Press, 1970.

Michael, J. A. The studio art experience: The heart of art education. *Art Education*, 1980, *33* (2), 15–19.

Morris, J. W. and Stuckhardt, M. H. Art attitude: Conceptualization and implication. *Studies in Art Education*, 1977, *19* (1), 21–28.

Pepper, S. C. *The Basis of Criticism in the Arts*. Cambridge: Harvard University Press, 1946.

Perry, W. G. *Forms of Intellectual and Ethical Development in the College Years*. New York: Holt, Rinehart and Winston, 1970.

Rockefeller, D. J. *Coming to Our Senses*. New York: McGraw-Hill, 1977.

Stuckhardt, M. H. The development of a scale to measure attitude held toward the visual arts. (Doctoral dissertation, University of Illinois, 1976.) *Dissertation Abstracts International*, 1976, *37*, 100A (University Microfilms No. 76–16, 203).

Stuckhardt, M. H. and Morris, J. W. The development of a scale to measure attitudes held toward arts education. *Studies in Art Education*, 1980, *21* (2), 50–56.

Sturr, E. Motivation with a rational twist. *Art Education*, 1982, *35* (1), 12–14.

SUPPLEMENTAL READINGS

Brouch, Virginia M. *Art Education: A Matrix System for Writing Behavioral Objectives*. Phoenix: Arbo Publishing, 1973. Behavioral approach applied to art education.

Feldman, Edmund B. *The Artist*. Englewood Cliffs, New Jersey: Prentice-Hall, 1982. Process of becoming an artist at various time periods including the present.

Linderman, Earl W. *Teaching Secondary School Art: Discovering Art Objectives, Art Skills, Art History, Art Ideas* (2nd ed.). Dubuque, Iowa: Wm. C. Brown, 1980. Textbook, with emphasis on objectives, art history, and studio concerns.

Mager, Robert F. *Preparing Instructional Objectives*. Palo Alto, California: Fearon Publishers, 1962. Definitive statement concerning behavior objectives in teaching.

Saunders, Robert J. *Relating Art and Humanities to the Classroom*. Dubuque, Iowa: Wm. C. Brown, 1977. Aesthetic education described, including goals, values, background, and methods.

Silverman, Ronald (ed.). *Art, Education, and the World of Work*. Reston, Virginia: National Art Education Association, 1980. A discussion of careers in the arts.

Tyler, Ralph W. (ed.). *Educational Evaluation: New Roles, New Means*, Part II. Chicago: The University of Chicago Press for the National Society for the Study of Education, 1969. Aspects of evaluation in education addressed by leaders in the field.

Zernich, Theodore (ed.). *Careers in the Visual Arts: Options, Training, and Employment*. Reston, Virginia: National Art Education Association, 1980. Various art/art-related fields explored.

CHAPTER 3

THOSE WE WORK WITH
Adolescents

To many adults, who look upon adolescence as a period of great joy, exuberance, and exploration, it may come as a surprise that many times early adolescents feel alone and isolated. Coming from the warm, restricted, and secure environment of an elementary school where everything has been planned for them as a group, they enter a larger, new school environment where, after a brief homeroom period, they spend the rest of the day on their own, each having a different schedule of classes. They now have to relate to many new teachers and fellow students. Classes and extracurricular activities, conducted by different teachers, all seem unrelated to one another. Attitudes change at home. Many parents feel that the important formative years of childhood are over—when it was time for instilling values and the teaching of right and wrong—and greet their youngster's entry into junior high with a sense of accomplishment and also relief—feeling they have done all they could. Unfortunately, some parents relinquish all their responsibility at once during this period. Parents do not feel they have to be home or make any provision for when a junior high son or daughter returns from school. Thus the youngster returns to an empty house, drops his or her books and is free on the town. No longer are parents so concerned with a continual monitoring of the youngster's whereabouts and activities. Some early adolescents develop new and positive responsibilities in extracurricular school activities such as sports, the arts, the school newspaper or yearbook, or a part-time job; but for others, there is a vacuum—an empty void. Youngsters may feel isolated from both family and school.

However, for many teenagers, parents are not entirely out of the picture because they push to have their children achieve more in grades and sports and the like so that the adolescent feels that he carries not only his own problems but also the aspirations and ambitions of his parents. Many teenagers are "expected" to go to college, to become an engineer or whatever, to continue in the family business, and/or to "make it" where mom and dad never did.

Under such isolation and pressure to achieve, many adolescents turn to peers who become another pressure group insisting upon a particular behavior or a level of behavior to remain as a member of the group. In 1960, parents had the greatest impact upon a teenager's values and behavior; by 1980, friends and peers replaced mother and dad in this capacity as shown in a survey by Robert Johnston for the National Board of Junior Achievement (Rice, 1980). Perhaps this shift is a result of more parents relinquishing their responsibility over their children because of emphasis on personal freedom, civil liberty, and the general permissiveness of society, especially concerning clothes, sex, and drugs. In addition, many parents have become unsure of the values they inherited because of a feeling of a lack of governmental response and concern, the threat of nuclear war, the economic situation, the lack of opportunity for blacks and women, and societal ambivalence. Parents have become afraid that their children will resent them or that they will distort their children's personalities if very much authority is exerted. Benjamin Spock (1974) notes that this parental hesitancy is much more prevalent in relation to adolescents than to any other age group. Economic conditions and the Women's Liberation Movement have resulted in both parents working, allowing little time for their children, which may force adolescents to relate more and more to their peers. Researchers (Fornaciari, 1980) found that the average family with teenagers spends about fourteen minutes a day in parent–child communication. Of that, twelve minutes is spent on such business as "What's for dinner?" and "Who's using the car?" That only leaves two minutes for open communication and forming relationships. No wonder adolescents turn to their peers.

However, in turning to their peers, they spend an awful lot of time and effort trying to be like other adolescents. The resulting peer pressure can lead to healthy, constructive behavior, as well as destructive behavior. Peck and Havighurst (1960) believe the peer group is a positive influence in that it provides a basis for learning the major social loyalties needed in our society. If adolescents get along well and enjoy the peer group, they are likely to approach all groups with the expectation of liking them. Probably loyalty to the nation, to a community, and to a professional or a working group depends upon learning loyalty to the smaller and more intimate groups of the family and peer group. The peer group has such a long-lasting effect upon the adolescent that most of us consider "home" to be wherever we lived during our adolescent years, especially if we were associated with a strong and influential peer group. Friendships established within the group at this time tend to last throughout one's lifetime. Therefore, the importance of the peer group should not be discounted. The pressure to conform/perform is reflected in the significance the group has for the adolescent at the time.

Schools are under pressure from parents and universities to upgrade academic content. High school students are now studying what their parents learned in college. Elementary/junior high school students are often introduced to geometry and algebra. Certainly the upgrading of subject matter content is not bad if the concepts presented are not beyond a student's maturity level; otherwise, tensions are created. Some schools add to this pressure by offering material incentives based upon performance. Sometimes a successful student is awarded points that lead to prizes.

One can easily see how the carefree days of adolescence can become days of worry, self-doubt, and aimlessness—if not isolation—because of the pressures of parents, peers, and school.

STRIVING FOR INDEPENDENCE AND RESPONSIBILITY

Parents of a fourteen-year-old son noted that he had suddenly become very out-spoken and argumentative after having been compliant, well-behaved, dependable, and affectionate. In one day it all seemed to change and he refused to do what he was asked to do without some kind of argument. The parents were taken aback by this negative type of behavior and wondered if this is normal. Yes, these are normal changes that take place when a child reaches puberty. He is telling us that he is no longer a child, has a mind of his own, and wants the same respect and recognition that adults show each other. The adolescent is striving for his inde-pendence and wants responsibility.

Frequently at this time, there seems to be a need on the part of some ado-lescents to create a kind of disturbance within the home as if they wanted to make the home a place of conflict and unpleasantness in order to leave it more easily (Blaine, 1962). It may be less difficult to leave home if they first make it an unattractive environment characterized by conflict.

As a result of this breaking away from childhood and their parents, some adolescents become moody and contradictory; some become terrified and even more pious and parent-fearing; some try to remain children, often becoming hurt in accidents as a result of the wild things they try to do; and some immerse them-selves in an all-engrossing activity like a part-time job, working on an old car, or participating in drama, sports, music, and even art. The more normal ones find a substitute for their parents in their peers upon whom they become dependent. A 1975 survey of 15,000 high school students by the Educational Testing Service found that the overwhelming majority would go to someone other than their parents for help with a serious personal drug or drinking problem.

Two other means of escaping parents and asserting independence are provided by technology: the automobile and the telephone (Group for the Advancement of Psychiatry, 1968). The automobile provides privacy, defiance, and escape. It offers mobility and freedom from restraint and supervision. The telephone provides a wonderful means of fulfilling the need for flight from parents to peers without ever leaving the house. The adolescent is transported out of one world and into another, escaping the parents by turning to others in the same predicament.

In addition, each generation of adolescents seems to develop its own language: slanguage. Terms may vary from region to region and from school to school but the result is the same: a rapport among their peers and an escape from adults who may not understand or condone their behavior, particularly in relation to drugs. No listing of terms is given here because the teenagers' own language and terms come and go with bewildering speed and vary greatly from region to region.

This relinquishment of parents and the striving for independence and respon-sibility often serve to lower the adolescent's self-esteem; it becomes a period of mourning. Some subconsciously respond to the break as if it were a loss through death. Because in the past teenagers' views of themselves and of the world have been determined largely by the stability of their relationships with their parents, they now feel somewhat threatened and confused by cutting parental ties—the source of their value system, security, and approval. They are not sure of them-selves, having intense negative feelings and little confidence in their ability to cope.

They cannot imagine that everyone does not know how miserable they are. And yet the drive for individuality manifests itself in every adolescent.

Most junior and senior high schools add to this state of confusion experienced by adolescents, leaving them without a coherent identity. Schools typically inform students that they are expected to act like mature and responsible adults; but then these same students are closely supervised, conveying a more convincing message: "You are immature, irresponsible, and not to be trusted." Thus, we continue to hold the adolescent in a state of limbo.

SOCIETY AND ADOLESCENTS

In primitive cultures, the individual becomes an adult at puberty, usually by some initiation or rites of passage. When a child in Western societies reaches puberty he is in a no-man's-land called adolescence. For primitive societies, adolescence and adulthood appear to be identical (Mead, 1928). Western societies appear to have invented the adolescent period because their complex economic systems need highly skilled young people (statisticians, physicians, lawyers, analysts, teachers, engineers). Therefore, instead of letting children pass smoothly into adulthood, we insist they attend school, remain dependent upon their parents, be obedient, and keep themselves chaste.

Not only are adolescents forced by law to attend school, but they are constantly being informed that most employers will not give them a decent job unless they have a diploma and/or degree. Whereas the average American from 1880 to 1920 only reached the eighth grade, today 90 percent graduate from high school and more than 50 percent have a chance of going on to college (Coleman, 1973). Employable youths continue to be out of jobs more than any other age group. In 1910, 30 percent of all fourteen- and fifteen-year-olds were employed; one million youngsters under fourteen had jobs. Responsible work inside the home also has all but vanished. Years ago adolescents probably would have to help their parents on the farm or in the small family business. Today, there usually is no work in the home or outside the home for teenagers. They are suspended from any economic responsibilities.

The value of work for adolescents in their transition to adulthood has not been recognized by our society. The National Commission on Youth (1980, p. 80) perceives work to be the single most important factor in this transitional process. Work "teaches discipline and personal responsibility, provides a source of financial independence, expends time and energy in a purposeful manner, creates a sense of social identification and status, and constitutes a source of meaningful life experiences." Work also satisfies two human needs that are characteristic of everyone: "the need for self-respect and for the respect of others and the need to express one's self creatively." Since most adults organize their lives around their work and lose a sense of purpose without work, it is easy to understand the important place that work has in the lives of adolescents who are endeavoring to become adults. We, indeed, are a work-centered society. When adolescents are prevented from holding jobs, even part-time jobs, they are prevented from becoming integrated into society and become isolated and alienated. Schools, themselves, as institutions are becoming isolated from the people of the community—this and increased specialization of work have combined to separate youth from where the action is. Teenagers only associate with other teenagers in the isolated school setting and are held back from taking a place in the real world of work and life.

The law also insists that adolescents remain subservient to their parents. Teenagers are both indulged and oppressed. Although minors are accorded special considerations that shield them from the full legal consequences of their acts, many found in juvenile court are referred for conduct that would *not* be criminal if performed by adults; for example, running away from home, ungovernable behavior, and sexual relations. Until reaching ages prescribed by various state laws, young people are forced to attend school, excluded from many gainful employments, denied the right to drive a car, prohibited from buying alcoholic beverages and cigarettes, barred from some movies, deprived of countless pleasures and liberties available to adults, and judged delinquent for curfew violations, loitering, and trying to marry. The adolescent has no right to demand the particular protection of either due process or the juvenile administration procedure—the state decides. However, recently the Supreme Court did rule that adolescents appearing in juvenile court should have the same legal safeguards as adults.

Through television, films, and periodicals—all the media—adolescents are continually stimulated sexually but are expected to remain celibate. We do not seem to realize that the fourteen-year-old of today is the seventeen-year-old of yesterday. Modern medicine and diet have accelerated puberty by about three years over what it was at the beginning of the nineteenth century, an average of two to three months earlier each decade.

Concerning the adolescent in our society, sociologist Kingsley Davis (1949, p. 223) writes, "In terms of growth, strength, fecundity, and mental capacity, full maturity tends to be attained only a short time after puberty; but socially the adolescent still has a long way to go before full status is reached." Just when the teenager is at his peak sexually, he must remain celibate; just when he has the most strength and energy, he is given no productive, satisfying work to do; just when he is at his intellectual height and when his need for power is greatest, he is denied the right to participate in society's decision making. We cannot curtail the educational process just to let adolescents become independent and responsible earlier but we could speed it up. We might provide more jobs—part-time and full-time. We can give far more meaningful responsibilities at school and at home. We can get them out into the community via school-related activities. And as teachers, we certainly can show respect and build confidence in the adolescents in our classes.

ADOLESCENCE: A TIME OF CRISIS

While the pressure builds from within as a result of a drive for independence—to break away from childhood, from parents, and become what they are capable of becoming—and the need for finding a responsible place in the world, adolescents find themselves stymied by a society that shackles them to a long pre-adult period while educational/vocational goals are achieved. Those who shun the system usually end up jobless or with menial tasks and low pay. Indeed, this is a time of crisis for many adolescents and is reflected in various traumatic behaviors: suicide, use of drugs, promiscuity, and crime. Teachers must be aware of these possibilities because learning is virtually impossible during a time of trauma when emotions blur and may even obliterate intellectual and perceptual processes.

Suicide

Suicide is now the second leading cause of death nationwide for persons from ten to twenty years of age. The suicide rate for youth (ages fourteen to twenty-four) doubled between 1970 and 1980 to the present rate of 17 per 100,000 (National Commission on Youth, 1980, p. 79). These are tragic statistics. Male students are three times more likely than females to commit suicide. Perhaps this is because of society's less tolerant attitude toward emotional expression and failure among males and the fierce competition in schools and the job market. The suicide rate for all adolescents is more than the combined annual death rate from tuberculosis, meningitis, polio, influenza, bronchitis, and syphilis. For every successful suicide, there are at least ten (some believe fifty) unsuccessful attempts. Researchers have found no single reason why a young person would decide to end his life. The reasons are as complex as the personalities of the teenagers who see suicide as the only solution to the devastating situation in which they find themselves.

Although the first suicide attempt usually comes as a surprise to parents and friends of the person attempting suicide, it can never be dismissed as an impulsive act, the result of a temporary upset or an insincere gesture independent of the teenager's usual life pattern. In most cases, the teenager considers the suicide in advance, weighing it against other alternatives. Many behaviors are tried to no avail—peers, parents, and teachers being oblivious or rejecting such overtures. Some adolescents adopt the drastic measure of an attempted suicide as an attention-getting device but find that this, too, fails to open an avenue to possible solution of their problems. At this point, adolescents become convinced that death is the only way out after having failed in all other attempts to cope with the difficulties at hand—there being no one else to turn to or talk to.

Suicides resulting from the pressures of society are sociologically based, and adolescents responding to such pressures may develop any one of three suicidal personalities (Durkheim, 1951). Some are egotistic and may be described as "loners" who are not integrated into society and who feel alienated. The more these individuals are thrown onto their own resources, the higher the suicide rate. These teenagers usually have weak peer, family, school, and religious ties. Others are altruistic and have overidentified with a particular group so much that they are willing to sacrifice themselves for the group. This is understandable since group loyalties can become very strong and group pressures are difficult to resist during the adolescent period. A third type is the anomic suicidal personality, which comes about when individuals are so upset that their horizon is broadened beyond what they can endure. Sudden and unexpected changes in one's personal or social life create a confused state and alienation. A failing grade in a final exam, an unwanted pregnancy, a poor showing in a sports event, rejection by a girlfriend or boyfriend may trigger an attempt at suicide.

Another viewpoint considers suicide to be more psychologically based rather than sociologically based. Suicide herein results from high personal ambition, keen rivalry, and the discrepancy between opportunity and meager results with inevitable disappointment, guilt, and depression (Smith, 1976). From unsuccessful attempts, a feeling develops that one is incapable and is no good.

Studies by J. T. Barter et al. (1968) of adolescents hospitalized for suicide attempts reveal that school adjustment is one of the variables definitely related to self-destruction. School performance was almost uniformly poor for these students. Low grades, truancy, and discipline problems were typical of students dropping out of school at the time of hospitalization. At high school age, 30 percent of suicides occur among drop-outs. Schools must face up to the potential danger of the competitive, single-dimensional atmosphere they create when so much emphasis is placed upon grades and academic achievement. Grades reflect just one small facet of one's total development. According to government studies, there is considerable evidence that nonschool factors may be more important determinants of educational outcomes than are school factors (Jencks, 1972), with academic achievement (grades and standardized test scores) having *no* relationship to success in later life (Gintis, 1971; Holtzman, 1971). Self-acceptance and self-confidence—far more important than proficiency in specific subjects—will enable adolescents to be the kinds of persons that they, parents, and the world want. It is interesting to note that proportionately more suicides occur in the spring when school problems come to a head.

The Center for Studies of Suicide Prevention (Smith, 1976) has developed a list of warning signs and distress signals of which teachers should be aware. Because art expression involves a projection of one's thoughts, feelings, and perceptions, the art teacher is in a particularly advantageous position to note these signs of distress. This list of behavior changes should alert teachers to the possibility of suicide:

1. Changes in personality and living patterns, such as extreme fatigue, headaches, and general aches and pains; crying, boredom, outbursts of anger; decreased appetite; lack of interest in personal appearance; preoccupation, and inability to concentrate
2. Absence of a significant personal relationship, no friends
3. A dramatic shift in the quality of schoolwork
4. Excessive use of drugs and alcohol (over half are involved in drug abuse)
5. Communication problems at home (most feel their families do not understand them)
6. Giving away prized possessions, getting affairs in order
7. Truancy
8. Open signs of mental illness, such as delusions and hallucinations—hearing inner voices commanding the adolescent to end his or her life
9. Direct and indirect verbal signals threatening suicide such as, "You won't have to be bothered with me much longer," and "You'll be sorry when I'm dead"

Most adolescents may show one or more of these signs but if they persist for a long time or several are evidenced at once, suicide may be imminent. The teacher is in a most strategic position to identify these adolescent suicidal behaviors—unconscious cries for help in solving some problems that appear urgent and hopeless—and to help the student. An art teacher can often get teenagers to express their problems/feelings in their creative art work, especially in drawing, painting, and sculpture. Being able to see their feelings, as depicted in their art work, will help adolescents see situations more objectively and therefore face up to life and reality. The art work makes it possible and easier for adolescents to talk about their problems. Often they will symbolize a problem in their drawing and will talk about it as if it did not relate to themselves. It is imperative to get them to talk. The teacher's job is to listen and probe gently by supportive questioning such as, "You seem to be kind of down. Is something bothering you?" or "You don't seem to be yourself lately." During such sessions the adult must not be judgmental or moralize. Never minimize the importance of a teenager's problems no matter how trivial they may seem to you. The teacher's role is to be accepting, open, and concerned; otherwise, the adolescent's sense of worthlessness will cause him to pull away.

After recognizing potentially serious suicidal behaviors, the teacher should relate such findings to the school counselor and/or administrator who can get in touch with parents and with agencies and specialists who can help. At no time should the art teacher act as a therapist but he or she certainly may provide human and emotional support.

Drugs

In the past twenty-five years, American society has become drug oriented, relying upon chemical substances that bring about physical, mental, and emotional changes. There are few homes where parents do not either drink or smoke cigarettes, use barbiturates to sleep or tranquilizers to get through the day. It is only natural that many adolescents, emulating adults, turn to drugs as a means of dealing with conflict and emotions, of coping with the pressures of growing up or just to feel good. Whether or not to become involved with drugs is a constant concern for all youth.

Harm in the use of drugs comes not only from the changed states of being but also from the user becoming dependent upon the drug, an overdose of which may even mean death. Disrupted family and school life frequently results from drug misuse and abuse which cross all social and economic strata. According to the 1979 National Survey on Drug Abuse (Fishburne et al., 1980), among students nationwide aged twelve to seventeen, it was found that 54 percent have at some time used tobacco (cigarettes) and 12 percent currently use it; 70 percent have experienced alcohol and 37 percent currently use it; 30 percent have experienced marijuana and 16 percent currently use it; 7 percent have experienced hallucinogens and 2 percent currently use them; and 9 percent have experienced inhalants and 2 percent currently use them. About three in ten report illicit drug experience with 8 percent saying they have used hallucinogens, cocaine, or heroin. And among high school seniors (Johnston et al., 1981), 93 percent have used alcohol; 60 percent have used marijuana; 13 percent have used hallucinogens; and 12 percent have used inhalants. As teenagers grow older, drug usage apparently increases dramatically. While the overall death rate for Americans dropped 20 percent from 1960 to 1978, the death rate for young Americans, aged fifteen to twenty-four, was up by 11 percent. Much of this increase was due to death from car accidents and murders attributable to drug and alcohol abuse and emotional problems.

The groundwork for drug dependency or avoidance is laid early in life, as early as infancy. Sometimes the knowledge that they have not done their job creates guilt in parents resulting in a defensiveness and helplessness when they come to deal with a problem in their adolescents. Building a trusting relationship based upon mutual respect and empathy should occur at the earliest possible time. It can be done during adolescence with patience and with tolerance of much testing, resistance, and rejection from teenagers. Loving, caring, sharing, communicating (listening to the adolescent and giving authentic information about drugs), clarifying values, and setting limits constitute a vital input into a healthy parent–child and teacher–student relationship. Consistently modeling these values is also an important aspect of the formula.

Drug usage and abuse may grow out of thwarted needs that teenagers face. For example, adolescents may feel the need to belong to a particular social group or to receive peer approval; to gain courage for sexual or other social participation; to offset boredom; or to experiment because it is the "in" thing to do. To cope with these pressures, adolescents may retreat into intoxication—and the agents of that intoxication are more and more alcohol and marijuana. This retreat now begins as early as eleven or twelve when the student enters junior high school. There, on their own, entering junior high school students gradually find themselves a new group of peers and begin experimenting with new life styles, a normal desire for teenagers breaking away from parents and trying to find themselves. Many, trying alcohol, marijuana and other drugs, become "hooked"—hooked, not only on the use of the drug, but also with the rituals of drug use and drug-using friends.

One of the most used drugs is alcohol. It slows down the central nervous system (brain and spinal cord), which is responsible not only for thinking, reasoning, and sensory powers, but also for vital functions such as breathing and the heart beat. If these are slowed down to the point of stopping, death, of course, would be the inevitable result. In 1977, the National Institute of Drug Abuse reported that more than one-third of high school students in the United States get drunk at least once a month; of approximately 13 million who have tried alcohol, about 1.3 million boys and girls between the ages of twelve and seventeen have serious drinking problems; 60 percent of those killed in drunken-driving accidents are teenagers—drunken driving being the number one killer of teenagers. Nearly 8,000 die in alcohol-related accidents every year. The number of teenagers arrested for drunken driving has tripled since 1960. By the time teenagers enter the twelfth grade as seniors in high school, most have used alcohol to some degree (Johnston et al., 1979). Five percent of all teenagers get drunk at least once a week, every week; 14 percent of high school senior males get drunk once a week, every week; 23 percent of all students, including 36 percent of male high school seniors, get drunk at least four times a year. Among seventh graders, 63 percent of boys and 54 percent of girls have at least tried alcoholic beverages. By the twelfth grade, it is 94 percent of the boys and 91 percent of the girls. Alcohol seems to be, by far, the drug choice of adolescents.

Another popular drug is marijuana. One-third of young Americans twelve to seventeen years old—64 percent of 1978 senior high school males and 53 percent of senior high school females—have used marijuana, twice the number in 1972. Marijuana appears to be following the tradition of alcohol and has the fillip of being different. Adolescents feel that it is important to distinguish their actions from those of their parents in asserting their independence. Marijuana is illegal, so it's the embodiment of the symbol of rebellion, of independence—of breaking away and doing one's own thing. Although the effects of marijuana have frequently been questioned, results of studies find that it impairs short-term learning, memory and recall; irritates the respiratory tract; causes a sudden drop in blood pressure with a tendency toward fainting, headaches, dizziness, and numbness; increases heart rate; and increases appetite. Less common effects include paranoid reactions and decreased concept-formation ability. Many other effects of marijuana use are still being studied.

Needless to say, with such a high level of drug indulgence by adolescents and the negative effects upon the body and behavior that are exhibited in the classroom, art teachers must be knowledgeable concerning drugs. Besides alcohol and marijuana, there are many more drugs of which the art teacher should be aware. The most frequently used are classified as the depressants, stimulants, narcotics, hallucinogens, and inhalants.

Since over half of the street drugs are not what they are alleged to be, it is difficult, even for the user, to know what has been ingested. And then, too, some drugs have unusual and unexpected effects upon people. Because of our lack of definitive knowledge of the drug(s) taken by a particular student and our lack of medical training, we teachers should not try medically to help but get professional help for any student who is on drugs or who has overdosed.

Recognizing that certain students are on drugs, teachers may feel a need to counsel such students so that learning in the art room can take place. The first rule in counseling is never to betray a confidence or put yourself in a position to do so. However, with drug counseling, there is a legal aspect which must be considered (Dell, n.d.). Teachers whose state law does not give them immunity in this regard must decide what course of action is best for them. You must first protect yourself. You cannot accomplish anything if you lose your teaching position. Students, also, must be aware of your position and decide how much they can confide in you. You must be sensitive and make yourself available to those who seek help but without losing self-respect. Always try to conduct discussions in private. This will encourage seriousness and honesty.

You should determine the personal and professional attitudes of your school principal and faculty with regard to drug abuse. School administrators should offer suggestions concerning what to do with drug victims and drug overdose in the classroom and in the school.

In counseling, a teacher can play the role of the unconcerned adult, someone who will not overreact, but will help the student gain perspective on his problem. The teacher is expected to be knowledgeable but should be unemotional in this situation. Never appear shocked at whatever you are told. Such evaluative behavior will immediately make the student feel he can tell you no more. A teacher who listens can be a great asset to adolescents who may know few other adults outside of their family. However, do not take responsibility for the condition in which you find the students. Drug abuse is both a personal and a social problem. As teachers, we should do all we can to help the student face up to the reality of the situation but do not get involved in arguing with students. Students may say, "I can stop anytime I want to; I haven't got any problems; marijuana is going to be legalized; I only get high once in a while; alcohol is just as bad or worse than pot; my parents don't understand me." The tendency is to respond with a convincing argument, but you will find yourself going round in circles with the student. Remember, *drug abuse is a symptom or a sign that something else is wrong somewhere.* Students are using drugs as a means of escaping some situation(s) they cannot face. Drug abuse is usually blamed on, or rationalized with, something outside the users themselves—school, parents, friends—and to argue about these topics is to miss the point completely. Every reason that can be listed for drug abuse can be restated to show that the fault lies with the drug users themselves. By keeping this in mind, you can help students see themselves and their motives more clearly. You will be able to avoid falling into the trap of sympathizing and thereby reinforcing the excuses, and you will be able to begin showing them what they need to do to change things for themselves.

Learning is, indeed, hampered by a mind and body that is handicapped by drug use; therefore, as teachers we must be concerned and do all we can to help the student who is on drugs.

Sex

With the advent of puberty and the accompanying physiological changes, similar needs and feelings involving sexual drive begin to manifest themselves in all adolescents, both male and female. These are natural developments in the life of mankind and are necessary for procreation.

With the increased sexual freedom in this country, the number of sexually active teenagers increased by two thirds in the 1970s according to a report from the Alan Guttmacher Institute (1981). Of twenty-nine million young people between ages thirteen and nineteen, seven million teenage men and five million teenage women are sexually active although the number of teenage marriages has continued to decline. By age nineteen, four out of five males and two out of three females have had sexual intercourse, with sixteen the average age for the first sexual experience. From a survey of many sexually active adolescents, it appears that most (80 percent) are not promiscuous but have remained with their original sexual partner over a period of one or two years.

As a result of this increased sexual activity, teenage pregnancies are increasing despite a rise in the use of contraceptives. Among fifteen- to nineteen-year-olds, nearly a million become pregnant annually (more than one in ten), in addition to 30,000 girls under age fifteen. Among the consequences of this high rate of teenage pregnancy are serious risks to the health of the mother and child, forced marriages, foreshortened education, dashed career hopes, increasing risk of dependency, and damaging social and economic results. For most adolescents, the principal issue is prevention or use of contraceptive measures. Although we may prefer that teenagers should have no need for birth control, the time is long gone for the pretense that they do not. Teenage sexuality reaches a fever pitch and is an issue we must face realistically. Experimentation with masturbation, homosexuality, sex play, and intercourse may create feelings of guilt that deepen depression and may become a cause of great concern. Adolescents are endeavoring to find themselves sexually, as well as in other aspects of their lives.

Crime

In the quest for independence, many adolescents turn to crime, which is increasing at the rate of six times that of the general population. According to 1975 crime statistics (*FBI Uniform Crime Reports*, 1976), eighteen-year-olds comprised the largest arrested group in the nation; the second highest group was seventeen-year-olds, then nineteen-year-olds, followed by sixteen-year-olds. Of all persons arrested in the United States for serious crimes, 62 percent were under twenty-one years of age; 43 percent were under eighteen years and 17 percent under fifteen years. More than two million adolescents under age eighteen were arrested in 1975. Self-report studies reveal that almost all young people at some point in their lives commit at least one act for which they could have been brought to juvenile court (National Commission on Youth, 1980, p. 100). This is entirely credible, because 65 percent of the seniors of 1980 report illicit drug use at some time in their lives (Johnston et al., 1981). In discussions with teenagers involved in crime, the teenagers usually ended up talking about their parents' reactions. The assumption is that part of the motivation may have been to create embarrassment for their parents and to demonstrate the emancipation of the adolescent from parental control.

About half of all criminal offenders are juveniles between seven and seventeen years of age. Most crimes committed by adolescents are on impulse or under the pressure of peers who taunt them. Often they are motivated by personal problems resulting from broken homes. The most significant clues to criminal behavior of early adolescents are school and social maladjustment, temper tantrums, and fighting.

Apparently our handling of adolescent crime offenders is not very successful since 90 percent of delinquents return to detention within a year after they are released. Certainly one solution in meeting the basic needs of teenagers would be to give them responsibility in the form of a job which could be a start in building lost pride. Most educators agree that "the antidote to detention is attention." Because of many activities in the art room, the art teacher can delegate many responsibilities from stacking the kiln to designing and constructing scenery for the school play. Through closure art experiences, positive attention can be given all adolescents via their art work. See chapter 5.

GENERAL CHARACTERISTICS OF ADOLESCENCE

Although there is no "average" adolescent at any given year, there are attributes that characterize teenagers in regard to growth and development. Awareness of these should aid the teacher in working with secondary students in the art room.

Physiological Changes

Adolescence can be described by its diversity in terms of the time during which physical changes occur, and by the great differences in the rate of these changes, resulting in a remarkable range among individuals of the same chronological age, especially during the earlier part of this stage. At the younger end of adolescence, most are in a stage of intense physical development, especially males. At the upper end some changes continue but at a much slower pace.

Most body organs and tissues undergo an adolescent growth spurt, although the extent and timing vary. Among boys, the normal range of ages for the onset of pubic hair growth is 10 to 15 years, and, for its completion, 14 to 18 years of age (Coleman, 1973, p. 94). Testes growth may begin between 10 and 13.5 years and end between 14.5 and 18 years. The comparable ages for penis growth are 11 to 14.5 years and 13.5 to 17 years. Some boys begin their height spurt at 10.5 and finish it by 13 while in others accelerated growth does not start until age 16. In girls the normal range is as great or greater. Pubic hair growth may start anytime between 8 and 14 years; breast development between 8 and 13 years; and the height spurt between 9.5 and 14.5 years. Menarche may occur between 10 and 16.5 years, the average being 12.8 years. As these age ranges suggest, most analogous adolescent phenomena occur about two years earlier in girls than in boys. Because of her earlier growth spurt, the average girl is taller than the average boy from about 11 to 14 years and heavier than he from about 9 or 10 until age 14.5. Late-maturing boys may be somewhat dwarfed by many girls for an even longer period.

The growth spurt so characteristic of early adolescence affects coordination, which is an intrinsic aspect of creating art. This "awkward stage" may appear as a regression to the art teacher, when students need more room to handle longer arms and legs, which sometimes seem out of control. No studio art experiences involving precise muscular coordination and control should be required at this time but, instead, flexible media (for example, chalk, watercolors, hand puppets) and studio art activities emphasizing expression and freedom of movement (for example, gesture drawing, paintings of dramatic topics) should be encouraged.

During adolescence changes occur simultaneously in internal organs and body chemistry. Accompanying enlargement of the larynx is a deepening of the voice in both sexes. Growth of the larynx is greater in boys, as is their voice change, but the process is gradual, beginning when penis growth is almost completed, often continuing until near the end of adolescence. Development of the apocrine sweat glands and increase in axillary sweating occur at about the time that axillary hair growth begins. Heart, lungs, and most other internal organs participate in the general adolescent growth spurt. The brain and other portions of the nervous system grow rapidly during early childhood but seem to share little in the adolescent growth spurt. Gradual maturing of function continues in the brain, resulting in faster reaction times.

Some individuals have completed their adolescent transformation before others of the same sex and age have even begun theirs. From about eleven through sixteen or seventeen years, the range of individual differences in physical structure at any given chronological age is greater than at any other time in the human life span. These differences include height, weight, body build, strength, motor coordination, reaction time, attractiveness of appearance, leadership, self-concept, and other aspects of personal and social behavior. Added to these variations within either sex are the differences in maturational rate of the two sexes. In a classroom of fourteen- or fifteen-year-olds, the diversity in size and function—with related variation in interest patterns and skills—can span the range from early childhood to adulthood. Individual differences in academic achievement may affect this variation. For example, although fourteen is the model age for ninth graders, a few pupils in a given class may be as young as eleven or twelve or as old as seventeen or eighteen. Some sixteen-year-olds are only in the seventh grade while others are in college; some are in the full-time labor force; and some are married and even parents.

The effect of such a variation of individual differences upon self perceptions and interpersonal relationships can be devastating. Among girls, it is the early-maturing ones who are most out of step with the model tendency of a mixed-sex age group. Their interests as well as their appearance are well in advance of their age peers of both sexes. Peers and adults may draw derogatory inferences about their moral character; their well developed figures may be a source of embarrassment among a class of childlike bodies. Because physical size and motor skills play an important role in social acceptance throughout the public school period, particularly for boys, some will be advantaged by age-grading while others are handicapped. Some late-maturing boys may not be able to compete successfully until the time has passed when skills linked to size, strength, endurance, and coordination have lost much of their social payoff. On the other hand, both boys and girls who mature very early are expected to exhibit adultlike behavior to go along with their mature bodies. Body changes bring about a need for psychological adjustment on the part of every adolescent who must learn how to handle his or her new body.

Intellectual Development

Barbel Inhelder and Jean Piaget (1958) note that adult mental processes, which they call "formal operations," begin between twelve and fifteen years—a most significant development. A formal operation is defined as a way of acting upon objects or ideas—the manipulation of hypothetical relationships involving clarity, precision, explicitness, and generality. The thinking process becomes dependent upon comprehension and abstraction. In other words, it becomes abstract. During childhood, thought processes are predominantly bound to concrete objects and phenomena, preceded by a background of direct nonverbal experience with empirical data. Small children see, taste, and handle or touch most of the things with which they come in contact. These direct concrete experiences result in naïve and idiosyncratic concepts being formed on a personal level wherein the child is not aware or conscious of the larger world and which are reflected in child-art expression. A variety of personal concepts (schemata) are gradually developed from the interaction with actual phenomena but a considerable number of variables cannot be considered at one time. A child draws a house and then a tree and then a fence—one thing after the other, ad infinitum—not consciously considering the whole. This approach may be characterized by $1 + 1 + 1 + 1 + 1$.

Beginning in junior high school, students become increasingly *less* dependent upon the availability of concrete objects and experiences. They become able to think abstractly without the necessity for concrete props, to reason with hypotheses involving multiple variables, and to conceptualize thinking per se, both their own and that of others. They can now envision the world as they think it should be rather than as it is. The idealism of adolescence is made possible by intellectual abilities now exercised for the first time. Adolescents tend to live very much in the hypothetical (abstract) future. With the advent of formal operations a self-centered egocentrism develops. Adolescents become concerned with their own thoughts and hypotheses. In the early phases of establishing these mental processes, about twelve to fourteen, the ability to test propositions exhaustively is not yet complete, nor are these young adolescents able to differentiate clearly between their own thoughts and those of others. However, by fifteen or sixteen the shift to the highest level of cognitive functioning is considered to be completed in the average person. The precise age when this shift occurs varies from one individual to another in accordance with cultural and idiosyncratic differences involving innate intellectual ability, experience, previous learning, personality, and subject-matter difficulty.

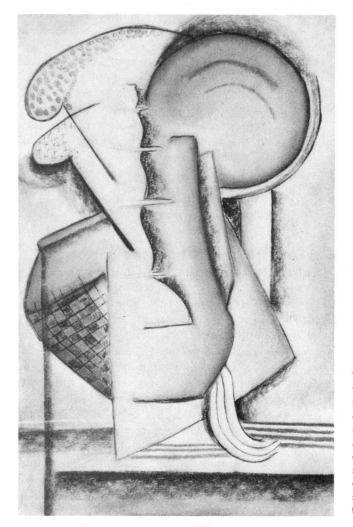

The transition from concrete to abstract functioning is reflected in the art work of adolescents. They begin to understand and appreciate abstraction in art. Some even enjoy working abstractly in art class, as in this example by a high school student concerned with synthetic Cubism.

Intellectually, every individual undergoes the same transition from concrete to abstract functioning in each new subject-matter area that is encountered, even after the abstract stage is reached on an overall basis. However, the transition from concrete to abstract functioning takes place much more readily since one is able to draw upon various transferable elements of one's general ability to function abstractly. In most teaching situations after the abstract level of thinking has been reached, concrete experiences with objects are primarily used for illustrative purposes—to clarify or dramatize abstract meanings. But in disciplines wherein concrete phenomena are an aspect in the adult world, such as in the arts, individuals who have reached the abstract stage of thinking apply hypotheses, understandings, philosophic approaches, and relational propositions to the concrete. A child may play with blocks and make a building, but an architect will apply his understanding of systems of construction, solar heating, wiring, plumbing, and building materials. Both are creating a building. The child works with concrete objects (blocks) in a direct, nonverbal manner from which some few abstractions may develop. The adult also works with concrete objects (building materials) but applies many complex abstract concepts and hypotheses to the materials and to the construction with which he is working. The scientist working in the laboratory, the engineer working with machinery, and the artist working with paint and canvas all apply hypotheses and previously learned abstract concepts to concrete objects and situations. These understandings and personal hypotheses may have been acquired via verbal expository teaching (Ausubel, 1962) at the adolescent/adult level by directly apprehending (verbally and symbolically) stated relationships between previously learned abstractions. This, then, differentiates child art which is based primarily upon concrete experience and adult art which is based primarily upon abstractions consciously applied to concrete experience.

In the visual arts, the expository verbal method of learning, wherein relationships are noted between newly learned and previously learned abstractions, is most appropriate in teaching art history and art concepts involving processes, tools, procedures, and the formal aspects of art. This means that at the secondary level there would be a great deal of verbalizing on the part of the teacher, even in the studio areas, to make students aware of various theories, philosophies, styles, periods, processes, and all other aspects of art. These abstract concepts, then, form a basis for art appreciation and for working upon the art project at hand. However, because of the nature of art, inductive discovery and problem-solving methods are also justifiable when secondary students are involved in studio work. Here, as artists, adolescents are reaching, discovering, and creating physical objects—their own art work. In so doing, they are also applying abstract concepts learned about art and art history to a concrete situation, the art work at hand. It may be said that artists, as well as scientists, engineers, and any other adult who works with concrete phenomena, consciously function in both the concrete and the abstract in their thinking but in a way very different from the naïve concrete operations of a child.

Research by Janet Sawyers (1979) suggests that adolescent girls have trouble with reasoning, integrating the parts, and seeing the whole—aspects of intellect—because their spatial ability is not as well developed as that of boys the same age. It appears that spatial ability (the manipulation of objects in space mentally, an aspect of abstract functioning) is more important than verbal ability in solving higher-level problems. When individuals reach adolescence, reasoning greatly develops but females do not seem to develop this ability as fast as males. Sawyers reasons that socially, females are channeled along verbal lines because they talk earlier, better, and faster, and, therefore, take a more verbal approach when it is not always best to do so. We encourage males to be more active: to manipulate toys, to build with blocks, and to have physical contact with things. As a result, when males reach adolescence and need to manipulate objects mentally, they have already developed an ability they can draw upon to help them reason with concepts because they have previously had so many concrete experiences with real objects. This underlines the importance of three-dimensional art experiences at the elementary level. Sawyers argues that males catch up with females in verbal ability because it is stressed at school. Males, then, are given many concrete experiences with objects as very young children, but also develop verbally so that when formal operations occur at the secondary level, they naturally perform at a higher level. (See Chart 2.)

CHART 2
Role of Intellect in Art Expression

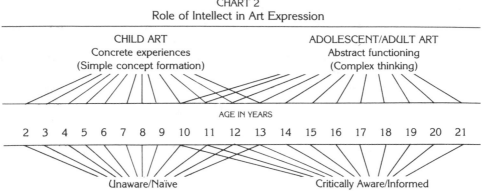

Social Awareness

To comprehend the social interactions of adolescents, it is necessary to be aware of their social development prior to the teenage years. Although the first indication of social awareness and willingness to cooperate generally takes place sometime during the six-through-eight-year period and is reflected in children's drawings by a baseline schema; it is around the age of nine that identification with others (usually peers) marks the beginning of what is commonly called the "gang age." At this time, children begin to look outside the immediate family to their peers and have the feeling that they can achieve more with others than they can alone. This is the basis for the formation of gangs and group friendships which continue throughout life. The child at the gang age is discovering the "self," as well as others—the beginning of social independence. Children realize they are an entity unto themselves; ego develops. Boys and girls usually discover that they have different interests; therefore the gangs tend to become all of one sex. Boys usually want to sleep outdoors, build hide-outs, go hunting, have codes, and play war; whereas girls usually want to play house, have parties, and wear fancy clothes (often their mothers'). As a result, we see Boy Scouts, Girl Scouts, and Campfire Girls—children are formally grouped according to sex by adults! In a study by Brian Sutton-Smith (Cook, 1977) to find out whether efforts to encourage youngsters, ages two to twelve, to expand beyond traditional roles had any impact on their play, no matter what toys were available, the girls played with toys having to do with domestic things—dolls and the like—while boys looked outside the house and to such things as war and space.

It is at this age, nine or ten, that overt sex roles emerge. Boys who relate to feminine activities are called "sissies" and girls who relate to masculine activities are called "tomboys." Strong feelings in this regard are frequently seen in junior high school students. This obvious differentiation and/or separation of the sex roles starting at the gang age continues in varying degrees throughout life and now, of course, is being challenged by the women's movement. It is interesting to note that the title of "sissy" carries a very negative and derogatory connotation in our society. On the other hand, "tomboy" carries a positive connotation, many fathers being proud of tomboy daughters. This suggests the much more difficult social role for boys than for girls in our society.

A differentiation between the sexes seems necessary so that young people are not sexually confused and do not develop problems of identity; however, traditional sex typing *does restrict* behavior. Men are reluctant to be gentle, sensitive, graceful, and women are reluctant to be dominant, competitive, assertive (Bem, 1975). Both types of qualities are needed to create art work. In the art program, there should be no sexual differentiation of activities. Girls should work at sculpture (wood, metal, stone, and clay) and boys should work in the fabrics area (weaving, sewing, stitchery, and printing). Regardless of sex, emphasis should be placed upon the expression, sensitivity, contribution, and cooperation of each individual.

After having discovered each other, their peers, and sexual differences during adolescence this development gradually—and sometimes not so gradually—manifests itself in a search for a mate. Much interest develops in the opposite sex. At the junior high level, punching, hitting, and verbal accusing usually ushers in this stage. These behaviors are the forerunners of flirting, eventual dating, petting, and going steady. About 50 percent of teenage heterosexual relationships now end in intercourse. By age twenty-one, 73 percent of the males and only 51 percent of the females have not yet married. More than 200,000 under the age of eighteen marry each year (U.S. Bureau of the Census, 1978).

Growing up socially is a continual reaching out for new relationships with others. Each child's/adolescent's universe is expanding into the adult world. During the gang age the first strong outside-of-home relationship is with peers. This identification continues, reaching a peak in the mid-adolescent years when there is often an extreme concern for the group. At that time there is a feeling of strong conformity and a concern for maintaining prestige among their peers. The adolescent peer group serves an important socializing function, including facilitating the transition from family dependence to independence; providing emotional security; providing an opportunity for the development of loyalties that extend beyond the immediate family; serving as models for socially appropriate behavior; and fostering the development of interpersonal relationships that become prototypes of adult relationships. Peer groups promote essential social skills related to conversation; to judging people; to interpreting verbal and nonverbal cues concerning one's own position and power in a group; and to determining what is appropriate and inappropriate in terms of behavior, dress, values, and ideals. Adolescents become critical and sensitive and frequently worry about the impression they are making on others. Being popular is very important.

In contrast and in contradiction to this desire for peer group conformity, there is also a desire for individuality—to discover one's own self, to develop self-esteem. These two opposing objectives seem to develop simultaneously, with conformity eventually giving way toward the end of adolescence to individuality when more definite personality patterns develop and there is an inclination to specialize in one type of interest. The mass media, particularly television commercials, have contributed greatly to the "do what the crowd does" syndrome. To be "in" means to have a particular shirt, sweater, or other attire, and to eat certain foods and to drink certain drinks exactly as everyone else does. In the face of this conformity, the art teacher tries to develop creativity—the uniqueness and personal expression of each student. Here, the art teacher must rely upon the student's contrasting desire for individuality. The teacher is also aided in a desire on the part of adolescents to compete in areas where they feel proficient. Skills and abilities in various art areas may be developed in the art room. These may be extended by the art teacher via praise, one-person exhibits, and artists-of-the-week designation. At this time, the uniqueness of the work of contemporary professional artists of the past may be pointed out in relation to the individuality of the adolescent's own work.

Concerning some social behaviors, adolescents realize they are not capable of making far-reaching decisions and actually welcome adult authority although they would never admit it. This is true whenever they encounter a situation they cannot handle. A correct decision by parents or teachers at the time may be face-saving and while condemning adult intervention, adolescents agree secretly that it was the best solution.

As children grow into adulthood, they begin to identify with adult structuring and phenomena. Instead of "going out to play," it becomes "going out to play with whom?" and then, "going out to play what?" They desire "rules for the game," an adult approach. Therefore, adolescents seldom if ever just "play"; they play baseball, tennis, basketball, and football. Socially, they desire a framework for operating. This may be perceived as applying the formal operations of abstract thinking—a formal structure—to social and recreational situations. Heterosexual relationships have also become something of a ritual. Adolescents have been made aware of these social innuendoes through movies and other media, as well as by their peers so that certain behaviors are expected on the first date, and at each succeeding stage of courtship.

In summary, we see that social development for the adolescent is a continuation of the process of reaching out to others that was begun in early childhood. Individuals identify with particular sex roles and eventually, for the most part, become attracted to the opposite sex during early adolescence—a development that finally ends in marriage. As adolescents identify with their peer group, there is a strong desire to conform while at the same time there is a search for individuality. As maturity takes place, more and more emphasis is placed upon adult structure and phenomena in life.

Emotional Development

Emotional development involves ability to adjust to new situations. Every adjustment implies flexibility; every maladjustment implies dependency and rigidity. An emotionally free and stable person is uninhibited, feels secure and confident, and identifies with his or her experience. Many adolescents suffer anxiety over their rate of physical development, sexual concerns, vocational concerns, intellectual ability, acceptance by their peers, and many other aspects of becoming adult. Such uneasiness is reflected in their behavior and in their art work. It is at this point that the emotional release, which is possible in art expression, is so important for adolescents. Such release is especially important during the adolescent period of great biochemical changes that create depressive states. Introspection becomes intensified as adolescents critically view themselves. This is accompanied by seeing the conflicting values of what they believe and what they see in the world—all of which leads to a period of great emotional stress. How adolescents perceive themselves and the world can be seen in such various statements as, "Most people think of me as . . . ," "When I'm thirty I expect to be . . . ," "The nicest thing about school is . . . " For a listing of such items by Edgar Z. Friedenberg (1959), see Appendix 4.

In early adolescence—sixth, seventh, and eighth grades—when individuals are experimenting, there is much fluctuation and instability as they try themselves in many ways: physically, intellectually, socially, and sexually. As a result of the growth spurt and other physical changes, they are usually restless and find it difficult to concentrate. Early adolescents tend to be spontaneous, enthusiastic, and show little foresight and judgment. Often, enthusiasm can overwhelm them to the extent that they become loud and lose control or revert to the opposite extreme.

In the late adolescent period—eleventh and twelfth grades—there is a growing ability to face reality and an obvious gain in security, self-confidence, and ability to adjust. Later adolescents show improved work habits, ability for sustained concentration, and ability to work on complex problems. They show much greater foresight, wisdom, stability, and penetration.

Perceptual Sensitivity

Perception is simply becoming mentally aware of something. Sensory perception deals with direct experiences of our senses—seeing, hearing, smelling, tasting, touching, and other body sensations. We would never be able to establish a relationship with ourselves or the environment without the ability to perceive. No learning is possible without perception. Initially, the intellect is entirely dependent upon direct sensory perception for its growth. Piaget's theory of human development relies heavily upon sense perception in the first three stages: sensorimotor, pre-operational (when children's thinking is dominated by their perceptions), and concrete operations (when children's thinking remains tied to real objects or to the potentially real) (Piaget, 1952). During these early stages, the child translates sensory perceptions into mental symbols. A symbol, or a concept, is a mental product based upon perception. As children grow toward puberty, the use of concepts continues but there is an increasing influence of visual perception and the representation of such in their art taken directly from experience. A survey (*Art and Young Americans*, 1981) of art achievement by 32,000 adolescents (in ages nine, thirteen, and seventeen) during the 1978–1979 school year labeled these students "artistic literalists" because they considered a work's resemblance to reality an important feature in its "goodness" or "badness." Although many art teachers promote an appreciation of abstract art, such as the work of Piet Mondrian, there remains a preference for more naturalistic work. Fifty-three percent of the thirteen-year-olds and 37 percent of the seventeen-year-olds agreed with the statement, "When a painting has horses in it the painting is usually good." This indicates a naïve but strong hankering for reality in art work. The marked degree of rejection of completely abstract/conceptual representations by adolescents is characteristic of the rapid change from the uninhibited, unaware reactions of the child to the critically aware reactions of the adult. It also means that for most pupils, from now on, perception is separated from intellect. Thinking involves abstractions and hypotheses. For the teacher, it means that some of the most appropriate stimulations in art are toward the direct and increasingly refined use of perception for art expression (Michael, 1964). However, such perceptions can now be combined with various art knowledges, concepts, and theories, in the production of art.

Of the various sense perceptions, it is the visual that becomes most significant for many adolescents. Visual perception cannot be developed in early childhood since the ability to see the effects caused by motion, distance (overlapping and

When visual perception develops, the drawing of expressive portraits of
classmates is not only possible but aids in bringing
about greater visual awareness and sensitivity.

perspective), light (shadows and shading), and atmosphere (sky and weather) does
not begin to develop until between eight and ten years. Bringing the sky down to
the horizon line (the overlapping of objects in the sky area) in their drawings is
one of the first indications of visual perception. A high level of development of
visual perception as expressed in drawing usually does not come about until late
adolescence or early adulthood and then only with training. Visual perception is
a very important aspect of adolescent art, as well as much adult art. More than
one half of all adolescents have a strong desire to express themselves in the visual
manner. However, some individuals gradually develop visually until about the age
of twelve and then return to other nonvisual modes of perception: touch, motions,
sounds, muscle sensations, odors, and taste—relying upon these body sensations
more than upon seeing. See chapter 5 for a discussion of visual/nonvisual perception
of adolescents.

It is important to reiterate that we can only relate to our environment through
our senses. How do you know where you are at the present time? Only by looking,
observing, listening, touching the chair you're sitting in, noting odors in the air,
and the like. These are all sense perceptions that we take for granted as adults.
To develop sensitivity to an ever higher level in all our senses that make us aware
of the environment is to become more alive, more sensitive, and more human!

Aesthetic Awareness

Aesthetic experience involves a harmonious ordering, organization, and structure. Such a harmony is brought about by a feeling of *consistency*—that all the parts belong; nothing is superfluous or needs to be added. There is a feeling of *balance*, of equilibrium; however, within the organization there is *rhythm*, a feeling of flow and movement which integrates the various parts of the organization. There is enough *variety*, *contrast*, and *opposition* of line, shape, texture, and color to hold one's interest. All the parts of the organization fit together, creating a feeling of completeness, a oneness, a *unity*. Such harmony may apply to an object, an environment, or a situation in time. There are always levels of quality within each aspect of an organization or composition that result in an over-all level of quality for a particular object or situation. The more experience one has in creating and observing these qualities, in all probability, the more sensitive and aware one will be of these qualities which go to make up the structure of an aesthetic experience.

Aesthetic experience is a basic phenomenon of our lives, of which many of us are not consciously aware. It is believed that our nervous system subconsciously orders our perceptions—what we see, hear, touch, smell, and taste—and assimilates these in an integrative way, filing them away in some manner so that we can effectively operate in the world. When perceptions come too rapidly, the nervous system cannot handle them. For example, whenever we are placed in a new environment in which we see many unfamiliar shapes, colors, objects, and hear unaccustomed sounds, we may become tired and even experience pain in the form of a headache. We are overtaxing the ability of the nervous system to organize these new perceptions. This ordering by the nervous system is the same process as the conscious ordering of lines, shapes, and colors by artists in their work and is one of the reasons for philosopher Herbert Read (1956) to write about the importance of education through art.

Everyone, therefore, has a sense of organization and ordering although it may be subconscious and undeveloped. In an experiment by the writer to compare nonart high school juniors and seniors (those who have never had art in any grade) with art juniors and seniors (those who had taken art courses continuously in elementary and high school) on ability to rank the art work of high school students for quality of their work, it was found that the high school nonart students could rank the art works almost, but not quite, as well as the high school art students. And the high school art students ranked the art work almost, but not quite, as well as the rankings of art teachers. It can therefore be assumed that everyone recognizes aesthetic organization and order to some degree, even if one has never taken an art course and does not have skill and knowledge concerning art. However, the nonart individual lacked confidence concerning art and felt inadequate in talking about art and in creating art work. Apparently, most adolescents do possess some aesthetic sensitivity but they are not consciously aware of this nor is it properly developed; therefore, they lack assurance in this area, a fact which is understandable since only about 10 to 15 percent of high school students are enrolled in art classes. For most Americans, conscious aesthetic awareness apparently is a latent aspect of their growth and development and results in their feeling inadequate in areas involving art.

As adults, we all make choices during our lives concerning material objects, the environment, and various other aesthetic situations. Adolescents need visual art experiences to make them conscious of qualities that contribute to harmonious structure and organization so that choices of an ever higher level will be made. Such awareness, in addition, helps one to experience the world more vividly, bringing about greater enjoyment of shape, color, texture, movement, feeling (mood), and other characteristics/qualities of every situation, whether it be a painting, a building, or an automobile. This latent aesthetic ability in all persons needs to be developed.

Creativity

Although most young children are creative—that is, they have a strong desire to investigate, explore, and imagine—by the time they have arrived at adolescence the school system and pressures for conformity in society have thwarted most of their creativeness. According to research by E. Paul Torrance (1962, p. 112) imaginative functioning or creativity declines to a low point between the sixth and seventh grades, after which there is a period of steady growth until the end of high school when a leveling off or a slight decline takes place. Other studies have found that the decline continues into the eighth grade before there is a period of growth (Simpson, 1922). As a result, many adolescents have little or no confidence in this area.

We can see the individual's creative ability as it functions at the present time, but we do not know an individual's potential. However, since creativity is a very important aspect of one's personality, we should make every effort to develop it. The National Commission on Youth (1980, p. 80) considers creativity to be one of two principal needs of all human growth and development. Calvin W. Taylor (1962, p. 182) writes:

> Creative persons are more devoted to autonomy, more self-sufficient, more independent in judgment, more open to the irrational in themselves, more stable, and more capable of taking greater risks in the hope for greater gains, more feminine in interests and characteristics, more dominant and assertive, more complex as a person, more self-accepting, more resourceful and adventurous, more radical (bohemian), more controlling of their own behavior by self-concept, and possibly more emotionally sensitive and more introverted but bold.

Because less creative adolescents may feel a lack of assurance, we should not be deterred but should try to develop whatever ability they have. Most students will be surprised at their accomplishments, via art experiences, in developing their ability in the eight components of creativity described in chapter 1.

Vocational Concerns

As adolescents look toward adulthood, they long for independence and responsibility which, for the most part, only education and a job can bring. There is, therefore, great interest in a vocation on the part of both junior and senior high school students. The art teacher is in a unique position to point out the many vocational areas where artists/designers contribute to our society via their aesthetic abilities and expertise. Herein, the art teacher can bridge the gap between the school, which tends to be isolated, and the real world of work. See chapter 2 and Table 6 for many art and art-related vocations and suggestions for classroom instruction in this area of career education.

WORKING WITH EXCEPTIONAL ADOLESCENTS

The underlying premise of this writing is that art experiences at the secondary level are valid for all students—including those who may be classified as exceptional. Usually under the heading of exceptional are students with various physical, mental/ learning, and emotional handicaps, as well as the gifted. In this country where we value so highly the life of each individual, exceptional adolescents should be given every consideration in the art room. No one has the right to determine which human beings should be given our attention and which are not worth the effort.

The underlying philosophic approach for working with these exceptional students is the same as for working with all secondary students in the art room. That is, we must always start with the individual student and try to meet his needs. Because they cannot excel without special assistance, handicapped students generally require more individual attention on the part of the art teacher than do the average or normal students.

The Gifted

Gifted or talented students in art at the secondary level are generally regarded as those who can perform at a high level as an artist as evidenced by their art products and art processes in contrast to the academically gifted as evidenced by high paper-pencil test scores. Giftedness in art is usually identified by the art teacher and/or jurors of art works rather than by paper-pencil tests of perception, creativity, and art/art history informational tests which are available in the field primarily for research rather than classroom use.

The art work and behaviors of gifted secondary students may be characterized by four traits:

1. Gifted students are *creative and imaginative*—nonconforming to rebellious—which is shown in the uniqueness of their work. They tend to be spontaneous and to sense intuitively what to do to improve their work. They have a high level of fluency, ideas occurring rapidly to them as they work.
2. They have a high level of *perceptual/aesthetic sensitivity*. They are very much aware of their environment and possess the ability to abstract and organize elements in a harmonious and unified manner.
3. Gifted art students are *very much involved with art* including both the subject matter and the medium. This involvement usually is reflected in their patience and skill/craftsmanship.
4. They are also characterized by *individuality and conviction*. Their work possesses a feeling of confidence, certainty, and purpose—reflecting a discipline of visual expression.

Gifted students are imaginative, perceptually/aesthetically sensitive, involved, and individual in their art expression as is seen in this work, "Fantasy Tree."

Gifted students are frequently ignored by teachers since it is obvious that they comprehend and master with ease that which is being taught. Many teachers, therefore, feel they should work with the average and less capable students, allowing the gifted to go their own way. Such apathy on the part of teachers may result in psychological damage and permanent impairment of ability. A laissez-faire approach toward the gifted in no way meets their needs to perform at an ever higher level of learning and development. (See chapter 5 concerning the needs of gifted students who are at the higher levels of performance.)

If one assumes that professional artists, who are at the forefront of their respective fields, are gifted, then it follows that an identification by these artists of factors in their childhood and youth that have influenced their work would be important considerations for gifted secondary art students and their teachers. In a survey of more than 350 outstanding artists (Michael, 1970, p. 21), 85 percent said that their childhood/youth experiences have had an effect upon their current art work. The experiences of gifted artists are probably valid in the education of gifted adolescent art students. The following are experiences identified by gifted artists as positively affecting their art work:

1. Exposure to art and music—art objects in the home and community; visits to museums; art books available; contact with artists
2. Encouragement by parents, teachers, and friends to do art work; art materials supplied
3. Producing art work; exploration of various materials; development of imagination
4. Adult acceptance and praise of art work created by the young person
5. Permissive home atmosphere
6. Many perceptual experiences; close contact with nature; development of awareness
7. An inner urge to do art

These behaviors, believed by gifted artists to affect their work as adults, are in keeping with the recommended methodology for all students in the art class as noted in chapter 5.

Mainstreaming

Federal mandates and various state mandates require that handicapped students be placed in the least restrictive educational/school environment. These laws have resulted in handicapped students being placed, where educationally feasible, in regular classes with nonhandicapped students, a practice which has become known as "mainstreaming." The federal law specifies that special classes, separate schooling, or other removal of handicapped students from the regular education environment may occur only when the nature or severity of the handicap is such that education in regular classes with the use of supplementary aids and services cannot be achieved satisfactorily. However, where a handicapped student is so disruptive in a regular art room that the education of other students is significantly impaired, the needs of the handicapped student cannot be met in that environment. Therefore, regular art room placement would not be appropriate.

Handicapped students are those evaluated as being mentally retarded, hard of hearing, deaf, speech impaired, visually handicapped, seriously emotionally disturbed, orthopedically impaired, other health impaired, deaf-blind, multihandicapped, or as having specific learning disabilities (Education of Handicapped Children, 1977, pp. 42478–9).

When evaluating a handicapped student for successful placement into a regular secondary art class, one must be cognizant of the individual's mental age, motor development, abstracting and creative abilities, and emotional and social development. Art expression at the secondary level makes heavy demands on perception, organization, integration and synthesis, symbolization, and physical energy. Since the majority of handicapped students are characteristically lacking in perhaps many of these, the art teacher must be very much aware of individual needs in order to plan for successful participation (DeChiara and Kaplan, 1981). Therefore, it behooves art teachers to obtain as much information as possible about the handicaps of particular students from experts trained in this area of special education. Art teachers should know the limits and expectations of each student with a particular handicap, each student being somewhat different from others with a similar handicap. Our goal, as for nonhandicapped students, is to help each student to actualize his or her potential in learning and development through art experiences.

Creative and expressive art activities are particularly meaningful for handicapped students because of the emotional trauma which may accompany the handicap. Art work can release, in an acceptable manner, the frustration, restricted energies, and emotional tensions caused by the handicap. Art experiences, particularly drawing, painting, and clay work, help these students to adjust and accept their handicaps. Art work strengthens their self images in relation to the social and physical environment. Learning in art aids in developing one's openness to experience. These students see themselves more positively and their handicaps more objectively/realistically when they realize they can create successfully and identify with themselves and their subject matter in their art work. The mirror of art may act as a reflection because of the projective character of the art process. Art work helps these students communicate and make contact with the social, cultural, and physical environment, overcoming a feeling of isolation due to the handicap. Art work also provides a means of developing compensating abilities in the remaining unimpaired senses and functioning body parts.

Generally, the approach to working with handicapped students is similar to that of working with nonhandicapped students. However, more sensitivity and a longer period may be needed in getting these students to identify with media. For instance, the temperature and plasticity of clay may be of great concern in working with blind students. If the clay is too cold or too soft and pliable, these students may reject it as a threat to their well being. After an acquaintance and acceptance of the medium, it is suggested that initial stimulations be directed toward the body/self. Most life experiences are related to and through the body. This, then, would be the aspect with which students are most familiar. Art expression by handicapped students may at first be diffused and unclear as they experiment with the medium, "find" themselves, and discover the problem of the artist—one's purpose in making art. As they become knowledgeable concerning these aspects of art, their art work will become more and more meaningful, personal, expressive, and aesthetic. Art experiences can do for these students what no other subject in the school curriculum can do—give them a personal means of visual expression/communication.

ADOLESCENT NEEDS AND THE SCHOOL ART PROGRAM

The particular needs and characteristics of adolescents *do* affect art instruction in many ways. The art teacher must consider and relate to these if there is to be an identification with the adolescent student and a meaningful art program. Objectives, stimulations, curricula, methods, media, art processes, and subjects must be seen in light of the following needs of adolescents. These needs are not necessarily listed in order of importance since importance varies from student to student and from one class to another. To summarize, adolescents need an art program that will help them:

1. Understand and accept their changing physical/sexual development
2. Develop more and more responsibility and become independent as they move toward adulthood

3. Become aware of the problem of the artist and creative aspects of art
4. Develop the unique and distinctive personality of each individual
5. Develop self-confidence in their own art work and in their own abilities so as to withstand critical evaluation
6. Relate to their peers of both sexes
7. Find a release of tensions brought about by this period of change and insecurity
8. Obtain recognition and praise of themselves and their art work (when merited)
9. Develop knowledges, skills, and abilities (perceptual, physical, aesthetic, intellectual, creative) as these relate to the visual and related arts (see Appendix 2)
10. Develop a knowledge of the history of art, as well as contemporary art
11. Discover many types of personal expression: naturalistic, expressive, and abstract, including an awareness of visual/nonvisual perception
12. Build a program from the elementary through the secondary level that is interrelated and integrated
13. Deal with individual interests and abilities
14. Deal with career education and vocational opportunities in the visual arts
15. Develop a good attitude toward visual art

REFERENCES

Alan Guttmacher Institute. *Teenage Pregnancy: The Problem That Hasn't Gone Away*. New York: The Alan Guttmacher Institute, 1981.

Art and Young Americans, 1974–79: Results from the Second National Art Assessment (No. 10-A-01). Denver: National Assessment of Educational Progress, 1981.

Ausubel, D. P. Implications of preadolescent and early adolescent cognitive development for secondary school teaching. *The High School Journal*, 1962, *XLV*, 268–275.

Barter, J. T., Swaback, D. O., and Todd, D. Adolescent suicide attempts. *Archives of General Psychiatry*, 1968, *19*, 523–527.

Bem, S. L. Androgyny vs. the light little lives of fluffy women and chesty men. *Psychology Today*, 1975, *9* (4), 58–62.

Blaine, G. B., Jr. *Patience and Fortitude: The Parents' Guide to Adolescence*. Boston: Little, Brown, 1962.

Coleman, J. S. *Youth: Transition to Adulthood*, Report of the Panel on Youth of the President's Science Advisory Committee (4106–00037). Washington, D.C.: U.S. Government Printing Office, 1973.

Cook, L. Little girls play house while little boys prefer war. *Cincinnati Enquirer*, March 22, 1977, B-11. Copyright Associated Press.

Davis, K. *Human Society*. New York: Macmillan, 1949.

DeChiara, E. and Kaplan, V. Mainstreaming in art. *School Arts*, 1981, *80* (8), 62–63.

Dell, L. L. *Suggestions for Drug Counseling by the Classroom Teacher*. Phoenix: Do It Now Foundation, National Media Center, n.d.

Durkheim, E. *Suicide: A Study in Sociology* (G. Simpson, ed.; J. A. Spaulding and G. Simpson, trans.). Toronto, Ontario: Collier-Macmillan, 1951.

Education of Handicapped Children: Implementation of Part B of the Education of the Handicapped Act. *Federal Register*, August 23, 1977, *42*, 42474–42518.

FBI Uniform Crime Reports: Crime for the United States, 1975. Washington, D.C.: Federal Bureau of Investigation, U.S. Government Printing Office, 1976.

Fishburne, P. M., Abelson, H. I., and Cisin, I. *National Survey on Drug Abuse: Main Findings 1979* (ADM 80–976). Rockville, Maryland: U.S. Dept. of Health and Human Services, National Institute on Drug Abuse, 1980.

Fornaciari, S. *How to Talk to Kids About Drugs*. San Francisco: Pacific Institute for Research and Evaluation, 1980.

Friedenberg, E. Z. *The Vanishing Adolescent*. New York: Dell, 1959.

Gintis, H. Education, technology, and the characteristics of worker productivity. *The American Economic Review*, 1971, *61*, 266–279.

Group for the Advancement of Psychiatry, Committee on Adolescence. *Normal Adolescence: Its Dynamics and Impact*. New York: Scribner, 1968.

Holtzman, W. H. The changing world of mental measurement and its social significance. *American Psychologist*, 1971, *26*, 546–553.

Inhelder, B., and Piaget, J. *The Growth of Logical Thinking from Childhood to Adolescence*. New York: Basic Books, 1958.

Jencks, C. The Coleman Report and the conventional wisdom. In F. Mosteller and D. P. Moynihan (eds.), *On Equality of Education Opportunity*. New York: Vintage Books, 1972.

Johnston, L. D., Bachman, J. G., and O'Malley, P. M. *Drugs and the Class of 1978: Behaviors, Attitudes, and Recent National Trends* (ADM 79–887). Rockville, Maryland: U.S. Dept. of Health, Education, and Welfare, National Institute on Drug Abuse, 1979.

Johnston, L. D., Bachman, J. G., and O'Malley, P. M. *Student Drug Use in America: 1975–81* (ADM 81–1066). Rockville, Maryland: U.S. Dept. of Health and Human Services, National Institute on Drug Abuse, 1981.

Mead, M. *Coming of Age in Samoa*. New York: W. Morrow, 1928.

Michael, J. A. (ed.). *Art Education in the Junior High School*. Washington, D.C.: National Art Education Association, 1964.

Michael, J. A. *A Handbook for Art Instructors and Students Based upon Concepts and Behaviors*. New York: Vantage Press, 1970.

National Commission on Youth. *The Transition of Youth to Adulthood: A Bridge Too Long*. Boulder, Colorado: Westview Press for the Charles F. Kettering Foundation, 1980.

Peck, R. F., and Havighurst, R. J. *The Psychology of Character Development*. New York: Wiley, 1960.

Piaget, J. *The Origins of Intelligence in Children*. New York: International University Press, 1952.

Read, H. *Education Through Art* (3rd ed.). New York: Pantheon Books, 1956.

Rice, J. Peers displace parents as teen's no. 1 influence. *Cincinnati Enquirer*, September 2, 1980, B-8.

Sawyers, J. K. Developmental study of sex differences in spatial, verbal, and logical reasoning ability. Unpublished doctoral dissertation. Oklahoma State University, 1979.

Simpson, R. M. Creative imagination. *American Journal of Psychology*, 1922, *33*, 234–243.

Smith, D. F. Adolescent suicide: a problem for teachers. *Phi Delta Kappan*, 1976, *57*, 539–542.

Spock, B. *Raising Children in a Difficult Time: A Philosophy of Parental Leadership and High Ideals*. New York: W.W. Norton, 1974.

Taylor, C. W. A tentative description of the creative individual. In S. J. Parnes and H. F. Harding (eds.), *A Source Book for Creative Thinking*. New York: Scribner, 1962.

Torrance, E. P. *Guiding Creative Talent*. Englewood Cliffs, New Jersey: Prentice-Hall, 1962.

U.S. Bureau of the Census. *Perspectives on American Husbands and Wives* (Series P-23,

No. 77). Washington, D.C.: Current Population Reports, U.S. Government Printing Office, 1978.

U.S. Department of Health, Education, and Welfare. *Suicide in the United States: 1950–1975*. Washington, D.C.: U.S. Government Printing Office, 1975.

SUPPLEMENTAL READINGS

Bachman, Jerald G., Johnston, Lloyd D., and O'Malley, Patrick M. *Monitoring the Future: Questionnaire Responses from the Nation's High School Seniors*. Ann Arbor, Michigan: Institute for Social Research, 1981. Detailed data concerning responses to many pertinent questions.

Berzonsky, Michael D. *Adolescent Development*. New York: Macmillan, 1981. A conceptual framework for viewing and interpreting adolescent behavior.

Betensky, Mala. *Self-Discovery Through Self-Expression*. Springfield, Illinois: Thomas, 1973. Understanding adolescents (case studies) through spontaneous art expression.

Burkhart, Kathryn W. *Growing into Love: Teenagers Talk Candidly about Sex in the 1980's*. New York: Putnam, 1981. An investigation of adolescent sexuality.

Dusek, Jerome B. *Adolescent Development and Behavior*. Chicago: Science Research Associates, 1977. Current theory and research on adolescent development centered around four themes: biological, intellectual, cultural, self perception.

Giovacchini, Peter L. *The Urge to Die: Why Young People Commit Suicide*. New York: Macmillan, 1981. An excellent review of adolescent problems that may end up in suicide, with suggestions for helping.

Guardo, Carol J. *The Adolescent as an Individual: Issues and Insights*. New York: Harper and Row, 1975. A "mini-course" in the psychology of adolescence and adolescent behavior.

Jacobs, Jerry. *Adolescent Suicide*. New York: Wiley-Interscience, 1971. Suicide accounts—intentions, motives, and morals—taken at face value and analyzed.

Lefrancois, Guy R. *Adolescents*. Belmont, California: Wadsworth, 1976. A textbook concerning biological, theoretical, psychological, sociological, and moral aspects of adolescence.

Meyerson, Simon (ed.). *Adolescence and Breakdown*. London: George Allen & Unwin, 1975. Authorities discuss problems of adolescence: dropping out, delinquency, rebellion, drugs, depression, and suicide—concluding with treatment and therapy.

Mosler, Ralph L. (ed.). *Adolescents' Development and Education: A Janus Knot*. Berkeley: McCutchan, 1979. A summary of current developmental knowledge of adolescents and new educational programs to stimulate their all-around growth.

Offer, Daniel, Ostrov, Eric, and Howard, Kenneth I. *The Adolescent: A Psychological Self-Portrait*. New York: Basic Books, 1981. The results of an eighteen-year study of the developmental path of normal adolescence.

Schwarz, Meg (ed.). *TV and Teens*. Reading, Massachusetts: Addison-Wesley, 1982. An analysis of the role of TV in relation to adolescents, including such subjects as health, entertainment/information, role models, careers, sex, drugs, crime, and suicide.

Silverman, Ronald H., and Hoepfner, R. *Developing and Evaluating Art Curricula Specifically Designed for Disadvantaged Youth*. Los Angeles: California State College, 1969. A research study that describes the positive effect of art experiences upon seventh-grade disadvantaged students.

CHAPTER 4

SELECTING ART EXPERIENCES
The Curriculum

The art curriculum consists of all the organized art experiences the student has in the school program. At the secondary level, these experiences are generally organized by the course. Whereas most courses are offered for the entire school year, others are offered for only one semester or one quarter depending upon the structural organization of the school.

Currently, much emphasis is placed upon curricula and curriculum development almost to the exclusion of other aspects of the teaching/learning process. This emphasis is a result of public concern for accountability and getting our educational money's worth. Many educators and a large segment of the public believe that if students perform certain intellectual/skill tasks and develop resulting competencies then, having experienced these activities (no matter how they are taught), education will be guaranteed or at least will be more apt to happen. Therefore, with emphasis upon what may be superficial behaviors, little attention is given to assimilation, internalization, or integration—and attitude, confidence, integrity, self-esteem, social-personal values (cooperation, responsibility), aesthetic sensitivity, creativity, and emotional stability are not even dealt with in most curricula.

BASES FOR CURRICULUM DEVELOPMENT

Curriculum guides are developed by teachers and supervisors of most school districts to aid teachers in planning art experiences for each course. Sometimes the curriculum guide, which is usually made up of suggested art activities, has become a required course of study with an agenda of certain art activities mandated to be rigidly adhered to by the teacher. However, for the most part, the art curriculum guides of a school system are generally thought of as being truly guides and aids for art teachers who, in the end, are responsible for selecting and developing the actual art experiences that go to make up the curriculum.

84

Guidelines

Art experiences should be planned with three considerations in mind: the students; the field of art; and the total art program of the school system.

Attention must be given to the needs, interests, attitude, background, and level of development of all students. It is important at this point to consider what the "needs" of students are. Teachers often glibly speak of meeting student needs without an understanding of the true meaning of the concept. Abraham Maslow (1970) noted several levels of human needs. First are the apparently unchanging physiological needs for food, water, air, shelter, and sex. Then he identified higher needs which appear as soon as the first set of lower needs, the physiological, are satisfied. These are the needs for safety and security followed by the love needs of self-esteem, respect, and approval from others. Topmost in Maslow's hierarchy are what he called "metaneeds" of truth, goodness, beauty, order, justice, simplicity, playfulness, self-sufficiency, and meaningfulness. Satisfying these needs results in a self-actualized individual—becoming all that one is capable of becoming, becoming fully human. William Glasser (1975) also noted that people must satisfy their basic needs for relatedness and respect. He equates personal responsibility with mental health. Viktor Lowenfeld (1957) stressed seven areas of human needs in which art experiences can be meaningfully involved: intellectual, emotional, social, physical, perceptual, creative, and aesthetic. (See Chart 6 and Appendix 2, item 3.) These needs (in reality, goals of education and of life itself), if not obvious to the reader, do underlie the objectives as promulgated in chapter 2.

Unless students are involved, stimulated, are made responsible, secure, and confident, and want to learn, little learning or development will take place, and certainly students will have a poor attitude concerning art. The bottom line of all curriculum planning should be the students. Without students there would be no schools. Therefore, the students' needs involving learning, growth, and development must be paramount in the mind of the art teacher when art experiences are selected for the curriculum. (Also see the listing of needs in chapter 3.)

Any student who is involved in art activity should become knowledgeable about some content that is significant to the art field and that is interesting to the student. The acquisition of such knowledge, as well as art skills, may be a concomitant learning as a result of involvement in studio and/or studio-related art experiences or may be a result of specific academic-type learning experiences that are conceptually oriented. Whatever the approach at the secondary level, the teacher should plan for the cognitive (content), the psychomotor (art skills), and the affective (art attitude) aspects of the curriculum, as well as meeting the needs of students, which may be the result of studio, isolated content, skill, or affective art experiences in the curriculum.

The art teacher must also be aware of how the curriculum of a particular course fits in with the curricula of all the other art courses in the school; otherwise, there may be repetitions and redundancies in the art program that may negatively affect student learning, attitude, and interest. Each experience of every course should take the student to an ever higher level and should be thought of as a block in the building of a total program of art education. For information concerning how the various curricula fit into a total program of art education, the art teacher may refer to the art curriculum guides of the school system, which indicate art experiences (required and suggested) for each course in the elementary and secondary art programs.

Tenets of Learning

For maximum learning and development to take place, various tenets of learning should be considered in planning any curricular art experiences, as well as in developing any methodology. The following are suggested as guidelines in developing and carrying out art activities for adolescents.

1. All learning is based upon one's perceptual/sensory intake: seeing, hearing, touching, tasting, smelling, and moving. Students learn more from first-hand experiences.
2. Needs and interests (based upon the life of the student) are the bases of learning experiences; classroom activities and materials must be meaningful; *students must be stimulated* and become enthusiastic.
3. Learning and development are stimulated by both security and adventure; the learning task should not be viewed by students as too easy or too difficult.
4. Learning involves some confusion and uncertainty because thinking takes place when one does *not* know what to do next. Learning begins with a lack of understanding (a question, a doubt, an uncertainty) with the student eventually achieving understanding and learning something new (Greenberg, 1969, pp. 34–35).
5. Learning is more meaningful when students are open to the new tasks, desire to learn, and have sufficient confidence in themselves to put forth energy and overcome obstacles.
6. Learning is more meaningful when students participate in determining objectives, in planning, and in evaluating.
7. Learning is more meaningful when students have self-understanding and direction leading to greater confidence and success.
8. Learning is increased when students are relieved of anxiety and pressure for competition; when failures are viewed constructively; when efforts are appreciated; when students are freed from distractions and personal problems; and when students are not restricted to the things the teacher already knows.
9. Learning involves some change in behavior, hopefully positive.
10. Skills and knowledges should be learned as aspects of art/art expression and life and not as isolated experiences.
11. Learning is most likely to occur when a conclusion or art product is reached before motivation is exhausted.

Benjamin S. Bloom (1976) believes it is possible for 95 percent of our students to learn all that the typical school has to teach at near the same mastery level. Bloom's research indicates that most students become very similar in regard to learning ability when provided with favorable learning conditions. However, when students are provided with unfavorable learning conditions they become more dissimilar in learning ability, rate of learning, and motivation for further learning.

The kind, quality of instruction, and the amount of time allowed for study must be appropriate for the *needs* of each learner; then the majority of students will achieve mastery. Mastery learning in art begins with the premise that all students are creative, have aesthetic ability, perceptual sensitivity, motor skills, and intellectual ability which enable them to attain a high level of art expression, art knowledge, and art appreciation if instruction is approached sensitively. Students must be motivated, helped when they have difficulties, given sufficient time, and given some clear goals to achieve.

ART CURRICULUM DESIGN

There are basically two design approaches to developing an art curriculum. One involves planning curricular experiences based upon the field of art and is usually done before classes begin—previous to meeting the students—and the other involves working directly with the students, letting the art activities that make up the curriculum evolve from the teacher interacting and working directly with the students and their concerns. The design approach selected depends upon the teacher's philosophic point of view, objectives, and how art and the art experience are perceived. However, because of various art teaching situations which may demand different curricular organization and sequencing, it is entirely possible for a teacher to use one design approach in one class and a different design approach in another class. Herein, the professional art educator considers all factors involved in the teaching/learning situation and arrives at a decision that is in accord with his philosophy and objectives. The following are three types of curricular organization based upon the above two design approaches and a combination of these. (See Chart 3.) It behooves the art teacher to know the meaning and purpose of each type of curriculum design and sequencing so that these may be applied when appropriate for the maximum student learning and development to take place.

The Preplanned Curriculum: Subject-Oriented

The art teacher following a preplanned, subject-oriented design approach organizes the art curriculum by relying upon the content of the field of art—art knowledges to be learned and art skills to be developed. Art is conceived as a subject, a content area, not unlike academic disciplines. Art is analyzed and dissected into elements, principles, skills, knowledges, and history. Art experiences are decided upon logically and usually before the teacher meets the students, which is possible since the students, in reality, are to learn about art as one would learn about math or history. After a rational and logical presentation of an art-class activity, all students generally work on the same activity, project, or problem at one and the same time. Models and examples to be imitated are frequently shown to the students when the lesson is first presented. Finished art products are conceived and visualized by the teacher before the lesson or lessons are presented to the students. Knowledges and skills the students are to possess are likewise predetermined. Sequencing is achieved by using one of the content-centered approaches described later in this chapter. For the most part, the art/design elements and principles, art media/processes, and/or the art history methods of sequencing

CHART 3
Curriculum Design

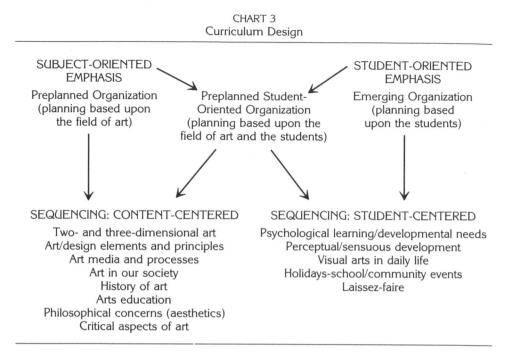

SUBJECT-ORIENTED
EMPHASIS
Preplanned Organization
(planning based upon
the field of art)

Preplanned Student-
Oriented Organization
(planning based upon the
field of art and the students)

STUDENT-ORIENTED
EMPHASIS
Emerging Organization
(planning based
upon the students)

SEQUENCING: CONTENT-CENTERED
Two- and three-dimensional art
Art/design elements and principles
Art media and processes
Art in our society
History of art
Arts education
Philosophical concerns (aesthetics)
Critical aspects of art

SEQUENCING: STUDENT-CENTERED
Psychological learning/developmental needs
Perceptual/sensuous development
Visual arts in daily life
Holidays-school/community events
Laissez-faire

are used by teachers who preplan an art curriculum based upon the discipline of art. Classes tend to be formal, with all activities becoming exercises that are assigned by the teacher. Students, who lack confidence and feel they lack ability to do the art work assigned, may show symptoms of anxiety and stress in their behavior in this type of curricular organization.

The Preplanned Curriculum: Student-Oriented

In using the preplanned, student-oriented method of curriculum design, the art teacher has in mind before meeting the students certain media and art experiences that are thought to be a necessary part of the curriculum and may be required in the course of study. However these required experiences are adjusted and timed to meet the needs and interests of the students. For instance, in an introductory art course, the teacher may be required by the course of study to involve students in particular art processes during the school year, such as drawing, painting, printmaking, lettering/advertising, ceramics, and art history. The schedule for sequencing these six activities is kept open and flexible to provide for stimulating events that may arise during the school year and for addressing the individual needs and differences of students. For example, closure experiences involving drawing and painting may be used at the beginning of the course to achieve student confidence and interest in art. Lettering, poster, and advertising activities may be introduced when these are needed by students for advertising a carnival, a play, a musical, or a sports event in the school. Holidays may also determine the most opportune time to carry out certain art experiences because of high student interest and involvement during the holiday period. Halloween may be an excellent time for figure drawing when students enjoy posing in costumes. This organizational approach may be described as being student-oriented with quasi student-centered sequencing since the teacher is concerned with the students and tries to introduce the required art experiences when they will be most meaningful in meeting student needs and interests. This may be an excellent curricular organization for an initial art course at the secondary level if teachers feel a need for teaching art fundamentals or for teaching specific introductory art experiences.

The Emerging Curriculum: Student-Oriented

The art teacher subscribing to the emerging curriculum design plans experiences after studying all the students' needs, interests, abilities, functional levels, backgrounds, and any other aspects that may affect learning and development. Art experiences are sequenced by any of the student-centered approaches that are included in this chapter. There is no prescribed art content to be covered. If interested, students may work on ceramics for the entire semester or even the entire year providing the teacher feels learning and developing on the part of the students is taking place with each new experience in the area of study. This approach requires teacher-student consulting and planning together for art experiences. Either the teacher or the student may suggest art experiences, the teacher's role being that of a guide or facilitator. Herein the teacher must be very sensitive to students and to what is happening to them in the art class. Although all the students in a class may be involved in a similar art activity in this type of curricular organization, it is also possible to have several groups within a class that are working with different media and processes. For example, one group may be involved in making woodcuts, another group in making effigy pots, and another group in painting a still life. This type of curriculum development may be appropriate for classes that have previously had a more structured art course, because it is important that students first learn about the problem of the artist, something about media, and classroom routines before attempting this rather free approach, otherwise chaos may result with an inexperienced teacher.

The emerging type of curriculum design may, perhaps, be used even more successfully on an individual basis. Herein, the teacher plans experiences after studying the needs, interests, functional levels, and backgrounds of each individual instead of considering all the students as a group. When this individualized emerging curricular organization is used, each student will probably be working with a medium/process/problem different from that of the other students. Obviously, this is the most flexible and personal approach to the teaching/learning process, and probably the most ideal.

A great variety of tools, materials, and pieces of equipment are a necessity for a rich program of art experiences when using this individualized organization; however, only a few tools are needed in each art area. One floor loom, one potter's wheel, an enameling kiln, a set of jewelry tools, a printing press, a few carving tools, a few oil paints, acrylics and watercolors, and art history books, may be sufficient for several classes using this type of curriculum. Students must be self-motivated, responsible, and cooperative in developing excellent classroom management procedures if each of the twenty or twenty-five students in a class is working with a different medium/process and with as many different art experiences going on as there are students in the class. The teacher must be very well prepared,

"Happy Hal" is one of a series of cartoons made by a student in an emerging curricular plan wherein each student works according to his or her individual needs and interests. This student was concerned with developing continuity in comic strips.

possessing a tremendous knowledge and background concerning both the field of art and the students. Each student must be counseled, problems/objectives decided upon, media chosen, procedures planned, and evaluative procedures considered. A lesson plan must be developed for each student. The teacher must keep abreast of the progress of each individual in the class and continually present new ideas, suggestions, methods, and stimulations, as these twenty or twenty-five lessons are simultaneously being carried out in the classroom. Some teachers keep a record by working out with each student a written contract. Each contract becomes somewhat like a lesson plan for that particular student.

Although the emerging type of curricular organization is tremendously challenging to the art teacher, great creativity, experimentation, and learning are possible for the students. It is ideal for self-motivated students because they can select, with the assistance of the teacher, the topic, media, process, or area of study that best meets their needs and interests. When each student is working in a different area, all the students in the class can become aware of what all the other students are doing. This extends the frame of reference of all the students far beyond what it would be if all members of the class were working in the same art area. However, one student still may not understand what another is doing in this type of organization unless the teacher calls for the attention of the entire class and makes all the students aware and responsible for knowing about the work of all the other students. A simple informational test concerning all the media/processes that are going on in the class will make the students aware of the seriousness of the teacher's objectives in this regard. Teaching for this knowledge and understanding is an important aspect when using the emerging type of curricular organization. When all students are made aware of all the art experiences going on in the class and become informed concerning all the particular art activities, students who want to pursue the particular art activity of another student can go ahead without the teacher having to repeat information over and over again. Students can also be utilized in the teaching process. For example, a student who has made a ring may teach a second student the procedure, allowing the teacher to spend more time discussing art/design and expressive aspects.

SEQUENCING ART EXPERIENCES

Art teachers may use various approaches and combinations of approaches in developing and ordering art experiences for any one of the three types of curriculum design previously discussed. *Art experiences must be ordered in such a way that there is an attempt to bring learning and development to a higher level as a result of each experience, each activity building upon the previous one.* A group of art experiences around a theme, medium, process, or historical period is called a unit. The desire of every art teacher should be to make all curricular experiences as meaningful as possible in achieving the objectives of the program. Therefore, in various situations, any one of the approaches to sequencing may be valid just as at times any one of the three curriculum designs may be appropriate. Only the teacher can make a decision as to where to use each type of organization and sequence depending upon his philosophy and objectives, the students, the total art program of the school system, and any other aspects which may have a bearing upon the teaching/learning situation. The many and varied approaches to sequencing that follow tend to be either student-centered or content-centered. Student-centered sequencing indicates an emphasis upon the importance of the student, his or her learning, growth, and development; the content-centered approach indicates an emphasis upon the importance of the student learning about the field of art, the content of the field being paramount.

Content-Centered Sequencing of Art Experiences

TWO-DIMENSIONAL AND THREE-DIMENSIONAL ART.   One of the simplest content-centered approaches is that of sequencing by alternating two-dimensional and three-dimensional art experiences. Some teachers require alternating experiences to be three-dimensional, the others being two-dimensional; other teachers require at least one three-dimensional work for every six-week term, all other work being two-dimensional. The rationale for this simplistic approach is that students must become proficient in flat work and work in the round for a greater understanding of spatial qualities in the visual arts.

Photo courtesy of Craig Roland

Art elements and principles are applied to an abstract painting emphasizing rhythmic growth, as in this example wherein art/design information is emphasized in a content-centered approach to sequencing.

ART/DESIGN ELEMENTS AND PRINCIPLES.   Art experiences may be sequenced and ordered around the art/design elements and principles, which are considered to be the basic language of the artist. The rationale for this approach is that students should first learn the grammar of art before they can express themselves meaningfully, creatively, and with aesthetic quality. Some schools require a semester or more of the study of these visual fundamentals before the student is permitted to try other art experiences. Therefore, many experiences with line, shape, value, texture, and color are planned. It is usually felt that art starts with line, which can produce shape. Value, then, is applied to shape creating form to which texture and color can be applied. These elements are generally taught as a series of many sensitizing/skill exercises, including a color wheel. Some teachers hold rigidly to a hierarchy of sequenced art experiences in this area. Teachers subscribing to this approach usually have tried many different exercises over the years, ending up with a few they feel are the most successful in developing sensitivity and knowledge of the art elements and skill in their use. After students have been grounded in the design elements, various art principles are then taught via a similar approach. Balance (formal and informal), rhythm, variety, opposition, contrast, and unity are some of the principles around which sensitizing experiences are planned. Lessons involving formal balance are usually the first in a long sequence of such experiences.

ART MEDIA AND PROCESSES.   Art experiences may be based upon types of art media and processes which are found in the typical art school program: designing, drawing, painting, printmaking, sculpturing, potting, advertising, metalworking (jewelry, art metal, enameling), and fabric designing (printing, dyeing, weaving). Some teachers believe it is necessary to develop drawing ability before one can paint. In fact, many teachers sequence drawing and designing before any

Printmaking is one of the art processes used in the content-centered art-media-and-processes approach to sequencing.

of the other art processes. Within some of these processes there are definite sequences that must be developed. For example, in throwing on the potter's wheel, it is necessary first to wedge the clay, then center it on the wheel, make a well, and finally draw up the clay before it can be shaped into a pot. Many of these teachers also believe it is necessary for students to have some experience with many art media, as well as art processes, within a course to ensure a broad experience. However, an opposite approach is seen in some secondary schools where semester-length or mini courses are developed around specific media/processes. Courses are offered in designing, drawing, painting, sculpturing, printmaking, and so on, in imitation of many university course offerings and give the student a depth experience with a particular medium and process.

ART IN OUR SOCIETY.   Art experiences may be selected and sequenced according to the uses of art in our society, such as art in the home, art in religion, art in industry, art in commerce, and art in the community (Faulkner and Ziegfeld, 1975). Art experiences are sequenced to give students insight into the social purposes of art—art used to satisfy human needs and to glorify human ideals and values. Units of work may involve advertising, interior design, industrial design, fashion arts, architecture, ecclesiastical art, city planning, and commercial art.

HISTORY OF ART.   Art experiences may be based upon the history of art. With this approach, art activities are usually sequenced according to the great epochs of history: the Egyptian, the Phoenician, the Sumerian, the Greek, the

Roman, and so on, up to contemporary times. Although art history is approached chronologically for the most part, art experiences may also be sequenced according to the periods of particular interest to the students and teacher regardless of any chronology. In addition, art history may be approached by studying particular facets of the visual arts such as architecture, painting, sculpture, or the minor arts. Another approach is that of sequencing according to themes such as love, war, and religion. This latter approach, in reality, becomes a humanities approach.

ARTS EDUCATION.   Recently, art experiences have been organized so as to include all the arts—an arts education approach. Various aspects of visual art, such as rhythm, balance, contrast, or pattern are taken as a point of departure in developing a sequence of arts experiences for students. For example, activities may be planned for pattern to be experienced in movement (dance); in sounds (music); with words (poetry and creative writing); and in repeated units in graphic design (visual arts). Pattern may also be shown in theatrical performance. Usually, the arts education approach requires team teaching or at least some involvement of specialists from the other arts since few teachers are prepared in all or even several of the arts.

PHILOSOPHICAL CONCERNS ABOUT ART.   Art experiences may be sequenced around philosophical concerns about art: that is, aesthetics. Various philosophic approaches, such as idealism, existentialism, pragmatism, and phenomenalism are studied, noting how these relate and concern themselves with beauty and the aesthetic. With this approach, the curriculum may be developed around a sequencing of questions such as the following: Why has art been important to most cultures? What is the role of the artist in our society? What are standards of art and who makes them? What is the role of an art critic? What is it about some works of art that makes them stand the test of time, and for generation after generation why have we considered them to be great works of art? Such a philosophical approach leads to academic classroom procedures that are characterized by lecture, discussion, critical papers, and assigned readings.

CRITICAL ASPECTS OF ART.   Art experiences may also be sequenced around critical and evaluative aspects. The writings of art critics are reviewed and works of art are studied, described, researched, discussed, compared, and evaluated. Herein, it is possible to organize critical experiences around various areas of the visual arts, such as painting, sculpture, and architecture; around various schools within an art area, such as painting—Impressionism, Fauvism, Cubism; and around the art of various historical periods. This approach to sequencing, like that of aesthetics, tends to be typically academic and is reflected as such in classroom procedures.

Student-Centered Sequencing of Art Experiences

PSYCHOLOGICAL LEARNING-DEVELOPMENTAL NEEDS.   Art experiences may be sequenced psychologically according to the learning-developmental needs, interests, and backgrounds of the students. Herein the teacher considers students' confidence in their own expression, their art background, attitude, emotional status, level of skill development, creative ability, perceptual sensitivity, knowledge/intellectual development, and perhaps their socioeconomic status. The teacher must determine priorities of student needs and plan experiences to achieve these. The emphasis, however, is placed upon the student's learning and development as a "whole" person in this psychological student-centered approach.

PERCEPTUAL/SENSUOUS DEVELOPMENT. Art experiences may also be sequenced primarily with regard to developing students' perceptual sensitivity. Art activities are selected and developed around sensuous experiences of students which usually involve seeing and touching although such experiences may also include hearing, smelling, tasting, and moving. Concerning seeing, many teachers emphasize getting students to observe depth, positive and negative shapes, idiosyncracies of an object, and the subtleties of nature. Perceptual awareness is accomplished in many ways but it is the sensuous aspects that are emphasized. Awareness and sensitivity of the student is always the concern of the teacher who subscribes to this perceptual/sensuous student-centered approach to sequencing art curriculum experiences.

VISUAL ARTS IN DAILY LIFE. Art experiences may be selected and sequenced according to contacts that students have with various aspects of the visual arts in their daily lives. Such an organization emphasizes art/design in clothing, jewelry, television and films, advertising, furniture, houses, cars, city planning, and whatever other art-related phenomena students find in their everyday lives. Such a curriculum would be made up of a sequence of art experiences involving an exploration of design, interpretation, and expression concerning these applied art areas.

SPECIAL DAYS/COMMUNITY EVENTS. Most students will naturally be stimulated by events and celebrations at home and in the community. Art experiences may be selected and sequenced around these home/school/community events, as

Halloween naturally stimulates the creation of masks, as shown by these simplified and expressive designs and is one of the holidays/community events that can be used for sequencing art activities.

well as holidays. Using this approach, the art teacher provides an opportunity for students to express their ideas and feelings concerning these happenings or to glorify these through art activities. More art curricula are probably influenced by special days and home/school/community happenings than most art teachers are willing to admit.

LAISSEZ-FAIRE.   This approach can also be used in sequencing student-centered art experiences. Herein, students are left to come up with their own sequence of art activities since teachers subscribing to this approach perceive themselves as being resource persons who provide materials, equipment, and information when students request them. Teachers holding this point of view are of the opinion that a more directed approach by the teacher will inhibit students and interfere with their creative aesthetic development.

SOURCES OF INSPIRATION FOR ART ACTIVITIES

Neither examples of a complete curriculum of the three types of curricular design organization previously presented, nor examples of a complete sequencing for any of the student-centered or content-centered approaches are offered here as specific models to be followed. Such models would not be appropriate for all situations and would thwart the creative thinking of an art teacher. Each art teaching situation must be analyzed, then the art teacher, working as a professional, must figure out the best possible curricular solution for that particular situation. For that reason— the professionalism of education—many possibilities for art activities (although somewhat fragmentary) are presented throughout this book; it is always up to the art teacher to add to these and to make them meaningful. The teacher must make the final decision as to how to bring about the most successful learning and development on the part of students in a particular classroom situation.

Now that the organizational framework for curriculum development has been presented, ideas for actual art activities must be conjured up by the creative and inventive art teacher. Teachers, as well as students, need sources of inspiration, and many of these are available to us.

Perhaps our greatest resources are the students themselves. Their activities, interests, and fantasies can be found right there in the classroom. All we need to do is to talk with our students to find out what they are involved in; what excites them; what their hobbies are; how they spend their free time; and what vocations they are interested in. As students work upon their art, problems usually arise and ideas evolve that can be used as inspiration for the next piece of art work. Closely related to the students and their activities are the holidays they celebrate, the changing seasons, and events taking place in the school, local community, and perhaps the world community. Local fairs, carnivals, and parades, as well as national and international happenings, such as space flights, Olympic games, volcanic eruptions and other disasters may be stimulating topics for art expression. In addition to curriculum guides, art/art history books and periodicals suggest many ideas for art experiences. A well stocked library of books is a necessity for the art teacher. Art supply catalogs, art suppliers who have display booths at professional conferences, and art/gift shops are sources that may suggest various media for use in the classroom. Many ideas can come from workshops at professional meetings and local universities; trips to art museums and galleries; and, of course, from one's own art work. Many teachers also get ideas from the other arts—dance, theater, music, and creative writing. Travel is another area that should not be overlooked as an exciting source for engendering inspiration. However, our most immediate source is ourselves. The creative teacher usually has so many ideas for art experiences that it is difficult to include all of them in the curriculum.

CURRICULUM CONSIDERATIONS OF PROFESSIONAL ARTISTS

In a survey of more than 350 professional artists in seven specialty areas—painting, sculpture, printmaking, pottery, weaving, jewelry, and enameling—there was a consensus pertaining to several aspects of curriculum development (Michael, 1970). Many of these artists are also teachers and are concerned with the teaching/learning process. Since adolescents are critically aware and tend to look at art as adults, it behooves us at least to consider the suggestions of those adult artists who are among the best in their particular area of art expression.

Importance of the Art Process

Since many professional artists (71 percent)[1] find that attending art exhibits and seeing the art work of others is very stimulating, such experiences should be included in the secondary art curriculum. Exhibits of local artists may be held in the school building itself. Some schools do have small art galleries where a schedule is maintained of continuous exhibitions by local artists. Trips to the studios of local artists and to local museums may also be regularly scheduled for all secondary art classes.

More than half of the professional artists (62 percent) in the survey note that thinking, feeling, and seeing (perceiving) are all important aspects of the art process but more emphasis is placed upon feeling. Art experiences that stress only drawing what one sees and correct naturalistic proportions would be out of keeping with the concerns of many professional artists.

Concerning working with tools, materials, and processes, most professional artists (87 percent) in this survey tend to enjoy these technical aspects and are stimulated by them. The art teacher, therefore, may want to give some consideration to the motivational effect of working with tools and equipment in planning art experiences. For many adolescents, as with professional artists, the mere handling of tools used in an art process is stimulating and no other motivation is needed.

Many artists (79 percent) in this survey feel that idea (topic, concept, inspiration) and media are equally important. Therefore, no curriculum should be based only upon topical ideas or upon media/processes; a combination of the two seems to be preferable. The art teacher should remember that ideas can and do grow out of experiments with media and permit an integrated combination of the two. Because fewer than half of the professional artists in this study are consciously concerned with an art vocabulary (45 percent) or the art elements (37 percent) as they work, perhaps a discussion concerning these aspects of art should be deferred until after the studio art experience has taken place when teaching art at the secondary

---

[1]Percentage of all artists agreeing on this concept.

level. If the teacher feels that art vocabulary and the art elements are important considerations, then they may be pointed out and discussed as these aspects are seen in the art work of students.

Most artists (85 percent) in this survey believe a sound training in drawing is necessary; therefore, drawing experiences probably should be given an important consideration in planning art experiences for adolescents. This may be an area the art teacher will want to return to several times in the course of a semester. Sketchbooks may also be required. Most of these artists (85 percent) also believe design is an integral part of drawing because one designs and composes as one draws. At the secondary level, perhaps drawing should be presented in such a way that design/composition is a constant consideration regardless of the art medium or process being used. It follows that many of these same artists (79 percent) believe a sound training is also necessary in design. Perhaps design should not be taught as a separate entity but should be a consideration in all art work.

Importance of Art History and General Knowledge

A knowledge of the history concerning the art area in which students are working is probably as important for many students as it is for many of the artists (62 percent) in this survey. Some historical background will aid students in their art production, extending their understanding of the medium, processes, subject matter, and artists who have worked similarly. This background in art history will give students a broader base upon which to make decisions concerning their art work.

Some students, as well as some professional artists (41 percent), may be aided more by a greater general knowledge and by developing a philosophy rather than by putting an emphasis upon the mechanics of making art. Both are important, but discussion about many subjects and value systems probably should be encouraged in the art class for the benefit of some students.

Introducing other arts experiences into the visual art class may be as inspiring for adolescents as it is for many of the professional artists (72 percent) in this survey. Experiences involving creative writing, dance, music, and theater should be planned as part of the visual art curriculum. Showing aesthetic relationships and making comparisons among the arts, again give the student greater understanding and a broader base for attacking his own art work.

The Contemporary World of Art

Most professional artists (84 percent) who were surveyed agreed that recent happenings in the professional art world indicate a breaking down of the lines between the various areas of the visual arts: paintings are becoming sculptural; paintings are appearing on ceramics; paintings are created on looms as weavings; and sculptural forms are created on the potter's wheel. Furthermore, various materials used by artists today were unheard of a few years ago. Art teachers now certainly are free to use all materials and processes in any combination and need not be concerned about teaching only painting, sculpture, ceramics, or any other art process. All materials and processes in any combination thereof may now be used in a creative and expressive manner in the art room at the secondary level.

Art experiences in the school curriculum may be multidimensional and all-encompassing.

REFERENCES

Bloom, B. S. *Human Characteristics and School Learning*. New York: McGraw-Hill, 1976.

Faulkner, R., and Ziegfeld, E. *Art Today*. New York: Holt, Rinehart and Winston, 1975.

Glasser, W. *Reality Therapy: A New Approach to Psychiatry*. New York: Harper & Row, 1975.

Greenberg, H. M. *Teaching with Feeling*. Toronto: Macmillan, 1969.

Lowenfeld, V. *Creative and Mental Growth* (3rd ed.). New York: Macmillan, 1957.

Maslow, A. H. *Motivation and Personality* (2nd ed.). New York: Harper & Row, 1970.

Michael, J. A. *A Handbook for Art Instructors and Students Based upon Concepts and Behaviors*. New York: Vantage Press, 1970.

SUPPLEMENTAL READINGS

Barkan, Manuel, Chapman, Laura H., and Kern, Evan J. *Guidelines: Curriculum Development for Aesthetic Education*. St. Ann, Missouri: CEMREL, 1970. Detailed account of developing art appreciation, behaviorally based.

Chapman, Laura H. *Approaches to Art in Education*. New York: Harcourt Brace Jovanovich, 1978. Textbook concerned with elementary and junior high, with emphasis on curriculum development in chapter 6 and Part 3.

Davis, Donald J. (ed.). *Behavioral Emphasis in Art Education*. Reston, Virginia: National Art Education Association, 1975. Behavior-oriented curriculum model presented in chapters 1 and 6.

Eisner, Elliott W., and Vallance, Elizabeth. *Conflicting Conceptions of Curriculum*. Berkeley: McCutchan, 1974. Many concepts concerning curriculum, which have been developed by outstanding persons in the field.

Feldman, Edmund B. *Becoming Human Through Art*. Englewood Cliffs, New Jersey: Prentice-Hall, 1970. Social/cultural/aesthetic theoretical background in chapters 1 through 5; curriculum development in Part 4. Although directed toward elementary level, applicable for adolescents.

Hardiman, George W., and Zernich, Theodore (eds.). *Foundations for Curriculum Development and Evaluation in Art Education*. Champaign, Illinois: Stipes, 1981. Many points of view concerning curriculum—some philosophical, some practical—by leaders in the field.

Hubbard, Guy. *Art in the High School*. Belmont, California: Wadsworth, 1967. Part 3 of this textbook deals with curriculum.

Mattil, Edward L. *A Seminar in Art Education for Research and Curriculum Development*. University Park, Pennsylvania: Pennsylvania State University, 1966. Philosophical statements by leaders in the field presenting a basis for art curricula.

Portchmouth, John. *Secondary School Art*. New York: Van Nostrand Reinhold, 1971. Stages of development at the secondary level are emphasized, including appropriate art curricular experiences.

Shultz, Larry T. A studio curriculum for art education. *Art Education*, 1980, *33* (6), 10–15. Up-grading an art program by means of a viable studio-based curriculum.

Tollifson, Jerry (ed.). *Planning Art Education in the Middle/Secondary Schools of Ohio*. Columbus, Ohio: State of Ohio, Department of Education, 1977. Primarily an aesthetic-education approach to curriculum development, with many examples and suggestions.

CHAPTER 5

IMPLEMENTING ART EXPERIENCES
Methodology

As indicated in the preceding chapter, much emphasis has recently been placed upon the curriculum: the art experiences necessary to achieve desired objectives and/or learnings on the part of the student. The curriculum has come to embody the entire teaching process with all objectives being achieved solely as a result of assigned carrier art projects. In so doing, we have forgotten the teacher and what he or she actually does to bring about learning via these curricular experiences. A good art teacher does much more than simply tell students to paint a picture, read about Impressionistic painting, carve a piece of sculpture, throw a pot, or make a block print. The manner in which curricular experiences are brought about in the classroom is the method of teaching—the level of education and the quality of the educational experience of the student being a result of a very effective method employed by the teacher. Research of Dwight Webb (1971) and data collected by him indicate that the way teachers behave, not what they know, is probably the most important aspect in the teaching/learning process. The art teacher, in reality, serves as a catalyst-guide-director-stimulator in bringing about learning, development, and a positive attitude concerning art on the part of the student via experiences involving art.

METHODOLOGY: A CONTINUUM

Methods may be placed on a continuum progressing from a rigid, authoritarian, "Do as you're told" approach to a free, laissez-faire, "hands-off" approach reflecting the type of curricular organization being used. A teacher's philosophic outlook and purpose concerning art/art experiences as noted in chapters 1 and 2 will determine the method as well as the curriculum. Philosophically, teachers may be concerned with formalistic and conceptual aspects of art, perceptual and sensuous awareness, art history and culture, art media and skill development, and creative/expressive purposes, using the art class and art experiences as a means, an instrument, for developing these and/or various other points of view or combinations thereof. Between the two methodological extremes—authoritarian and laissez-faire—lie various alternative approaches which may be employed according to one's philosophic stance. Let us consider the various methods from one end of the continuum to the other.

The Authoritarian-Dictatorial Method

The teacher using this method perceives the teaching act as one of telling and giving out information, dictating exactly what is to be done in a step-by-step manner and offering much direction/criticism at each step. Of great concern to teachers using this approach are usually formalistic aspects which involve art concepts and fundamentals; chronological art history via slides and reproductions; good conventional versus creative student art products; skill and craftsmanship; ability to follow directions; and responsibility. In completely authoritarian situations, ideas are controlled, as well as media, organization of the art work, and rate of progress. Somewhat identical products and ideas result from this convergent emphasis. Motivation comes about through fear of failure to conform, fear of being unable to meet the teacher's standard. The teacher is often viewed as someone to be emulated as master artist and authority on art. Negative criticism is often given to challenge students to do better. This authoritarian method is usually used when the teacher is working with a preplanned and rigidly structured curriculum wherein art, including studio, is viewed as a body of knowledge/concepts and skills to be mastered.

Teachers who require students to memorize, to read the next chapter, to follow precise directions, and to copy examples and imitate—reproducing a painting or an object as an exact facsimile; teachers who use prepared outlines, as in paint-by-number exercises; and teachers who use patterns designed by someone else, as found in many leather-tooling kits, are employing the authoritarian method. Although this approach does *not* permit students to express much of their own individuality in solving aesthetic problems and in discovering their own forms of expression, it may be used more legitimately when teaching certain factual information, art fundamentals, processes and procedures involving media, tools and equipment, as well as aspects of art history. Knowledge and skill in soldering; the initial procedures of throwing on the potter's wheel; applying value (charcoal) to geometric forms; and knowledge of a particular style of painting, such as Impressionism, are examples. Fortunately, most teachers view these simply as extra-art activities or exercises and *not* as art.

In a study of this convergent approach involving memorization, skills, accumulation of facts, and a conventional (all alike) end art product, Stanley Madeja (1967) found that only students rated low in art ability tend to learn about art via this method. However, for all students their self-concept was better when a creative, divergent approach was used in the art class.

The Assigned Topic, Student-Oriented Method

Herein the teaching act is generally perceived as one of helping students become motivated to express themselves and, as a result of this art experience, develop their abilities and knowledge concerning art. Of great importance to teach-

"The Parade" was the topic assigned to students as a result of a military parade near the school. The use of community events is an appropriate motivational method for implementing art experiences in the classroom and may be used in part for developing a curricular sequence.

ers using this method are usually students' confidence, creativity, perceptual sensitivity, aesthetic awareness, art knowledge, skill/craftsmanship, and a good attitude as shown by the art product and other behaviors. In this approach the teacher and/ or students decide upon a topic, subject, or idea, and the art medium—the medium being of secondary importance. In the studio area, for example, many teachers give assignments such as designing a travel poster for the Orient, painting a stormy landscape, making a coil vase for flowers, designing a stained-glass window for Christmas or other occasion, and drawing from memory dried grasses and weeds of winter.[1] Similarly in the area of art history, a topic is selected, such as art works depicting certain subjects (clowns, animals, sports, portraits, landscapes), or schools or periods or styles. In such instances, the teacher generally selects the area and/ or topic and hopes that it will be appropriate for the entire class; that it will meet

[1]See Appendix 7 for a listing of suggested topics.

art program objectives and class needs; that students will be interested and become involved in the activity. With this method, students are usually free, if not encouraged, to organize in their own personal manner the studio art work or study of art history concerning the assigned topic. To be most successful in using this approach, the teacher needs to stimulate the class concerning the topic in such a way as to get students involved to the point of developing a feeling, if not a strong point of view, about it. In other words, emotionalize the experience. Many teachers try out a topic on one or two students before presenting it to the entire class.

Successful teachers generally create an atmosphere and feeling for the topic when it is initially presented. If the topic is to be a "Mexican Bullfight" for a studio art experience, mariachi music may be played as the students enter the room. Banners and flags would visually create a festive atmosphere. A short film may be shown concerning the pageantry and the symbolic meaning of the bullfight in the Spanish culture. Members of the class may dramatize the fight with a few props, such as a red cape or hat. When the whole class has "the feel" and are inspired by the topic, actual expression with the art medium can begin. The teacher must do much more than simply state the topic or write it on the chalkboard. Creative teachers will give an unusual twist to the topic, which will intrigue the students. For example, the students would be asked to paint the bullfight from the bull's point of view. Questions and suggestions by the teacher soliciting divergent responses are important here. "What if . . ." questions are especially successful in developing imaginative thinking. A similar approach may be used for art history. The above example may be used as an introduction to the bullfight paintings of Goya or Picasso. To teach effectively via the assigned-topic method involves a great deal of preparation, creativity, and imagination on the part of the teacher.

After the class has become motivated and has started to work, the teacher should continue the mood and feeling of the topic throughout the initial class and all the classes that follow via music, dramatizations, assigned readings, various visual aids, and verbal comments in order to maintain a high level of student identification with the topic. The teacher must be very much involved with the topic and the students as they work. Praise and the showing of student work in progress with appropriate suggestions/questions are stimulating and encouraging to the students, the teacher becoming an integral part of the art class experience (Clements, 1976). It is during the work period of each class that the teacher attempts to achieve his or her objectives by pointing out students who have achieved them—whose work is creative, sensitive, expressive, well organized. Timing is another important aspect throughout the art experience. Most successful teachers hold something back from the original topic stimulation to be used if interest begins to lag. Topics that extend over several class periods usually require additional stimulation, especially at the beginning of each class period. A teacher must become sensitive and aware, anticipating the ideal time to introduce any new aspect, make a comment, give praise, or ask a question to keep momentum and learning progressing at a high level in the classroom.

The Media Method

Teachers using the media method primarily approach teaching via art materials, the subject matter being secondary. For teachers using this approach the following are of particular concern: knowledge about a certain art medium and artists who specialize in the medium; skill and craftsmanship with the medium; creative handling of the medium; aesthetic considerations of the medium; personal expression via the medium—the art product, a good attitude and confidence in working in the medium. Herein, the teacher and/or students decide upon a medium with experiences centered around it. Most minicourses, currently popular in secondary schools, are developed around particular media, for example, ceramics (clay), oil paint, leather, jewelry (metals), and watercolor. Teachers using media as a reference point tend to operate in one of two directions: the art-product approach (an assignment to make a piece of art work involving various procedures or processes with the medium); or the art-process approach (a type of closure-discovery experience that leads the students into knowledges and skills involving the medium). Forming an eight-inch clay bowl via the coil method is an example of the product approach whereas rolling out clay coils, experimenting with size, joining together, and so on, in creating a ceramic piece is an example of the process approach.

Teachers using the media approach rely on the art material and the relevant procedures, and sometimes the product, to interest and stimulate the student. Here again, as in the assigned-topic method, the successful teacher is usually concerned with holding interest and keeping the student motivated so that learning and aesthetic development continue. Selection of appropriate art media, meaningful experiences with the medium, and the timing of suggestions, questions, praise, and criticism is of paramount importance. The successful and creative teacher will hold back particular materials for the most opportune time to present them, such as the use of gold overglaze in making ceramic jewelry or a special paper for watercoloring or printmaking. Timing is equally important when emphasizing procedures. In making a bowl, a student's interest may be aroused again by a demonstration of turning a foot. In making a piece of jewelry, it may be the oxidizing procedure

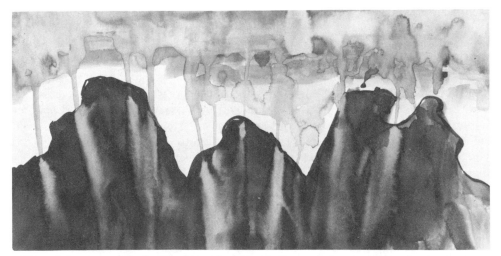

This painting is a result of using the method wherein the curriculum is developed around various media. Emphasis is placed upon the medium/process, a type of closure-discovery experience, that leads students into knowledges and skills. Here the student is learning to control the flowing qualities of watercolor so as to express a feeling concerning these mountains.

that would bring renewed interest when timed right. In the media method, it behooves the teacher to keep the student involved with the medium in order to maintain the necessary motivation for learning.

Media may be used as a means of approaching art history wherein the teacher wants students to learn about artists who work in a particular medium or art process. For example, the use of watercolor could lead to a study of the work of John Marin, Winslow Homer, and other watercolorists. In this method, studio work serves as an introduction to the aspect of art history to be studied. In reality, working with the art medium provides more than an introduction because the student learns about the problems of artists who work with the particular medium and become involved and knowledgeable, wanting to continue a study of the area.

The Guide-Facilitator Method

In this approach, ideally, the students choose their own topic, idea, or subject matter, and their own art media; they plan their area of study, organize and design their art work, and express themselves in their own manner—all with the support, guidance, and help of the teacher. Some students, more than others, will need stimulation, art knowledge, assigned readings, development of skills, aesthetic/perceptual sensitivity, awareness, creativity/imagination, self-confidence, and a better attitude. In this method, the teacher is concerned with all of the above as these aid in developing the ability, learning, and individuality of each student. Divergence and personal qualities along with experience are emphasized. The teacher views the teaching act as one of actualizing the uniqueness and learning ability of each student as may be seen in and through art experiences. The successful teacher, then, necessarily must be aware of each individual in the class. Many times students are not aware of why they are having difficulty in the art room. The perceptive teacher must prescribe activities, experiences, media, and/or readings for the student which will aid in his or her learning, growth, and development. The teacher becomes a facilitator in the classroom. Success generally depends upon the teacher's art experience and sensitivity to the needs of adolescents. This individual approach requires small classes because the teacher must come to know each student to be most helpful as a teacher.

This guide-facilitator method is usually carried out in a classroom via individual and small-group work, two of the most effective teaching styles (Olson, 1971). In this method, students generally decide in a conference with the teacher upon art experiences, areas of study, and products which meet their needs and interests. Most teachers keep a record of these conferences by developing a card-file system. The cards become contracts for the student to carry out certain art activities. When each art activity, area of study, and/or product (contract) is completed, a student-teacher evaluation conference takes place wherein the original objectives are considered in light of what the student has done, and new objectives are formulated for another aesthetic experience, that is, a new contract.

Since this is an individual, or at best a small-group approach, it is not appropriate for the teacher o stimulate the entire class around a topic or a medium. Therefore, teachers who prefer a more traditional class/teacher situation may find this approach to be frustrating. On the other hand, teachers who prefer to work individually with students will find this approach rewarding. This method is appropriate for students who are somewhat self-motivated and have previously had a more formal introduction to art/art experiences.

The Laissez-Faire Method

This method is used by teachers who perceive teaching as that of letting students learn, grow, and develop on their own with little or no extrinsic considerations that are thought to be interferences to a student's learning. The aims of teachers using this approach are usually natural learning and natural development concerning art knowledge, media, skill and craftsmanship, personal expression, perceptual and aesthetic sensitivity, and a good attitude. This is a completely unstructured method. Teachers who subscribe to this method believe they should in no way inhibit the student. The learner decides on the topic, subject, area of study, on media, and on everything else that is involved in the art experience. The teacher only offers suggestions and information when he is asked to do so. Students are assumed to be self-motivated. Art media, equipment, and art history materials are usually made available to students by the teacher; however, all students select their own. Students have complete freedom in this situation, which is at the opposite end of the continuum from the authoritarian-dictatorial method. This laissez-faire approach might be thought of as being without any method because the teacher exerts no direction for the student to follow or pursue. Stimulation, timing, leadership, and many other classroom methodological considerations are ignored.

Teaching Styles

In addition to method, there are many styles of teaching that may be employed by the teacher regardless of his method and philosophical position. Most teachers use several styles. However, some are more appropriate for one method than another, but all may be used. The teacher's basic method will determine the manner in which the style is developed in the classroom.

The choice of teaching styles is an important one. In a study involving 20,000 public school classrooms Martin Olson (1971) found that the style of teaching is the single strongest overall predictor of the quality of a school system. The following styles at the secondary level are listed in order of importance according to their mean scores: small-group work (9.80); individual (8.76); laboratory work (8.42); discussion (7.63); pupil reports (7.50); library work (6.68); and demonstrations (5.60). Lowest scoring styles were lecture (1.09); tests (1.16); movies (1.32); seat work (2.17); and questions/answers (3.69). Of all the styles of teaching, Olson found more secondary teachers using questions/answers (19 percent); individual work (14 percent); discussion and seat work (11 percent each); and lecture (10 percent). Teachers can significantly improve their teaching by increasing the frequency and/or skill with which they employ the higher scoring styles.

CHARACTERISTICS OF GOOD TEACHERS

Because it is the responsibility of the teacher to bring about achievement of program objectives involving art/personal learning and development and because it is the teacher who is in the classroom directly interacting with the students, the personality of the teacher is very important in any consideration of methods. *Teaching is the process of personalizing learning.* Certainly everyone would agree that it is possible to have two teachers of equal intelligence, training, and proficiency in art who nevertheless differ greatly in what they achieve with students. What kind of person, then, is needed in the classroom? We *do* know the effect of a teacher's personality on the learners and we *do* know the qualities that go to make up the successful and competent teacher.

From a great deal of research[2] over the years, characteristics of an effective teacher's classroom behaviors and interaction patterns can be summarized as follows:

Ability to personalize teaching and to view learning as an active, on-going process

Willingness to experiment; psychologically open; perceives the unknown as a challenge, not something to be feared

Compassion for and identification with the individual student; patience

Flexibility, ability to be direct or indirect as the situation demands

Ability to provide fresh perceptual/aesthetic experiences

Perceptually sensitive, providing experiences that increase student awareness

An appreciative attitude as evidenced by nods, comments, smiles

Stimulating, bringing about student involvement in a dramatic way

Warm, friendly, with a sense of humor

Skill in offering suggestions and asking questions (as opposed to seeing self as a kind of answering service)

Knowledge of subject matter and related areas, with ability to demonstrate and communicate clearly

Fairness and understanding in evaluation

Underlying most of the above criteria for good teachers is teacher enthusiasm, which should be emphasized here. The word means stimulating, animated, energetic, and mobile. A teacher who presents activities with demonstrative gestures, dramatic body movements, variations in voice, emotive facial expressions, animated acceptance of ideas and feelings, eye contact, and exuberance will have students who achieve at a higher level than teachers who do not behave enthusiastically (Cruickshank, 1980, p. 212). These nonverbal behaviors send forth messages that are just as important as verbal content. We learn much by watching others—we watch how other people behave, store these ideas, and later use them as models for our own actions. An art teacher who paints so that students can see it and exhibits locally will be very convincing. Your students will be moved by your personal interest in the art field. It is important to show enthusiasm for your students and their art work. If you are committed to helping your students, to learning about art, and to producing art and you display such commitment, you probably will be an inspiring and powerful force for your students.

Table 7, developed by Mary L. Collins (1976), will aid you in determining just how enthusiastic you are by using the eight enthusiasm behaviors. The most effective method would be to videotape several lessons and rate yourself. Another

---

[2]See, for example, Hart (1934); Witty (1947); Cogan (1958); Flanders (1960); Heil, Powell, and Fiefer (1960); Edmonston (1962); Spaulding (1963); and Olson (1971).

TABLE 7

Enthusiasm Rating Scale

DEGREE OF PERFORMANCE

	LOW (1)(2)	MEDIUM (3)(4)(5)	HIGH (6)(7)
1. Vocal delivery	Monotone, minimum inflections, little variation in speech, poor articulation.	Pleasant variations of pitch, volume, and speed; good articulation.	Great and sudden changes from rapid, excited speech to a whisper; varied tone and pitch.
2. Eyes	Looked dull or bored; seldom opened eyes wide or raised eyebrows; avoided eye contact; maintained a blank stare.	Appeared interested; occasionally lighting up, shining, opening wide.	Characterized as dancing, snapping, shining, lighting up frequently, opening wide, eyebrows raised; maintained eye contact while avoiding staring.
3. Gestures	Seldom moved arms out toward person or object; never used sweeping movements; kept arms at side or folded, rigid.	Often pointed, occasional sweeping motion using body, head, arms, hands, and face; maintained steady pace of gesturing.	Quick and demonstrative movements of body, head, arms, hands, and face.
4. Body movement	Seldom moved from one spot, or from sitting to standing position; sometimes "paced" nervously.	Moved freely, slowly, and steadily.	Large body movements, swung around, walked rapidly, changed pace; unpredictable and energetic; natural body movements.
5. Facial expression	Appeared deadpan, expressionless or frowned; little smiling; lips closed.	Agreeable; smiled frequently; looked pleased, happy, or sad if situation called for.	Appeared vibrant, demonstrative; showed many expressions; broad smile; quick, sudden changes in expression.
6. Word selection	Mostly nouns, few descriptives or adjectives; simple or trite expressions.	Some descriptors or adjectives, or repetition of the same ones.	Highly descriptive, many adjectives, great variety.
7. Acceptance of ideas and feelings	Little indication of acceptance or encouragement; ignored students' feelings and ideas.	Accepted ideas and feelings; praised or clarified; some variations in response, but frequently repeated same ones.	Quick to accept, praise, encourage, or clarify; many variations in response; vigorous nodding of head when agreeing.
8. Overall energy level	Lethargic; appeared inactive, dull, or sluggish.	Appeared energetic and demonstrative sometimes, but mostly maintained an even level.	Exuberant; high degree of energy and vitality; highly demonstrative.

The Enthusiasm-Rating Scale was developed by Mary L. Collins (1976). Reprinted by permission.

possibility is to have a colleague observe you. In general, a score of 8 to 20 indicates a dull or unenthusiastic level; 21 to 42, a moderate level of enthusiasm; 43 to 56, a high level of enthusiasm. Try improving your enthusiasm in the art room by practicing those enthusiasm behaviors listed in the "High" column. Maxwell H. Gillett (1980) found that teachers who had undergone enthusiasm training had an immediate effect on students by increasing their attentiveness to instruction.

How one sees and feels about one's self also have an enormous effect on how one functions in the classroom. Combs (1965, pp. 70–71) and Ryans (1960) found that there are differences in the ways good and poor teachers perceive themselves. Good teachers typically see themselves as:

Identifying with people rather than withdrawn, removed, apart from or alienated from others

Feeling basically adequate rather than inadequate, able to cope with problems

Feeling trustworthy, reliable, dependable

Seeing themselves as wanted, likable, personally attractive

Having dignity, integrity, and confidence

The same research also confirmed that not only do good and poor teachers view themselves differently, there are also characteristic differences in the way they perceive others. Good teachers have a positive view of colleagues and administrators; have a favorable view of democratic classroom procedures; have ability to see things from the other person's point of view; and see students as persons capable of doing things, being respected and valued.

Holding a positive attitude toward students appears to be an important aspect of student achievement. Two researchers, Robert Rosenthal and Lenore Jacobson (1968) found that students tend to live up to the expectations held of them. When teachers believed their students were high achievers, even when they were not, those students tended to learn more, living up to the expectations. Rosenthal and Jacobson called this phenomenon the self-fulfilling prophecy: people tend to become what they believe they are. If students believe they are capable and competent, they tend to behave in those ways; if they believe they are good, they tend to become good. It must be remembered, however, that these expectations on the part of the teacher *must be genuine and must be communicated effectively to students*. Students tend to be more successful when teachers expect them to be successful, illustrating the importance of the self-concept.

In a study of 420 high school art students by Ellsworth (1969, p. 30) "teacher aliveness" was considered of highest significance in determining the worth to them of all school experiences. It is not surprising, then, that this group placed "dullness in teaching" as the greatest block to personal progress encountered in high school art classes. Students were proud when they felt they had helped to make a good art department.

They were proud of the teacher who had a reputation as a fine instructor, who was without question their friend, and who commanded the respect of the community. . . . They appreciated the dynamic teacher who "invited us to learn," who created a climate "where everyone accomplished," who "challenged us to think and to explore," who was "flexible," and "who adjusted problems to our needs." They were grateful for the teacher who "emphasized originality," "was a master counselor," "helped us to meet failure," "gave a feeling of significance to our work," "increased the quality of our work constantly," and "was always willing to help us out of school hours." Students repeatedly mentioned serious frustrations they had endured due, in their opinions, to shallow course content, grades given for nothing, habitual teacher absence from class, appalling disorganization, uncertainty caused by insecurity, and just plain old boredom.

In summary, good teachers view teaching as a human process and are aware of the complexities of personality structure, group dynamics, and counseling processes. Good teachers are confident, enthusiastic, and have a positive view of themselves and others. They are competent in their field (art) and are able to communicate what they know in an innovative and creative manner which their students understand. Communication is more than a process of presenting information. It involves discovery and development of personal meanings. There is no one best kind of teaching because there is no one kind of student. Good teachers are skilled in human relations and are able to influence both student feeling/attitude and achievement in positive ways.

ADOLESCENT ART ORIENTATIONS: STUDIO METHODS

If art involves three primary human processes—thinking, feeling, and perceiving as these relate to the visual organization of experience—then these processes are necessarily of great concern to art teachers. Generally, emphasis is put on one or the other of these three aspects in most art expression. For example, in Impressionism, emphasis is placed upon seeing (visual perception); in Expressionism, emphasis is placed upon feeling; and in Cubism, emphasis is placed upon thinking. However, perception, especially seeing and touching, does underlie most visual art and art experiences even though emphasis may be placed upon thinking or feeling. Education in art involves the development of these three basic human processes in the art experience. The process or production of art involves organization and communication in one's own unique and personal manner with great reliance upon intuition. It is the teacher's role, then, to make students aware of these three processes. Quality art work is achieved when students are involved in thinking, in feeling, and in perceiving at the highest level their ability will permit at the time. Any one of these aspects that is neglected needs to be developed so that a student's life will be fulfilled. Keeping this in mind, let us turn to adolescent art, the work created after the unaware expression of the child but before the work of a professional artist. Adolescents are consciously and critically aware and know that they are attempting to create art and are having an aesthetic experience.

As a result of research by Burkhart (1962), Beittel and Burkhart (1963), and Michael (1970), various adolescent orientations and strategies for doing art have been discovered. These are simply ways of working and approaching the art experience and are not presented here to type or to categorize students but to aid the teacher in arriving at an appropriate method of instruction. Just as a physician must understand his patient, the illness, and the drugs prescribed, so the art teacher must understand the student—the student's perception of the art experience and the student's needs—and the art media, processes, and concepts that are prescribed to satisfy these needs. As a result of understanding the four art orientations into which most adolescents can be grouped and the additional considerations noted at the end of this chapter, the secondary art teacher can be more effective in bringing about aesthetic learning and personal growth on the part of the student. Some students may *not* be classified as having all of the attributes of any one of the following orientations because students may be moving from one orientation to another. They may be in between. However, the teacher will now know where the student is in relation to these four orientations and be able to adjust the method of teaching accordingly.

Mechanical Orientation

Art work by these students is stiff, rigid, awkward, and poorly organized. It is very simple in structure and tends to be imitative, if not stereotypical in nature. There is some sensitivity toward texture which is usually expressed in the work.

ATTITUDE TOWARD ART EXPERIENCE   These students are pleased and secure with a mechanical and imitative type of work. In fact, they crave mechanical devices (rulers, compasses, and specific rules/directions), which serve as crutches for them in making art. They do not attempt things they are afraid to do and are generally discouraged about art. They believe they have few ideas and lack involvement. They are highly dependent, are concerned about the opinion of their teachers and their peers, and worry about getting passing grades. In making art, they try to get a clear picture in mind of the final product before drawing, painting, or whatever the art activity may be. On many occasions, they will sit for long periods of time saying that they cannot get an idea. They try to preconceive a final product (generally representative), which is all they are interested in. Once they conceive of what they want, they desire to be given an exact procedure for achieving it, and they want to achieve it quickly! They want a safe and known approach to proceed to a known goal.

These mechanically oriented students work in a step-by-step manner with a fixed idea of the final product in mind—a static strategy wherein everything is under control. They generally start drawing in a precise manner, such as with a contour of an object, having no intention of changing or varying it once it is down. They mechanically apply texture using no extreme lights or darks. Rarely do they purposefully exaggerate. As they work they are generally discouraged about art and feel they cannot express a mood or feeling. They feel stiff and rigid and want a successful art product and a known standard against which to judge it but are unwilling to risk loss of it by experimenting and trying something new.

As they work, mechanically oriented students differentiate between the concept they hold of themselves as a person and that as a potential artist. Failure is only as an art student, not as a person. Therefore, it is possible to give severe and negative criticism about their work without affecting them emotionally. In fact, they will agree with any negative criticism, agreeing they know the work is not good! These students usually do not elect to take art but rather are "placed" in the art class.

PERSONALITY STRUCTURE.   These students tend to have a rigid personality structure, as their work suggests, being resistant to new learning experiences. They are generally socially immature, somewhat naïve, dependent, with a low perceptual

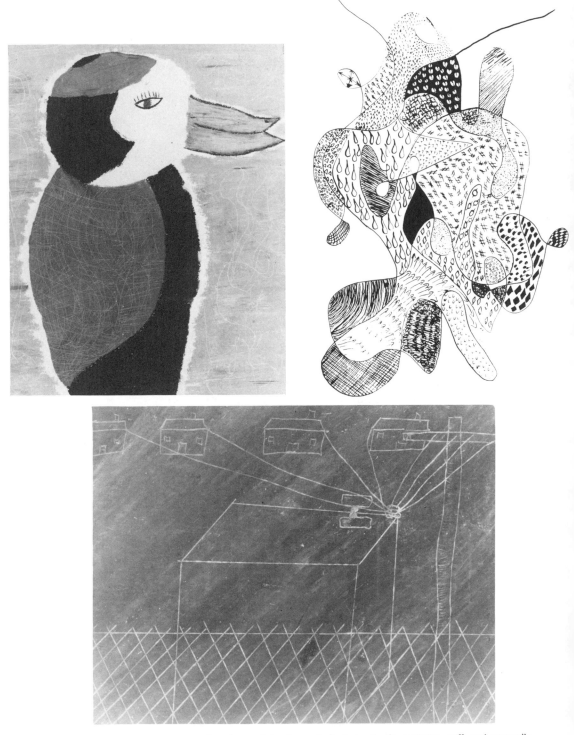

Mechanical orientation examples. Art work by these students is simple, imitative, stiff, and generally poorly composed. These students desire a mechanical means and specific directions for making art work.

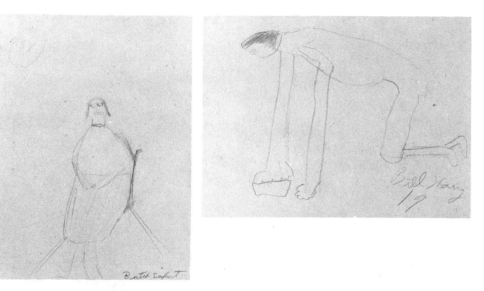

These drawings of people by mechanically oriented students are typical, revealing a lack of visual perception and compositional sensitivity. One can readily see why these students believe they cannot draw and produce art.

aptitude. They lack organizational ability but are of average intelligence. Being fearful of change, they prefer clear distinctions between right and wrong, typical of the authoritarian homes they generally come from where parents assume responsibility for all decisions. Achievement is a means of recognition or acceptance by someone in authority. In this way they seek security.

SUGGESTIONS FOR THE TEACHER.   These students are readily identified by the art teacher because of their unusual insistence on mechanical aids and crutches for making art and because of their strong preconception and rigid personality structure which make them difficult to instruct. However, there are many approaches open to the teacher.

First of all, all art experiences which involve imitating and copying should be avoided, as well as so-called drawing (that is, perspective), design, and color exercises wherein these students may continue with a closed, impersonal approach. These students need to be forced to identify with personal, thoughtful, and expressive considerations. Many do not want to reveal their true feelings or thoughts in any manner in their art work. Stimulations, then, for these mechanically oriented students initially need to be very exciting and dramatic so as to bring about a personal involvement and reaction rather than an impersonal, objective report (Kielscheski, 1974). These students need to identify with subject matter, media, and expression. Because of their rigid and closed approach to art and life, they need a variety of experiences—a breadth approach—with subjects, media, concepts, and procedures being changed frequently so they cannot rely on old, rigid work habits and ways of thinking. Use media that promote flexibility and produce bold effects rather than details. Such media as soft chalks, clay, wire, tempera, and watercolors are appropriate.

Painting with a sponge, as in this work, prevents mechanically oriented students from relying upon rigid work habits and promotes flexibility and bold effects. The sponge also necessitates some experimentation.

Emphasize experimentation for its own sake—get them to risk the loss of their work by trying something new, to develop tolerance for frustration. Explain what art/art expression involves—the problem of the artist. Put these students in creative situations wherein established patterns cannot be used. For example, drawing with sticks, bones, rocks, and rags tied to sticks help students to forget that "they can't draw." Students usually laugh and feel that no one could draw with these unusual, if not bizarre, materials. Start out by simply having students make marks on a sheet of paper with a stick and India ink or black tempera. This approach is even more effective if the sticks are three or four feet in length requiring students to stand up to work, the paper being placed on the floor. As the students continue to make marks, point out the variety and quality of the lines made. Note how each stick produces a different type of line. Eventually some student will see something—a head or tree or part of an animal—in his strokes. Then the teacher should encourage all the students look at their marks on the papers for recognizable forms and insist that they try to develop a picture around whatever they see. In other words, they complete the picture. As a result, the student temporarily forgets his inhibitions and becomes involved in his own expression, something he has rarely done. As he works and desires more control, the sticks may be broken, making them shorter and shorter. Eventually, brushes may be used when students feel the need for them. A similar approach may be used with the bones, stones, and a rag tied to a stick.

The procedure described above is a *closure* experience wherein the teacher begins the experience via strong direction and students close it or complete it in their own manner. For extremely tight, rigid, and closed students, many such closure experiences are usually necessary before students feel secure and comfortable working in a personal, expressive, and creative manner. Blotto pictures, scribble pictures, wet paper watercolors, chalk drawing on wet newspaper, and squeezed clay sculptures are other closure experiences based upon a media approach. As students work through a closure experience, the teacher should help them *think* and *feel* about what they are doing. Questions should be asked about the subject, the medium, and the procedure, forcing these students to think about their work. The teacher should also help them experience and express feelings about their art work. Get them to relate to their own experience. Encourage them to verbalize what they are trying to express. Similarly, they should be made aware of perceptions. Certain specific and limited creative art goals should be planned for each closure experience. The teacher should be adamant about students achieving these, making students aware of goals and praising their specific achievements.

For the mechanically oriented, it is necessary that successful creative art experiences be brought about wherein these students become psychologically open and personally involved and expressive. *With this action* (brought about via the closure method) *will come the accompanying emotions*, the feeling of satisfaction, of accomplishment, of being sensitive and aware to shapes, colors, of all that goes with successfully producing art work and having an aesthetic experience. Any progress in either work or attitude should be pointed out to these students so as to make them aware that they are moving in a positive direction. The mechanical student needs continual reinforcement; however, commendation and praise should be merited and must be genuine on the part of the teacher.

Primitive Orientation

Primitive expression of feelings, usually accomplished by a naïve simplification of nature forms, characterize the art work of these students. Simple schematic forms tend to be repeated in symmetrical arrangements. Compositions range from depicting rather rigid symbols to showing somewhat limited and superficial expression of immediate feelings and moods concerning subject matter.

ATTITUDE TOWARD ART EXPERIENCE.   These students are concerned with expressing simple personal moods and feelings, are able to identify with the subject matter on a somewhat superficial level, and are also able to identify with various qualities of a medium. However, they lack confidence in their own expressive powers. These students do have capacity for taking advantage of accidents as they work and are somewhat interested in what they are expressing. They are flexible in regard to the art experience—willing to experiment (trial-and-error approach), unafraid of making mistakes or losing the art product. However, experimentation for these individuals means primarily dealing with accidents that occur as they work.

Primitive orientation examples. Art work by these students is superficial, naïve, somewhat free, and often rather schematic. These students express simple personal feelings and are flexible in regard to making art.

Primitively oriented students differentiate between the concept they hold of themselves as persons and that as potential artists. Failure is only as an art student, not as a person. Therefore, it is possible to give somewhat severe negative criticism about their work without affecting them as persons. Because of their lack of confidence in their own art ability, they generally will agree with any negative criticism. They tend to become discouraged easily if the problem of art becomes very involved, requiring much control or is perceived by them as being very difficult.

PERSONALITY STRUCTURE.   These students have a tendency to be rigid and lack openness to new art experiences beyond a superficial level of involvement. Feelings tend to dominate their thoughts. A wide range of possible emotional responses to subject matter and media is possible; however, intellectual responses during the art process are somewhat limited. These individuals have some perceptual aptitude, tend to be socially immature, are dependent, and usually come from an authoritarian home background.

SUGGESTIONS FOR THE TEACHER.   First of all, the art teacher needs to show respect for the feeling, though it may be limited, that primitively oriented students bring to the art experience. Depth should be given to this aspect via working over a period of time involving a particular subject and a flexible medium (Mattil et al., 1961). In working with these students, then, the number of art areas pursued will necessarily be limited. Try to get these students in the mood of the art work rather than expressing a temporary feeling; for example, get them to do religious paintings rather than a picture of Christ on the Cross. This will necessitate a series, doing more than one piece of art work about a particular subject and with a particular medium. Students must be kept interested and stimulated while increasing their degree of control and depth of expression.

In addition to pursuing depth concerning feeling, the teacher must work for an increased perceptual sensitivity and an increased intellectual awareness, a refinement of the total experience. This may be done by many open-ended "if" questions concerning work habits, media, and subject matter. Encourage students to explore the sensuous aspects of an experience (Madenfort, 1972). Get students to observe minute details of objects via contour drawings and the use of a finder,[3] a magnifying glass, and colored transparencies. Get them to analyze problems that result from the art experience, and to relate their work to the field of art. Complexity of expression should gradually be increased by requiring additional objects to be included in compositions (a drawing of ten objects, half of which overlap, instead of the one or two objects these students usually draw when left on their own) and increasing the variety of emotional meanings (make these bottles or objects appear sad, excited, or dreamy in your painting). Encourage flexibility by emphasizing the trial-and-error approach—a creative-discovery method. Help students set specific goals to be achieved as they work.

---

[3]A finder is simply a piece of cardboard with a small rectangular hole in the middle through which a person may "frame" a particular aspect of the environment.

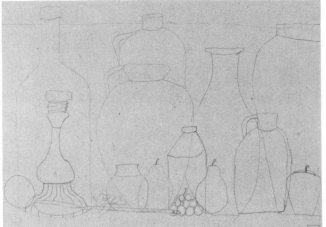

Contour drawing forces students to observe details by moving the pencil as the eye follows the various contours of an object.

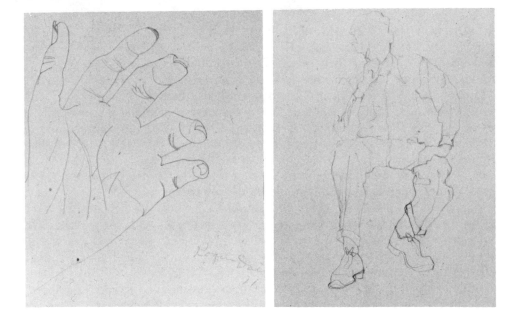

Intellectual Orientation

The work of intellectually oriented students who tend "to think out" their art work is characterized by preciseness, objectivity, detailed emphasis of subject matter, facility in drawing, visual sensitivity, prominence of textures, and usually complex compositions. Emphasis is on a static placement and, for the most part, all edges are sharp and clean. A great deal of reliance is placed upon opposition and contrast. These students tend to express a single mood or idea and lack deep involvement in feeling. Often their work is so skillful and technically proficient that this rather superficial expressive aspect of their work is overlooked.

ATTITUDE TOWARD ART EXPERIENCE. These intellectually oriented students describe their way of working in terms of "thoughts" rather than "feelings."

Intellectual orientation examples. Art work by these students is carefully *thought* out, one part being completed at a time. Preciseness, skill, visual sensitivity, and objectivity characterize their approach.

They generally think out or preconceive what they are going to do. Great orderliness is seen in their approach and work habits. They usually begin drawing with a controlled contour of a single element that is chosen as a theme to be developed through variation. A direct statement is important: each part being exact, right, and clear at any one point. One part is completed at a time and it has to work before moving on to the next. Each step is conceived with clarity, but at any one time these students do not know exactly which step will follow. Any freedom lies in the organization, the putting together of the parts. A great deal of reliance is placed upon opposition and contrast. This is a synthetic approach wherein the work gradually becomes more complex as more parts are completed. Unity is achieved at the conclusion of the art product when all the parts are finished. These students vary the goal rather than the procedure; they control the process in order to search *intellectually* for ideas which will lead to new discoveries, and discovery comes through elaboration. Enrichment is the objective.

These students have enough flexibility and control over media to take advantage of mistakes. Although they can use the trial-and-error approach as they work on each part, they lack a sustained interest in experimentation. For them the process is not very creative. Creativity comes at the end when all the parts are completed and the object is seen as a whole for the first time. The students feel insecure when attempting an unplanned approach to the whole art work.

Because many of the intellectually oriented students have so much control over the process and usually have rather keen powers of observation, they develop great skill in using media. This proficiency frequently brings prestige, and *some* students become concerned with gaining recognition and making a good impression with their skillful art work, which tends to take the place of genuine expression and personal values. They become other-directed. To make a good impression, then, becomes an important aspect of doing art.

Intellectually oriented students differentiate between the concept they hold of themselves as persons and that as potential artists. This is probably a result of a lack of deep emotional involvement with the art experience. Failure is only as an art student, just as one may fail in any academic subject area. It is not failure as a person. Therefore it is possible to give somewhat negative criticism about their work without affecting them as persons. Generally, they are not easily discouraged, even being self-critical at times.

PERSONALITY STRUCTURE.   Intellectually oriented students have a desire to learn and a capacity for great involvement. They have a fairly high perceptual aptitude and good organizational ability. They are somewhat creative and are open to new ideas on an intellectual level. They are socially mature but have a limited emotional reaction, a lack of expressive feeling. However, they possess enough ability and skill/craftsmanship to become very competent in art expression. These students work deliberately and may have visual tendencies (Gutteter, 1972, p. 22).

SUGGESTIONS FOR THE TEACHER.   Intellectually oriented students need many spontaneous closure experiences to develop a flexible and creative approach to the entire art experience, not just at the end. Closure experiences should be followed by depth experiences to develop an increase in feeling, sensitivity, and desire for expanded personal and expressive possibilities in their art work.

The process needs to become creative. These students need to value imaginative and original aspects as they work by developing a greater willingness to risk the loss of their product. Goals need to be shifted from product to process by emphasizing the joys and satisfactions of the doing, making, creating. For example, emphasize throwing on the potter's wheel rather than the finished bowl; emphasize the painting process—the excitement of watercolors running and blending together, forming new shapes and colors—rather than the framed painting; emphasize stretching and forming the metal rather than the finished *repoussé* piece. These students should be given no specific answers to questions; they need to think things out for themselves. Get them to accept failure as being a natural part of the creative process. Put them in situations wherein they cannot rely on previous step-by-step patterns of working. Gesture versus contour drawing, wet paper versus dry paper watercolor procedure, pinch versus coil pots are examples.

Intellectually oriented students need to become involved with the process, emphasis being placed upon feeling and movement, as seen in this painting of "City at War."

These students are beginning to plan the whole surface area by using a few sketch lines to suggest the position, proportion, and shape of each object, not completing any one object before going to the next and thus moving away from a consideration of only one part at a time so characteristic of students with an intellectual orientation.

Greater expressive quality may be brought about in the art work of intellectually oriented students by emphasizing verbs rather than nouns in any art experience. Instead of a tree, people, or objects in a still life, insist on expressing growing, reaching, extending, flowing—words that denote action and movement. According to a research study by Sharon Hendrix (1966), there is a significant positive correlation between movement and aesthetic quality in drawings by persons beginning to learn about art—the more movement a person puts into his work, the more aesthetic it becomes. Emphasis upon feeling and movement tends to bring about a more intense expression. Through many open-ended questions and suggestions concerning the meaning, feeling, and purpose of the subject matter, the teacher can also develop a higher level of expression. This should be a very personal expression having real meaning for the student. This means no superficial snow-capped mountains in back of idyllic lakes surrounded by palm trees. Some of these students will resist a public display of their personal feelings in their art work, a reflection of the social mores that frown on men crying and on responding emotionally in public. Recognition should be given for genuine expression, not just for facility and skill in handling media.

If at all times the problem of the artist (personal expression involving thinking, feeling, and perceiving that is harmoniously organized) is kept before these students, the art product will reflect more creativity and expressiveness. These students must especially be made to face the problem of formulating their own expressive purposes and to act independently on their own decisions in every part of the art experience. They must be made to realize that art experiences can be important aspects of self-discovery, self-realization, and knowledge of the adult world of art. The teacher should use the intellectual ability of these students to find imaginative ways of bringing new personal meaning to art experiences.

When these students begin to plan the whole page or area with a few sketch lines, they are moving away from the intellectual one-part-at-a-time, step-by-step approach toward a more flexible creative and expressive way of working and should be praised. (See Appendix 5, "Freehand Drawing.") Security and confidence are then developing in their capacity to deal with new problems within the whole area of art.

Intuitive-Emotional Orientation

Feeling and the facile handling of movement permeate the art work of these students who are emotionally oriented. Little use is made of contours, preplanned sketching, or elaboration—much reliance being placed upon suggestion. Nonessential details are eliminated. Great diversity, originality, directness, sensitivity to media and subject matter, and good organization characterize their work. Some of these students have difficulty with representative skills and visual perception, but their work always suggests a mood and feeling often achieved by expressive exaggeration. Traces of the development of an individualistic style are evidenced.

ATTITUDE TOWARD ART EXPERIENCE. These students have great tolerance for frustration and describe themselves as being involved, flexible, free, loose, praising, rational, and self-seeking as they work. They are interested in

Intuitive-emotional examples. Art work by these students is characterized by movement and feeling, with little use of contours and a great reliance upon suggestion. They work over the whole surface, their objective being vitality of expression.

creating personal expression based upon their own experience. Intuitive-emotionally oriented students, being procedural and process oriented, are concerned with pursuit, the approach—problem solving. They are open but are negative to extrinsic restrictions involving the process. They desire a concept of the whole at the very beginning; however, this is more a general idea, a sense of direction, than a preconceived or meticulously thought out plan. They generally start a drawing or painting with a centrally placed, vaguely defined whole that is analytically and organically developed via expressive movements through voids encircled by big dark forms. There is great concern for freedom of movement as they work over the whole area of the art piece. Their objective is vitality of the whole but allowance is made for interaction with the medium; therefore, they can easily take advantage of mistakes. The trial-and-error approach is a natural way of working for them.

Through exploration and discovery, these students are trying to find themselves in their art work. They identify with all their art activities to the extent that, as they work, there is no separation between the concept they hold of themselves as persons and as potential artists. Failure or success in art work is failure or success as a person; therefore, the teacher must be very careful in giving negative criticism. See Appendix 6 for an example of the sensitivity of an intuitive-emotionally oriented student in the class of an authoritarian teacher as she expressed her feelings in a poem. Inner response—feeling—concerning subject matter is most important to these students. One can easily see why they are excited about and involved with the art work they are doing.

PERSONALITY STRUCTURE. Intuitive-emotionally oriented students tend to be independent, confident, and determined. They seek inspiration and often develop an intense emotional identification with the subject matter. They may feel both tight–tense and loose–relaxed while working on one art product. They have strong feelings of satisfaction toward experiences they feel are desirable. These students are socially mature and are only slightly higher in intelligence and spatial aptitude compared with students of the other three orientations. Being open to new art experiences, they are highly creative and original. They are concerned with the process and not the product. Organization is not a problem for them. Most of these students come from permissive homes where they cannot rely on parental authority for guidance; therefore, they see life as problems to be solved by their own actions. They may even sense a problem before it is clearly defined. In fact, they prefer intangible problems, working to find a problem and to clarify it (Getzels, 1981). Achievement is necessary for self regard and self acceptance. These students work spontaneously and may have nonvisual tendencies (Gutteter, 1972, p. 22).

SUGGESTIONS FOR THE TEACHER. Intuitive-emotionally oriented students need a depth experience wherein they can continue the expression of feeling and movement. They also need experiences that help them think more about their work; that help them become more perceptually sensitive to essential details; and that help them develop greater skill and control. Introducing new subject matter and new ways of discovering and perceiving the environment will encourage thinking and extend their sensitivity to details. The use of a magnifying glass, cardboard finders, colored glasses, and texture boxes are methods of rediscovering one's environment. These students should return to a subject upon several occasions so that time is provided to think and to study details and character (mood). Using a flexible medium for a period of time will develop greater control and skill. Many of these students are capable of handling the quality materials of the professional artist. Such media will provide great inspiration and also aid in bringing variety to a depth experience. However, no tedious media and no activities of a tedious nature (demanding careful repetition) should be insisted upon as these may require a control which is beyond these students at the time. For most, a high level of skill and control will come slowly; the teacher must be patient.

A few deadlines may be necessary to help some of the intuitive-emotionally oriented students overcome the "unfinished-product syndrome." Because they are so interested and involved in the process, in discovering problems and solutions to these problems, some tend to jump from one art experience to another, feeling no need to complete anything.

To maintain openness, flexibility, and creativity, no one art procedure or approach (such as Impressionism) should be allowed to become fixed and rigid. This may be accomplished by ensuring a knowledge of the importance of flexibility in the creative process. Assigned art experiences not only must provide challenge for these students but must also open up new alternatives they might not have been aware of because of lack of experience. By working out learning goals with these students, a sense of direction will be given to them and their work. However, the process of working should be kept problematic via a nondirective type of guidance in which no specific answers are given, the students being forced to make their own decisions; but technical knowledge should be shared freely since the students have the ability to adapt, relate, and alter technical information for their own purposes.

Showing a personal interest and sharing in their art experiences will give intuitive-emotionally oriented students incentive to continue and move forward. Any criticism and suggestions that are made should help students set new goals and higher standards for themselves. By encouraging work to be done on the student's own time outside of art class, individuality and independence can be reinforced, bringing thinking, feeling, and perceiving to a higher level in the art experience.

ART HISTORY/APPRECIATION METHODS

While the preceding adolescent orientations primarily involve studio work, art history and art appreciation are two additional concerns of the teacher. Whereas art history involves cognitive aspects (knowledge of the field) and art appreciation involves affective aspects (attitude toward the field), it is difficult to separate knowing from feeling since both tend to happen simultaneously. Likewise, it is difficult to separate doing (studio art considerations) from feeling and knowing and, hopefully, certain appropriate art concepts and attitudes will also be developed during studio art experiences. In art education, the teacher must deal with all three considerations: knowing (art history and art concepts); doing (making art products); and feeling (art appreciation/attitude).

Although art history, which many think of as the cognitive aspect of our field, may be taught as a separate course, aspects of art history and a concern for art appreciation should be introduced in conjunction with studio art experiences in the typical secondary art class. However, the over-all interest and involvement of the student in art must not be jeopardized by a series of unrelated and juxtaposed studio, art appreciation, and art history activities or by an overemphasis on cognitive aspects of art history (the memorization of names and dates). Ideally, *activities in the art room should be integrated and meaningful*, presenting a unified, consistent, and meaningful series of art experiences for the student. This does not rule out spontaneous activities that tend to grow out of the interaction of students and teacher in the art room.

Attitudes toward the visual arts fall within the affective domain, which involves objectives emphasizing feeling and emotions—a valuing, a degree of acceptance or rejection (Krathwohl et al., 1967, p. 7). Since most teachers and curriculum workers who state objectives do make distinctions between the cognitive, content aspect and the affective, attitudinal aspect and employ very different techniques to evaluate and appraise these, it is appropriate that we consider particular *methods* both for developing positive attitudes and for teaching content concerning the visual arts in our classes. At the present time, the field of art education seems to be deluged with objectives, few of which are truly affective and attitudinal, probably because we have so very little information concerning methods of teaching for achievement in this area. However, both cognitive and affective or appreciative objectives may be achieved via two methods: logical and psychological.

Logical Methods

The logical methods of developing knowledge of art history and art concepts are usually those which are considered traditional and are based upon a common-sense approach and the intellect. Herein, art appreciation tends to be a concomitant aspect of the teaching/learning situation. If we study about art, view works of art, compare one work with another, and finally attempt to make art work ourselves, it is only reasonable to assume that an *understanding* and *appreciation* of art/art history will develop.

INFORMATION.   Knowledge of art/art history can be brought about by reading and study, particularly concerning the time and place of production, the aim and technique of the artist, media and processes, aesthetic qualities, and influences. Although knowledge of art history is a goal in itself for the understanding of the field of art, achievement of cognitive objectives as such does not mean there will be a corresponding development of appropriate affective behaviors (Jacob, 1957). Research evidence suggests that appreciation develops when appropriate learning experiences are especially provided for it. Under some conditions, the development of cognitive behaviors may actually bring about negative feelings toward art (Krathwohl et al., 1964). Research by the writer (Michael, 1959, pp. 101–102) resulted in a similar finding. Using an introductory high school art class, the writer experimented for a six-week period by displaying and discussing, every day, twenty cubistic-to-abstract reproductions; by student reports on cubistic artists and theories; and by students voluntarily producing art work in a cubistic-to-abstract style. It was found that the students rejected more intensely cubistic-to-abstract art work after the experimental period than before the experiment began. Although they

Photo courtesy of Craig Roland

Aspects of a logical approach to developing art appreciation are observing and comparing works of art. Trips to galleries to view art are invaluable.

knew much more about cubistic art after the experimental period, students preferred it less!

OBSERVATION.   Contact with art work in galleries and museums and viewing art films and slides will also bring about knowledge of art. Collecting and cataloging reproductions will provide the student with art facsimilies conveniently at hand for observing and analyzing.

COMPARISON.   By analyzing, evaluating, and comparing the art work of one period with that of another; one style with another; one artist's work with another; art of one area or country with another; one of the arts with another; one medium with another; and one purpose/function of art with another the student will have a better understanding and knowledge of the field. Such comparisons force students into an awareness they may not otherwise be able to grasp and, therefore, extend their frame of reference.

PRODUCTION.   By actually doing art work with a particular medium in the manner and style of a particular artist and/or period as an *exercise*, students will develop an understanding and knowledge of the difficulties, peculiarities, satisfactions, and relationships of the particular art work under consideration. Herein, students can identify with the artist, style, concepts, and period because of the impact of the art experience if the teacher provides for this through creating an appropriate and stimulating environment.

Psychological Methods

The psychological methods are those that relate to personal considerations of the self and usually attend to the development of art appreciation with knowledge of art history and art concepts being secondary considerations. These psychological methods primarily have to do with one's feelings, rather than the intellect and tend to emotionalize experience.

A SINGLE INTENSE EXPERIENCE. Through an intensely vivid and meaningful experience, which has an emotional impact, the teacher can get the student to value, accept, and internalize the desired aspect of art. Experiences involving surprise, suspense, challenge, anticipation, conflict, mystery, awe, and/or wonder tend to involve us emotionally in such a way that our interest and feelings are aroused. Many such experiences are possible in the classroom, for example, not admitting a regularly scheduled class into the art room will cause emotional concern. If the art room is darkened, the students will wonder, "What is happening?" "What is going on inside our room?" "Why can't we go in as we usually do?" Finally, when the teacher opens the door to admit the students, they enter a darkened room; soft music is playing. At the end of the room in front of a velvet drapery is a large painting that is spotlighted. The students quietly take their seats as the teacher, in a low voice, asks them to look at the painting and note what mood or feeling it communicates. What is the artist attempting to say? Do they feel this in the painting? How did the artist convey this? Did he use exaggeration, unusual colors, or facial expression? George Szekely (1980) believes that "creative entrances" are very important, conveying a message to students that art involves creativity, inventiveness, and challenge; however, the form of entrance must always relate to the visual concepts being presented.

We tend to remember those instances that were intense, vivid, and charged with feeling. What experiences do you recall from high school? Winning a particular game; your first school dance; a part in a play; an accident in the chemistry lab; receiving an award or recognition for special work. Teachers can plan art appreciation experiences that are meaningful and vivid for their students through an imaginative and creative approach to teaching. Such experiences do take time and much preparation; however, the positive response of the students toward art makes the extra effort worthwhile.

ACCEPTANCE OF THE OPINION OF ANOTHER. Whenever we are confronted by a problem in an area of which we have little knowledge, experience, and confidence, we tend to seek out authority figures, those in leadership roles, and rely upon their suggestions and opinions. We assume the value system of persons we look up to as experts in a field. When art teachers have gained the confidence of their students by exhibiting their own art work, discussing art, or in any other way have shown that they are competent and knowledgeable concerning the field of art, students will assume that the teacher really is an expert in the field and will accept his opinion concerning art. Therefore, if the teacher says that cubistic art is very important because much of contemporary art is based upon Cubism and the theories developed by these artists, students will accept this opinion as valid and believe it themselves, greatly valuing cubistic art work. Because of this identification and acceptance of the teacher's point of view and discriminatory taste, as a teacher you have a tremendous responsibility to yourself, your classes, and the field of art because you have become a model to be emulated by the students.

SPECIFIC RESPONSES OF A SIMILAR NATURE.   One may become aware of a work of art by many separate and individual experiences with it, each experience giving a new and different aspect and enlarging upon one's previous perceptions. A painting must be seen many times and perhaps under many different circumstances for us to become fully acquainted with it and for us to accept and value it. For example, the art teacher displays a reproduction of one of Van Gogh's paintings in the art room for a week; then, the reproduction is moved to another location in the school building. Students will observe it in many environments and will begin to know and enjoy the colors, subject, feeling, and composition of the work. The student is presented with the opportunity to become acquainted with the art work in different situations. A reproduction of the painting may be seen in an art book, on the wall at the doctor's office, and in a friend's home. Soon, to view this painting will be like a reunion with an old friend. The student will have a feeling that this painting is important because it has come to give so much pleasure.

ADDITIONAL METHODOLOGICAL CONSIDERATIONS: MODES AND TYPES

As a teacher, one must be aware of additional considerations as one works with adolescents in the art room. Brain research has determined interesting and unique hemispheric functions or modes that have many ramifications for the art teacher. These plus visual and nonvisual perception, must not be overlooked. Methods of professional artists and methods with new media are other considerations of importance and have a direct bearing upon art education at the secondary level.

Hemispheric Modes

Research has shown that specific functions reside in each of the two hemispheres of the brain and by means of the *corpus callosum* that connects them they work in a complementary manner (Rennels, 1976). Functions of the left hemisphere appear to be verbal, rational, linear, analytic, objective, symbolic, on-time, and logical (having to do with the cognitive aspects of life); functions of the right brain are nonverbal, visual, spatial, perceptual, intuitive, global, imaginative, subjective, time-free, and sensitive (having to do with the creative, aesthetic, and affective aspects of life). Most nonarts school experiences deal with left-brain functions. Since arts experiences, for the most part, are right brain in nature, such experiences bring about a balance in the growth, development, and education of an individual and are sorely needed in the school curriculum. Robert Masters and Jean Houston, researchers in this area, argue that a child without access to a stimulating arts program "is being systematically cut off from most of the ways in which he can perceive the world. His brain is being systematically damaged. In many ways he is being de-educated" (Williams, 1977, p. 14). Many others agree, noting that students have particular artistic aptitudes which, if not developed during critical growth spurts of the brain, may go forever undeveloped—brain circuitry being difficult to achieve at other times (Hollingsworth, 1981). These growth spurts correspond for the most part with Piaget's classical stages of intellectual development: 3–10 months; 2–4 years; 6–8 years; 10–12 years; and 14–16 years. Such findings tend to substantiate "readiness" and "timing" as important factors in learning.

With such emphasis placed upon development of the brain, it behooves the art teacher to be aware of both right- and left-brain modalities (growth patterns) and the effect these have upon art instruction. (See Table 8.)

For drawing and painting experiences depicting what one sees, it is necessary for students to shift to the right-brain mode. This shift is somewhat difficult for most students who have grown up in our culture, wherein emphasis is placed upon the verbal, linear, rational, and logical rather than upon the visual, spatial, perceptual, intuitive, sensory, and creative. A shift to the right-brain mode is achieved in drawing by placing students in a situation in which they are required to draw shapes, spaces, angles, curves, and lines without any recognition, naming, or categorizing of the objects or parts of objects to be drawn—perceiving abstractly. (See Table 2, Part B.) Betty Edwards (1979) prescribes specific exercises for bringing about this right-brain mode in drawing, such as drawing face-vases, copying from upside-down drawings, and drawing contours of things without looking at the paper. Persons involved in the right-brain mode in drawing become locked into an object; perceive lines, shapes, and forms with great clarity and sensitivity; become unaware of the passage of time; and have a pleasurable, relaxed, and refreshing experience. The right-brain mode appears to be necessary for the development of visual perception, which results in naturalistic drawings. Since many adolescents, especially at the beginning of adolescence and often before (10-to-12-year-olds), have a strong natural desire to draw realistically, the art teacher needs to understand how to develop visual perception so that their work comes up to their critical expectations of what art should be.

TABLE 8
Left and Right Hemispheric Characteristics

LEFT	RIGHT
Verbal: using words to describe, to name	Nonverbal: awareness of lines, shapes, forms, colors of things
Analytic: figuring out things in an orderly fashion	Synthetic: putting things together to form a whole
Symbolic: using a symbol to stand for something	Concrete: seeing things as they are now
Abstract: simplifying down to the essence	Analogic: seeing similarities between objects, relationships
Temporal: keeping track of time; doing one thing after another	Nontemporal: without a sense of time
Rational: arriving at conclusions based upon reason and facts	Nonrational: not requiring a basis of reason or facts
Numerical: using numbers as in counting	Spatial: seeing where lines, shapes, and colors are in relation to other lines, shapes, and colors
Logical: arriving at conclusions based upon logic, one thing following another in a logical order	Intuitive: making leaps of insight, often based upon incomplete patterns, hunches, feelings, or visual images
Linear: thinking in terms of linked ideas; one thought directly following another, leading to a convergent conclusion	Holistic: seeing whole things, all at once; perceiving the over-all patterns and structures often leading to divergent conclusions

Adapted from Betty Edwards, *Drawing on the Right Side of the Brain*, p. 40. Copyright 1979 by Betty Edwards; reprinted by permission of Houghton Mifflin Company.

However, objective and precisely observed drawings with correct natural proportions and perspective do not necessarily ensure a work of art. The teacher must keep the problem of the artist before students, remembering that art is not "the thing" no matter how well delineated, but art is a visual organization and an expression/interpretation of one's experience with the thing. Thus, both hemispheric modes are involved (Youngblood, 1981).

The left-mode/right-mode of experiencing also affects how one perceives the art work of others. Those who favor the left hemisphere tend to prefer literal, naturalistic/logical, and conceptual/symbolic art expression whereas those who favor the right hemisphere tend to be more interested in color, abstractions, expressive forms, surrealistic forms, and tactile (texture) sensations in art work (Virshup, 1976). Art teachers need to understand these two ways of experiencing the world and to realize that these types of modes tend to be merely dominant and not fixed. For a better understanding of art expression, students should not only learn to view their own work, but they also need to view the work of other artists who are oriented to both of these two types of brain functions.

Visual and Nonvisual Types

Viktor Lowenfeld (1957, pp. 264–266) popularized two perceptual/psychological types, the visual and the nonvisual, the latter being called "haptic" from the Greek word, *haptikós*, able to grasp. He described these two types as follows.

VISUAL TYPE

The visual type, the observer, usually approaches things from their appearance. He feels as a *spectator*. One important factor in visual observation is the ability to see first the whole without an awareness of details, then to analyze this total impression into detailed or partial impressions, and finally to synthesize these parts into a new whole. The visual type first sees the general shape of a tree, then the single leaves, the twigs, the branches, the trunk, and finally everything incorporated in the synthesis of the whole tree. Starting with the general outline, partial impressions thus are integrated into a whole, simultaneous image. This is true not only psychologically, but also for the act of creating. Thus, we will notice that visual types usually begin with the outlines of objects and enrich the form with details as the visual analysis is able to penetrate deeper into the nature of the object.

This visual penetration deals mainly with two factors: first, with the analysis of the characteristics of shape and structure of the object itself; and second, with the changing effects of these shapes and structures determined by light, shadow, color, atmosphere, and distance. Observing details, therefore, is not always a sign of visual-mindedness; it can be an indication of good memory as well as of subjective interest in these details. For visual-mindedness, it is necessary to see the changes these details undergo under the various external conditions as mentioned above.

Visually minded persons have a tendency to transform kinesthetic and tactile experiences into visual experiences. If, for instance, a visual minded person acquaints himself with an object in complete darkness he tries to visualize all tactile or kinesthetic experiences. "How it looks" is the first reaction to any object met in darkness. In other words, he tries to imagine in visual terms what he has perceived through other senses. A visually minded person who encounters an object in darkness thus tries immediately to visualize the object he has met. From this analysis it becomes evident that the visual approach toward the outside world is an analytic approach of a sepctator who finds his problems in the complex observation of the ever-changing appearances of shapes and forms.

HAPTIC TYPE

The main intermediary for the haptic type of individual is the *body–self*—muscular sensations, kinesthetic experiences, touch impressions, and all experiences which place the self in value relationship to the outside world. In this art, the self is projected as the true actor of the picture whose formal characteristics are the resultant of a synthesis of bodily, emotional, and *intellectual* apprehension of shape and form. Sizes and spaces are determined by their emotional value in size and importance. The haptic type, therefore, is primarily a subjective type. Haptically minded persons do not transform kinesthetic and tactile experiences into visual ones, but are completely content with the tactile or kinesthetic modality itself, as experiments have shown. If a haptically minded person acquaints himself with an object in complete darkness, he would remain satisfied with his tactile or kines- thetic experiences. Since tactile impressions are most partial only (this is true for all impressions of objects that cannot be embraced with the hand, where the hands have to move) the haptic individual will arrive at a synthesis of these partial impressions only when he becomes emotionally interested in the object itself. Normally, he will not build up such a synthesis and will remain satisfied with his haptic experience. If he encounters an object in darkness, he will merely withdraw, perhaps, with some feelings of the surface structure of the obstacle or with partial impressions of those parts that he has touched. Since the haptic type uses the self as the true projector of his experiences, his pictorial representations are highly subjective; his proportions are proportions of value.

In art education it is therefore of prime importance to consider these attitudes toward the world of experiences as significant as the visual approaches toward art. Thus a stimulation will be effective only if it includes haptic sensations as well as visual experiences.

Others have also been aware of these ways of viewing the world. Max Verworn discussed physioplastic representation (naturalistic-visual) and ideoplastic repre- sentation (predominantly haptic) in *Zur Psychologie der primitiven Kunst* (1908) and developed these types more fully in *Ideoplastische Kunst* (1914). Carl Reed (1957) called these types "emotive" and "reportive," and Herman Witkin (1962) called them "field dependent" and "field independent." They have also been called "objective" and "subjective," as well as "expressionistic" and "impressionistic."

Haptic and visual drawing styles appear to be related to differences in psy- chological makeup. Lee Gutteter (1972) found that students who are visual tend to be moderate, patient, steady, realistic, industrious, and conforming whereas students who are haptic tend to be impatient, restless, changeable, complicated, imaginative, opinionated, rebellious, spontaneous, resourceful, and have internal conflicts. However, these drawing styles are not significantly affected by differences in sex. Witkin (1962) found that the parent who dominates a child produces de- pendency—dependency upon environment and lack of sensitivity or respect for bodily cues in space—by constricting the child's growth. Likewise, the field in- dependent (who tend to be psychologically similar to haptic) are sensitive to bodily positioning and weight and are more aware of the body generally. Witkin felt the "growth-fostering" parent was primarily responsible for this identification. A. Dean Howell (1973) cautions that whereas visual and nonvisual attributes are primarily psychological in nature, much of the writing in this area tends to emphasize the physiological—a fallacy since blind persons are of both orientations.

Lowenfeld (1957, p. 263), found that a great number of students show both visual and haptic characteristics but more commonly there is a preference for one over the other. Of every four persons of an average population, Lowenfeld noted that 47 percent are clearly visual, 23 percent are haptic and 30 percent are not identifiable, having no dominant tendency. Therefore in a typical class, approximately one fourth of the students appear to depend more on subjective reactions, such as touch, movement, and body sensations, and work in a synthetic, part-by-part manner whereas about one half of the students depend upon vision and benefit from visual stimuli. These latter students work in an analytic, holistic manner. About one fourth are unidentifiable, working both ways. In a survey of professional artists (Michael, 1970), 31 percent reported they work synthetically—the part method—and 76 percent work analytically—the whole method. Some few artists indicated they work both ways at various times. These proportions appear to reflect somewhat the findings of Lowenfeld's nonart population and give us all the more reason to become aware of these two approaches. Gutteter (1976) found a significant difference between students whose drawings are strongly visual or nonvisual and students whose drawings are lacking in any precise style, that unidentifiable 30 percent whom Lowenfeld found neither visual nor haptic. The dominant characteristics of these unidentifiable students are confusion, lack of consistency, internal conflicts, vacillation, uncertainty, and lack of self direction. They seem to be unable to express themselves through any strong approach or to act upon the

Visual and haptic orientations are demonstrated in these two drawings, in which eating candy was used for stimulation. The visual type draws the total visual image of the head, while the haptic type, more concerned with autoplastic sensations and feelings, draws only the body parts involved: lips, teeth, tongue, and, of course, the candy.

conviction of their feelings because of a lack of confidence. Mary Rouse (1965, p. 51) came to a similar conclusion, observing that these "indefinites," as she called them, display "an unsureness and lack of confidence in their own ability which forces them to remain stylistically uncommitted, afraid to venture to either extreme." She felt our teaching efforts should be directed more toward these rather than toward the strongly visual or haptic students because the unidentifiables need the most help in arriving at a more efficient perception. Gutteter (1976, pp. 59–60) also argues that "our responsibility may well be to encourage our students to choose the style (visual or haptic) they feel most comfortable with and work to continue developing it. Positive reinforcement from us might well do more to develop confidence in their art ability and thereby turn them on to art."

The visual/haptic phenomenon is *not* a dichotomy with visual at one end of the continuum and haptic at the other as many have thought. Practically everyone possesses both qualities. Therefore, it is logical to assume that the teacher should devise methods for the development of both qualities, realizing that some students can naturally develop a high level of expertise in visual considerations and others in haptic considerations. Lowenfeld argued that these two types must not be dissociated by a method which presents concepts and situations that are completely incomprehensible to the other type—allowance for both orientations must always be made by the teacher.

Beginning with stimulation, both types are motivated by the inclusion of both environment (the visual, actual and remembered) and dramatic action (subjective body feelings vividly expressed). Although the teacher may use one stimulus, such as a still life, students' attention should be called to the visual qualities: the whole or unity of the arrangement; the form created by light, shadows, and color changes; and placement of one object in front of another (depth). Attention should also be called to the haptic qualities: texture, emotional feelings about the objects or parts of objects—moods, movement, tension, dynamic qualities, and personal meanings concerning various aspects of the objects in the still life. For most teachers, stimulation of subjective and personally expressive qualities of objects in a still life seems to be much more difficult than the stimulation of visual qualities. Emotional feelings may be developed by creating a still life around a topic or theme such as the Victorian period, Halloween, or the beach. A still life may also be created by emphasizing a quality such as delicacy, abruptness, boldness, lightness, and the like. Colored spotlights and even music may aid in conveying and/or developing a feeling or quality about a still life. Students who find it difficult to identify with the objects in the still life should pose or move in such a manner as will express the feeling or concept they have concerning a particular object of their choice. To heighten interest in this experience and to bring about greater identification with the objects, let the other students guess which object in the still life the student is expressing with his body and body movement.

In figure drawing, as in still life, in addition to pointing out the visual aspects, subjective (haptic) aspects must also be developed by giving meaning, purpose, and feeling to each pose. The visually minded will draw what they see and the haptically minded will depict feelings about the pose that will probably result in exaggerations, Picasso's *Guernica* being an excellent example. At this time the teacher should make clear the difference between observed proportions of the visual student and proportions of value (exaggerations) of the nonvisual student, noting that both are appropriate and are present in various great works of art. Various props and bits of costumes, such as musical instruments, hats, baskets, and swords not only will stimulate visually but also will give meaning and purpose for the action to the nonvisual student. The same is true for landscape/seascape wherein the teacher should develop a mood via topics such as a storm over the city, the quietness of the forest, and evening at lakeside. Such stimulation may be accomplished by verbal descriptions and stories, poems, films, music, dramatic role playing, and movement/dance.

After students are stimulated and have started on their art work, the teacher should help them clarify their expressive purposes. What are they trying to say, to communicate, to express, to accomplish in their work? Such clarification will give the student a sense of direction and confidence and may be accomplished through a series of open-ended questions concerning the subject matter and the student's purpose.

When the work is completed, it must be evaluated in part, at least, according to the student's own goals, purposes, and orientation. If such an evaluation is done in a group or class situation, each student will begin to appreciate the different approaches and purposes in the work of all the other students, as well as the work of professional artists which may be introduced by the teacher at an appropriate time during the evaluation period.

The teacher must always be aware of these two types or ways of looking at the world—the visual and nonvisual (subjective)—in the art class so as to provide opportunity for both types to become stimulated and work in their own natural direction. However, *there is no necessity for the teacher to identify students as being either visual or nonvisual so long as both types are provided for in all phases of instruction* (Michael, 1982, p. 345). Although students should not be forced to work in a manner that is foreign to themselves, they should become aware and develop whatever ability they do possess, both visually and nonvisually.

METHODS OF PROFESSIONAL ARTISTS

In the previously mentioned survey (Michael, 1970) of over 350 professional artists in seven areas, a consensus was found concerning many aspects of methodology. These methods, in all probability, are also appropriate for those adolescents who are beginning to consider art experiences in the same manner as professional artists.

Stimulation

Problems that artists discover in their art work stimulate them to continue on the work at hand (94 percent).[4] This suggests that teachers should help student artists identify problems in their work as stimulating challenges and offer suggestions for solutions. Furthermore, many artists (95 percent) get ideas while working on one piece of art for working on another. The teacher must watch students as they work to discern new ideas that evolve and then encourage an exploration of these stimulating ideas in new works of art. Teacher demonstrations may stimulate

---

[4]Percentage of all artists agreeing on this concept or behavior.

some students just as they stimulate some artists (44 percent), while other students, like artists, become stimulated when preparing art materials (58 percent). Some artists (38 percent) survey their past work for inspiration and as a means of knowing where to start and what to do in their art work at hand. Some students may want to keep a portfolio of their work for this purpose. Cluttered studios, where many objects are found, serve as stimulating visual cues for many artists (51 percent). Teachers may collect and display objects such as shells, bark, dried plants, interesting stones, bones, skins, and feathers to stimulate and inspire students.

Various subjects, aspects of life, and art inspire professional artists and may also stimulate secondary students. Such listings by artists may be categorized into the following: nature and human forms; man-made objects and buildings; city life; the space age and contemporary life; color; moods and feelings; visual art work of the past in museums or in publications; related arts areas, such as literature, music, dance, and drama; materials and tools; processes of creating art involving experimentation, communication, discovery, technical problems; the desire to improve; association with fellow artists; preliminary sketching and drawing; one's previous art work; public admiration and encouragement; and economic considerations—sales and commissions. Many of these may prove valid for stimulating secondary students as the need arises. (See also Appendix 7.)

Methods of Working

Professional artists suggest that for students the best way of working is to develop their own approach by producing art in a manner that is most comfortable and right for themselves (91 percent). Students must do a great deal of exploring and learning about art before they can arrive at their own personal approach. However, this exploration on the part of students must not include imitating and copying the work of others (94 percent) or even producing art work in the manner of some other artist, school, or historical period (75 percent). In fact, students should not even try to identify with a particular art movement in their work (95 percent), but should work in their own manner. Should teachers feel the need to have students work in a particular style to understand an approach such as Cubism, Surrealism, or Abstract Expressionism, the resulting work should be considered as an experimental exercise and should not be thought of as art—their own expression.

Since many artists (80 percent) enjoy discussing art with other artists, it behooves the teacher to encourage students to talk about art with each other, as well as inviting professional artists to talk with the class. The teacher needs to develop a dialogue among the students about art. Such discussions can be triggered by newspaper articles, art happenings in the community—local as well as national—the colors selected to paint the school, and any other pertinent art-related event or consideration.

Students should be given the opportunity to mull over ideas before they begin their art work in the same way that professional artists do (87 percent). According to research by Dorothy V. Hunter (1967), students who pondered over ideas did significantly better on creative art work than did classmates who worked directly and immediately from the stimulation. This did not hold true when the same students were drawing from what they actually saw in the art room, such as a still life or a posing model. Apparently for imaginary work, students need some time to think, to consider feelings, and to conjure up past perceptions before doing art work of quality.

Producing a series of art works, all of which explore a similar theme, subject, color, and technique, is the typical approach of most professional artists (81 percent) and is a method the art teacher may seriously wish to consider. Many works of a similar nature permit more exploration, expression, and understanding. Not only do artists produce a series but they also have many different pieces of art work in process at one time (71 percent). Therefore, as with professional artists, it should not be necessary for a student to finish one piece before starting another, perhaps rather starting several before any one piece is completed. Some artists have as many as fifty pieces in process at once.

Artists use many different methods when beginning their work, and the art teacher should be aware so that these may be used whenever the need arises. Most artists use more than one of these approaches. Some artists (31 percent) work from preliminary drawings or plans which are complete and precise; but most artists (81 percent) using this approach try to think in terms of the medium in which the piece will finally be developed, and note that they do deviate from the precise drawings in the final product (79 percent). According to research by Kenneth Shelley (1963) and by the writer (Michael, 1959), students who mentally preconceive, produce creative art work of lesser quality than those who do not preconceive. Suggestions made by the teacher were shown to be more helpful for students who did *not* preconceive their work. These students appear to be more open and flexible in their approach.

Many artists (59 percent) work from preliminary sketches, doodles, or drawings that are vague and general and even more artists (65 percent) work without any sketches but only with a general idea in mind. Some (48 percent) approach their art work without any sketches or even vague ideas and work directly with the medium getting inspiration from what happens as they work with the material. Whenever the art teacher introduces a medium, the student must work directly with it so as to become acquainted with its characteristics. These four approaches provide the secondary teacher with a variety of methods for initiating a work of art with students.

Most artists (92 percent) find that the art elements require shifting and relating as they grow into a structure that is satisfying. In other words, artists *do* work in a flexible manner. Getzels and Csikszentmihalyi (1965) found that the more change in the early stages of a drawing the better the quality of the product. These findings suggest that the teacher should help students look for possibilities of changing their work, especially in the early stages. Perhaps teachers should insist upon an initial exploration and brain-storming period when students try various ideas and approaches.

Some artists (53 percent) move back and forth from one medium to another as a means of holding onto awareness, sensitivity, and a fresh quality in their work. Likewise, students should be encouraged to try a new medium and possibly start a new art piece when they lose interest and involvement in a work. However, when working with a particular medium, students should be encouraged to consider its characteristic qualities as they work, as do professional artists (84 percent).

Some artists (48 percent) keep systematic work schedules and others (44 percent) set deadlines for themselves. For some students, then, the teacher may follow the example of these professional artists.

METHODS INVOLVING NEW MEDIA

When students are asked to work with a new medium, it is only natural that time must be set aside for experimentation. (See Table 9.) Students need to discover the various characteristics and the processes or procedures necessary for working with the new material. Two methods are possible.

In the first, the teacher may introduce a new medium via an experimental period that is structured in such a way that certain particular learnings occur. At this time, a rudimentary knowledge and sensitivity concerning qualities of the medium and appropriate basic procedural skills are developed. The amount of time required for this experimentation will vary from student to student and from medium to medium. Some media may require only five or ten minutes while others may require several class periods. Although most students are stimulated by a new material, the experimentation period must not be so long and drawn out that students lose interest. For example, in an experimental period involving metals, students need to become aware of the metal's hardness, malleability, finish, color; procedures for sawing, bending, hammering, drawing, twisting, fusing or attaching

TABLE 9
Experimental Period: Approach to a New Medium

EXPERIMENTATION PERIOD: OBJECTIVES	STIMULATION	WORK PERIOD: PRODUCTION, EVALUATION

1. Qualities of the medium are discovered
 	
2. Procedures concerning the medium, i. e., processes and tools are presented; skills are developed
	1. Ideas come from the media—intrinsic (media method)
	    Ideas come from an explanation of procedures, i.e., processes and tools (media method)
	
	2. New ideas are introduced—extrinsic, such as using a story to stimulate (assigned topic method)
		1. Production: Qualities of the medium are pointed out in relation to expressive purposes and the student is questioned concerning these
		    Procedures again are explained concerning the medium, i.e., processes and tools
		
		2. Problem of the artist is kept before the student: an aesthetic organization and expression of one's thinking, feeling, perceiving
		    The relationship of the art product and art experience to the world of art (art history and criticism) is made
		
		3. Evaluation: Is there a harmonious, creative, and consistent organization of the elements of art?
		    Are skill and craftsmanship appropriate for the expression?
		    What do this product and experience mean to the student? What does the work express?
		    Where do this product and experience lead the student to next? Do they suggest something for the next art experience?

one piece to another; creating surface textures, shaping or forming, annealing, oxidizing, and polishing. Certainly not all of these aspects may be developed in one class period. The teacher will want to adjust the experimental period or periods in accordance with the level, interest, and sophistication of the students, as well as classroom considerations such as time, budget, and availability of tools and equipment. In time, students should become so well acquainted with the properties of the new medium and its related procedures that they are unconsciously aware of these as they work. It is only then that they can freely express and communicate through a particular medium. Although such a high level of identification cannot be achieved in the initial experimental period or periods, that is our ultimate goal.

While experimenting with a new material, most students will become stimulated, getting ideas for a piece of art work. For example, as students experiment with watercolors—dropping paints on wet paper—as the paints run together and the colors mix, certain objects will suggest themselves. At this point, the teacher can encourage the students to continue using the objects already found on the paper, to develop these and add more—thus creating a painting. This becomes the media method of teaching discussed previously in this chapter.

In a second method, experimentation with a medium occurs as students work directly on the art work at hand, no special initial time being given for experimentation. In other words, students simultaneously experiment and create a painting, a ring, a ceramic bowl, or any other art piece. During the process of making art, then, students must be made aware of the properties and special procedures unique to the medium in addition to expressing themselves in their work. As students paint on their pictures, they discover the properties of the particular paint and experiment with procedures, such as mixing, making washes or glazes, that are appropriate for that particular paint medium. With some media and for some students, such experimentation during the process of producing an art work may add to the uniqueness and the freshness of the expression while for others simultaneously expressing and experimenting with the media are overwhelming and inhibiting.

Regardless of the method used, students must be provided an opportunity to discover the characteristics and procedures necessary for working with a particular medium.

REFERENCES

Beittel, K. R., and Burkhart, R. C. Strategies of spontaneous, divergent, and academic art students. *Studies in Art Education*, 1963, *5* (1), 20–41.

Burkhart, R. C. *Spontaneous and Deliberate Ways of Learning in Art*. Scranton: International Textbook Company, 1962.

Clements, R. D. Encouragement: Toward CBTE in the art working period; five steps in giving students support. *Art Education*, 1976, *29* (4), 7–12.

Cogan, M. L. The behavior of teachers and the productive behavior of their pupils. *Journal of Experimental Education*, December 1958, 89–124.

Collins, M. L. The effects of training for enthusiasm on the enthusiasm displayed by preservice elementary teachers. Doctoral dissertation. Syracuse: Syracuse University, 1976.

Combs, A. W. *The Professional Education of Teachers*. Boston: Allyn and Bacon, 1965.

Cruickshank, D. R., et al. *Teaching Is Tough.* Englewood Cliffs, New Jersey: Prentice-Hall, 1980.

Edmonston, P. Conditions which enhance or inhibit creative teaching and learning. *Art Education Bulletin,* 1962, *19* (4), 9–22.

Edwards, B. *Drawing on the Right Side of the Brain.* Boston: Houghton Mifflin, 1979.

Ellsworth, M. How students react to high school art experience. *Art Education,* 1969, *22* (8), 29–30.

Flanders, N. A. *Teacher Influence, Pupil Attitudes and Achievement: Studies in Interaction Analysis.* University of Minnesota, U.S. Office of Education, 1960.

Getzels, J. W. "The Viktor Lowenfeld Memorial Lecture." Chicago: National Art Education Association Conference, April 12, 1981.

Getzels, J. W., and Csikszentmihalyi, M. Creativity in art students: Personality cognition, and the process of discovery. Paper presented at the annual meeting of the American Psychological Association, Chicago, 1965.

Gillett, M. H. Effects of teacher enthusiasm on at-task behavior of students in elementary classes. Doctoral dissertation. Eugene, Oregon: University of Oregon, 1980.

Gutteter, L. J. The relationship between the visual and haptic drawing styles and psychological variables, age, sex, and previous art experience. *Studies in Art Education,* 1972, *14* (1), 15–23.

Gutteter, L. J. The psychological functioning of early adolescents who have failed to develop a precise drawing style. *Studies in Art Education,* 1976, *18* (1), 55–60.

Hart, W. F. *Teacher and Teaching.* New York: Macmillan, 1934.

Heil, L. M., Powell, M., and Fiefer, I. *Characteristics of Teacher Behavior Related to the Achievement of Children in Several Elementary Grades.* Washington, D.C., U.S. Office of Education, Cooperative Research Branch, 1960.

Hendrix, S. The effect of movement upon the aesthetic quality of drawings. Paper presented at Research Seminar, Miami University, Oxford, Ohio, December 1966.

Hollingsworth, P. Brain growth spurts and art education. *Art Education,* 1981, *34* (3), 12–14.

Howell, A. D. An electroencephalographic comparison of Lowenfeld's haptic-visual and Witkin's field-dependent/field-independent perceptual types. (Doctoral dissertation, Ball State University, 1973.) *Dissertation Abstracts International,* 1973, *33,* 4941A (University Microfilms No. 73–6764).

Hunter, D. V. The effect of time to mull over a stimulation on the drawings of some eighth-grade students. Paper presented at Research Seminar, Miami University, Oxford, Ohio, December 1967.

Jacob, P. E. *Changing Values in College.* New York: Harper, 1957.

Kielscheski, C. J. Effects of aggressive art motivations on the overall aesthetic quality, identification/involvement, and creativeness of drawing. (Doctoral dissertation, Arizona State University, 1974.) *Dissertation Abstracts International,* 1974, *34,* 68–74 (University Microfilms, No. 74–9887).

Krathwohl, D. R., Bloom, B. S., and Masia, B. B. *Taxonomy of Educational Objectives: Handbook II: Affective Domain.* New York: Longman Company, 1964.

Lowenfeld, V. *Creative and Mental Growth* (3rd ed.). New York: Macmillan, 1957.

Madeja, S. The effects of divergent and convergent emphasis in art instruction on students of high and low ability. *Studies in Art Education,* 1967, *8* (2), 10–20.

Madenfort, W. J. Aesthetic education for the immediacy of sensuous experience. *Art Education,* 1972, *25* (5), 10–14.

Mattil, E. L., et al. The effect of a depth vs. a breadth method of art instruction at the ninth-grade level. *Studies in Art Education,* 1961, *3* (1), 75–87.

Michael, J. A. The effect of awards, adult standard, and peer standard upon the creativeness in art of high school pupils. In J. Hausman (ed.), *Research in Art Education, Ninth NAEA Yearbook.* Kutztown, Pa.: National Art Education Association, 1959.

Michael, J. A. *A Handbook for Art Instructors and Students Based upon Concepts and Behaviors*. New York: Vantage Press, 1970.

Michael, J. A. (ed.). *The Lowenfeld Lectures*. University Park, Pennsylvania: Pennsylvania State University Press, 1982.

Olson, M. N. Research notes—ways to achieve quality in school classrooms: some definitive answers. *Phi Delta Kappan*, 1971, *53* (1), 63–65.

Reed, C. *Early Adolescent Art Education*. Peoria: Chas. A. Bennett, 1957.

Rennels, M. R. Cerebral symmetry: an urgent concern for education. *Phi Delta Kappan*, 1976, *57* (7), 471–472.

Rosenthal, R., and Jacobson, L. *Pygmalion in the Classroom*. New York: Holt, Rinehart and Winston, 1968.

Rouse, M. J. A new look at an old theory: A comparison of Lowenfeld's "visual-haptic" theory with Witkin's perceptual theory. *Studies in Art Education*, 1965, *7* (1), 42–55.

Ryans, D. G. Prediction of teacher effectiveness. *Encyclopedia of Educational Research* (3rd ed.). New York: Macmillan, 1960, 1486–90.

Shelley, K. The effects of pre-verbalization versus non-verbalization upon art work of students in grades five, six, seven, and eight. Paper presented at the Miami University, Oxford, Ohio, Graduate Club in Art Education Conference, June 1963.

Spaulding, R. *Achievement, creativity, and self-concept correlates of teacher-pupil transactions in elementary schools*. Urbana: University of Illinois, U.S. Office of Education Cooperative Research Project No. 1352, 1963.

Szekely, G. The art lesson as a work of art. *Art Teacher*, 1980, *10* (3), 12–14.

Verworn, M. *Zur Psychologie der Primitiven Kunst*. Jena: Verlag von Gustav Fischer, 1908.

Verworn, M. *Ideoplastische Kunst*. Jena: Verlag von Gustav Fischer, 1914.

Virshup, E. Art and the right hemisphere. *Art Education*, 1976, *29* (7), 14–15.

Webb, D. Teacher sensitivity: Affective impact on students. *The Journal of Teacher Education*, 1971, *22* (4), 455–459.

Williams, R. M. Why children should draw. *Saturday Review*, September 1977, 11–16.

Witkin, H. A., et al. *Psychological Differentiation*. New York: John Wiley, 1962.

Witty, P. An analysis of the personality traits of the effective teacher. *Journal of Educational Research*, 1947, *40* (9), 662–71.

Youngblood, M. Hemispheric amphigory. *Art Education*, 1981, *34* (4), 9–11.

SUPPLEMENTAL READINGS

Barr-Johnson, Virginia, and Brockmyer, James J. The art classroom as art teacher. *Art Education*, 1981, *34* (1), 12–14. Various art room environments that can be used to stimulate students.

Barron, Frank. *Artists in the Making*. New York: Seminar Press, 1972. Stages of personal and professional development of artists.

Beittel, Kenneth R. *Mind and Context in the Art of Drawing*. New York: Holt, Rinehart and Winston, 1972. Empirical study of the process of drawing.

Brommer, Gerald. *Discovering Art History*. Worcester, Massachusetts: Davis Publications, 1981. Text for use in secondary schools with suggestions for independent study.

Burkhart, Robert C. *Spontaneous and Deliberate Ways of Learning*. Scranton: International Textbook, 1962. Adolescent approaches to making art described and discussed.

Edwards, Betty. *Drawing on the Right Side of the Brain*. Boston: Houghton Mifflin, 1979. The effect of brain research on drawing methodology.

Lanier, Vincent. *Teaching Secondary Art*. Scranton: International Textbook, 1964. A textbook, with chapters on content and methodology.

McFee, June K., and Degge, Rogena M. *Art, Culture, and Environment: A Catalyst for Teaching*. Belmont, California: Wadsworth, 1977. Classroom approaches to seeing, drawing, and designing; followed by discussion of performance objectives.

Michael, John A. *A Handbook for Art Instructors and Students Based upon Concepts and Behaviors*. New York: Vantage Press, 1970. Methods of professional artists appropriate for secondary school art students.

Pappas, George (ed.). *Concepts in Art and Art Education*. New York: Macmillan, 1970. Several authorities contribute philosophical considerations on the practice of art.

Szekely, George. The art lesson as a work of art. *Art Teacher*, 1980, *10* (3), 12–14. The teacher is seen as a creative designer of classroom art experiences.

Wright, Jim. On caring and craftsmanship. *Art Education*, 1982, *35* (3), 33. Humanistic approach in working with students.

CHAPTER 6

MANAGING ADOLESCENTS
Discipline

For many years, a lack of discipline has been the most serious problem in the schools of America as indicated by the annual Gallup poll involving education (Gallup, 1982). Many teachers either quit or lose their jobs because of a lack of control of their classes. Little learning can take place in a class fraught with behavior problems. Therefore, serious attention must be given to this aspect of classroom management.

DEFINITION AND PURPOSE

First, concerning discipline, we must ask ourselves, "What do we want; what is our purpose, our goal?" In a democracy where we govern ourselves, most people want self-discipline wherein individuals behave in a socially acceptable manner (being responsible, cooperative, courteous, and unselfish) because they want to, not because they are forced to do so by some external authority. We recognize that we must behave in an acceptable way so that we can live together happily, so that we can do whatever we feel we need to do so long as it does not threaten and interfere with the well-being of others. Many times art students must work alone or in small groups that require self-discipline. The teacher cannot be the control of every student all of the time. Self-discipline, therefore, is necessary and a very important educational goal. *Webster's* (1976) defines discipline as "conduct in accordance with a self-imposed rule or set of rules: self-control, self-restraint," and as "training or experience that corrects, molds, strengthens, or perfects especially the mental faculties or moral character." It may also be "control gained by forcing obedience or order." It is the hope of most teachers that we will not have to "force obedience," but at times even this may be necessary.

Classroom student behavior may be thought of as being on a continuum—complete freedom and permissiveness at one end and dictation and regimentation at the other. Most Americans would probably opt more toward freedom. Freedom, however, must be qualified. Erich Fromm (1941, p. 258) notes that freedom in its highest form "consists of the spontaneous activity of the total, integrated personality," a harmonious organization akin to aesthetics, which he calls "positive freedom." He then describes negative freedom as being chaos and anarchy—freedom without responsibility. For the most part, then, discipline means self-control in a free society.

In a democratic situation, we control ourselves by purpose. The successful teacher stimulates adolescents in an art class so that they have a purpose. They are motivated to do something—to produce a mural with a social message for the front hall; to design a ring for a special person; to make a block print for the school annual; and to illustrate a poem or story written for English class. After students are motivated to create something in art class, then the teacher should question them to find out if there is anything that will not let them achieve their purpose. They must be able to do all those things that will let them reach their goal. Discipline, then, grows out of the work itself. The teacher's initial role is to get students involved, interested, and wanting to do something in the art area.

The types of experiences in the art room are in themselves a kind of discipline. There is a discipline in the use of an art medium in that we can do with it only that which is possible. Clays must be used differently than metals and both are quite different than wood. And within each of these media classifications there are

Photo courtesy of Craig Roland

The best means for developing self-discipline are purpose and involvement in art experiences. Tools and processes are intriguing and bring about a keen interest on the part of students.

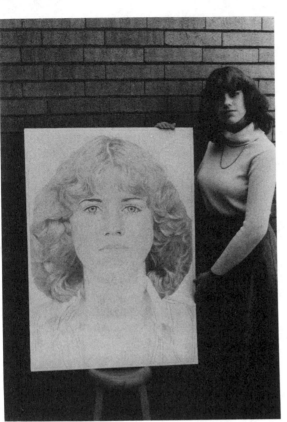

Consistency and control of the medium are aspects of discipline as
shown in this large portrait in pencil.
Note the sensitive observation of
every detail and the control of dark
and light to emphasize expression in
this self-portrait.

materials that possess unique characteristics that must be taken into account. For example, porcelain is different than stoneware; pewter is different than silver; teak is different than pine. The student, in a way, is disciplined by the media. There is also discipline in aesthetic discrimination by being consistent in making choices of lines, shapes, colors and in composing these into a unity. There is a discipline in comparing the work of one artist with another; one art style or period with another; one manner of working with another. There is even a discipline in selecting aspects from one's own experience for expression in a work of art. All the above aspects involve purpose, choice, control, and a perfecting of our sensitivities as we work on our art. When students are busy and involved in any of these aspects of art, there is harmony and a sense of purpose in the classroom. The best solution for avoiding disciplinary problems is an excellent art program wherein students are involved, interested, and busy and all their efforts and behaviors are directed toward their art class activities.

Whenever you plan your work and life, this in itself is a discipline, both for students and teachers. People without a plan in life are confused and do not know what they want. As teachers, we must have purpose as we teach, as well as thoughtful planning in our own lives. According to Layman H. Jones (1965), a successful teacher has a strong sense of direction and does not bend with every whim.

Glenn E. Tagatz (1969) proposes four disciplinary principles that will assure maximum self-control on the part of students. The first is a relaxing of restraints on individual behavior and ultimately allowance of complete self-determination. This he calls "freedom," without which self-discipline cannot take place—discipline would remain a result of external force, the student's behavior not being a function of his own determination but rather a function of the teacher's demand. Tagatz's second principle is "acceptance," when the student as a person is accepted and respected by the teacher. It may be difficult to accept some students who use street language, whose clothes and even bodies are dirty and not well cared for. But only through such acceptance is reciprocity of acceptance possible. Students must view their teacher as accepting and concerned for them. The third principle is "restriction," a limitation of the student's freedom. Secondary schools handle large numbers of students who work with many teachers (usually five to eight) each day in a limited work area (usually thirty by forty feet per class of thirty or more students). It is obvious that some rules are necessary but these should develop naturally and be few in number. Some behaviors in the classroom, as in society, must be forbidden. Teachers must prohibit these behaviors in a straightforward way, feeling no sense of guilt or timidity in doing so. Many students will test teachers to find out the teacher's limits and any feeling of timidity or unsureness on the part of the teacher. The fourth principle is consistent application of the previous three: freedom, acceptance, and restriction. Resentment always results from inconsistency, which is one of the main reasons for negative feelings on the part of students. Teachers must be judged as being fair and just by students.

Self-discipline also involves a belief in your students: they are valuable and responsible. This is nurtured by treating students with civility, dignity, and respect— all within a framework of positive expectations. Such an attitude on the part of teachers will bring about similar self-perceptions on the part of students who will then behave in ways that are mutually beneficial to themselves and others. Students who are consistently treated with courtesy, respect, and positive expectations are less likely to exhibit negative behaviors. Students tend to see themselves as others see them and behave accordingly ("Discipline, an Overview," 1981).

PREVENTIVE DISCIPLINE: MANAGING THE CLASSROOM

Some teachers never have any discipline problems because they manage their classrooms in a manner that prevents disruptive behavior from occurring. Successful teachers stop problems before they start by a keen understanding of adolescents and group dynamics and a strong feeling concerning the type of behavior deemed acceptable. Let us consider some aspects of managing the classroom that prevent behavior problems.

Atmosphere of Acceptance

Every human being has a desire for acceptance and a need for self esteem. The acceptance by the teacher of each and every student should be apparent to all the students in a class. Such interest in students must be genuine and positive and is conveyed, in part, by talking with students about themselves and what they are doing: their activities in the art class and their activities outside the art class.

Praise of art work and/or positive comments about personal life, clothes, sports, and school life will make students know the teacher is interested in them as persons. Students must feel respected. They must also have pride in themselves. A belief in one's self can be developed through art work. If personal and creative art work is to take place, there must be the freedom to try new things, to experiment without an immediate—and especially a negative—evaluation. The teacher may point out strengths and also problems in the work and ask for the student's point of view concerning solutions. In doing so, we imply an acceptance of students and their ideas and opinions while trying to raise the level of quality of their work. There must be praise for effort, perseverance, and any improvement of abilities on the part of the student, all of which will convey the message that the student is respected and accepted by the teacher.

Teacher Involvement and Interest

Students tend to become interested in art areas in which teachers themselves are very much interested and involved, especially if the teacher is somewhat overtly enthusiastic, beginning each class promptly with a suggestion of vigor and excitement. Someone who is greatly involved in an area usually enjoys telling others about it and the more other people become interested, the more enthusiastic such a person becomes. Teacher interest in art may also be shown by teachers taking their art work to school and displaying it—even having a one-person show. Some teachers occasionally work on their own art during class time, becoming a role model for their students.

In addition to conveying involvement and interest in art, the teacher should demonstrate his or her knowledge and ability in the field to gain the respect, if not the admiration, of students. Expounding at length on some aspect of art and displaying one's art work in the art room is usually sufficient. It is difficult to misbehave in the presence of someone whose ability we highly respect and whom we accept as a role model.

Teachers must also be involved with and interested in students. One indication of concern for students is learning their names quickly. Name tags or at least names on art work on which they are working will help in the beginning. For teachers who have difficulty remembering names, it may be necessary to take a few minutes of each class and review the names as you study their faces.

The art room environment can reflect the involvement of the teacher with art and with the students' work. Exciting visual displays and a continually changing and aesthetic environment may keep student interest high and motivate students, giving them a sense of pride and purpose.

You may use special occasions to convey the idea to the students that you are interested in them as human beings. You may want to attend sporting events, school plays, concerts, and other school functions. Many teachers do not recognize what an opportunity they have when one of their students is ill. In such cases a note or telephone call will work wonders in getting across the feeling of your interest and concern. Lee Canter (1980) suggests that teachers write notes to parents praising those students who are most cooperative and good citizens. In fact, he recommends that teachers select outstanding students in every class and regularly send complimentary notes to parents.

In every situation the teacher should be courteous with students and be a role model. Avoid baby talk, sarcasm, and favorites; do not insist on apologies. Such avoidance will show that you care about all your students.

Teachers should take advantage of the drama of the teaching situation. As teachers, we communicate our interest, as well as our approval or disapproval, to our students just as the actor communicates his feelings to the audience. The teacher tends to be "the star," with the students becoming the audience. In academic subject areas, teachers usually stand at the front of the class while all the students are sitting in rows at their desks. After experiencing this arrangement in elementary school for many years, students are "trained" to look to the teacher as being "on stage." Teachers can use this audience-performer situation in a very positive way to emphasize their interest, concern, and respect for students. For example, the teacher who is at the door of the classroom waiting for the students to enter conveys a message to the students that "this teacher is on duty" and is really interested and concerned. This point can be emphasized if the teacher praises students who enter the room nicely, who bring their art materials, or whatever is important for learning at the time. Such positive comments to a few students (by name) will engender a desire on the part of other students for recognition and attention. Therefore, they will all begin to assume the desired behavior the teacher feels is necessary for learning on that particular day.

Leadership in the Classroom

The classroom is a small social system of complex elements in mutual inter-action. Part of this system is a response to external factors such as the physical (room, location, temperature) and the social (school, community) environment. And part of the system is also in response to internal factors, such as the things people do in the art room; how the interaction of one person influences another; and the likes, dislikes, and feelings of the individuals in the class. Concerning interaction, the more you interact with a person, the more you tend to like that person; the more liking (sentiment) increases, the more interaction occurs. An increase in activity among individuals in a group results in cohesion and growing sentiment (liking) for the group. Art teachers can use this knowledge and take a leadership role in developing class and school spirit—and especially in developing a favorable attitude and respect for the art teacher. A class unit concerned with advertising a school function can develop much interaction between the teacher and the class, as well as among the class members themselves. In developing advertising campaigns with small groups of students working together, much interaction will take place. A successful campaign will result in the students feeling they have accomplished much together, the same feeling as students on a winning athletic team. They will feel, "We have been through this experience together; look what we did!" and thereby develop a very positive feeling for the group and especially for the teacher who has been responsible for making it all possible. There are many such opportunities for this type of leadership and interaction in an art program: designing and making scenery for a school play; producing five hundred silk-screen posters for a school function; designing and building booths for the school carnival; creating holiday decorations for the school building; producing a puppet show; and putting on an art exhibit or arts fair.

Group norms in a social system—in a class or in a school—are the group's ideas of how things should or ought to be. Conformity to the group's norms is rewarded; nonconformity is punished, even in radical groups. Each group is different and sets norms for itself. The higher the person's social rank in the group, the more he conforms to the norms. A teacher usually begins with an above average rank. It should also be noted that there may be subgroups within a group. The subgroups should be prevented from competing with one another, which can usually be accomplished by separation of subgroup members within the class. Geography does have an affect upon subgroup interaction. For example, if the sexes are separated by a seating arrangement in the seventh grade, competition between girls and boys will probably develop. The leader of a group understands what the group wants and takes the group where they want to go. An emerging leader gains power and authority only by conforming to group desires. However, after the leader is established, he can deviate from the norms. The emergent leader is viewed by the group as having credits—the more critical the situations the leader reacts to in the way the group thinks he should, the more credits are built up in the plus column for norms. When the leader has enough plus credits in the norm column, the group can then be moved in other directions. The leader also has the strongest influence in establishing the social ranking of others in the group.

A teacher is an *appointed* leader and can identify group norms and assume the role of the emergent leader, but the teacher must first conform to the norms of the group and become sensitive to the personality of the group. But the teacher must discover what the school community and the class thinks a teacher should do and be (the norm for teachers) and at first must conform to this role.

The feelings of the group affect the quality of work done. When feelings are negative, the work will be done because it is required but quality may suffer. The cohesiveness of the group is therefore related to self-initiative. The greater the inward solidarity of the group, the greater the outward hostility. A substitute art teacher may find it difficult to take over a class in which the class identifies and wholeheartedly accepts the leadership of the regular art teacher. In such a situation, members of the class will feel the substitute is intruding upon a somewhat sacred relationship they have developed with the regular art teacher. However, when such group-class spirit has been developed by the art teacher, the class may be led into fantastic high-level learning experiences not otherwise possible.

Routines in the classroom established by the art teacher become group norms; for example, the procedures for the students to receive their art work and materials at the beginning of class and the procedures for clean-up and putting materials away. These may serve to regulate behavior and manage the class more efficiently and permit the teacher to spend more time on learning aspects with students. However, the essence of art is the unexpected and the unpredictable. George Szekely (1981) recommends that creative variations in routine should be in keeping with art and can awaken interest and stimulate students. Such variation is possible in initiating a class, in preparing materials, in communicating with students, in discussing art, and in assigning homework. Student expectations should be *not knowing* what to expect in the art room, thus keeping students attentive.

When becoming an emergent leader in the classroom, the teacher must keep in mind various considerations concerning the students and the techniques used to manage the class and support self-control on the part of the students. The teacher should ask, "Why is the student acting that way?" "What does the class think of this behavior?" "What is the student's relationship to me, the teacher?" "How will the student react to the method I use?" "How will it affect the student's relationship with me, the teacher, and the class?"

There are many techniques and methods which the teacher may use in assuming the leadership and control of a class. Teachers should be aware of these and select the approach they feel is most appropriate for the situation.

Nonverbal Techniques

The teacher is provided here with a means of leading a class by nonverbal behaviors, which have the added attribute of saving the teacher's voice. Teachers who are assigned many classes per day must learn to conserve the voice, as well as energy. Many times, not all students are consciously aware of the teacher's leadership by these quiet means.

Body actions and location of the teacher in the room are controlling factors. Standing or sitting in front of the class create entirely different feelings on the part of students. The teacher who stands erect and looks students in the eye conveys a feeling of "all business," whereas the teacher who casually sits on the desk and leisurely talks creates a relaxed and permissive atmosphere with students reacting accordingly. The teacher must keep in mind the type of behavior that he wants from the class. There are many body actions the teacher can use that are controlling. Standing stiffly erect with folded arms and no smile communicates a definite message to students!

Teachers can give the impression that they are in charge and leading the class by *eye contact* and facial expression. In the early weeks of school, it may be appropriate for the teacher to remain in one area of the room, preferably in front of the students, and observe the class. The teacher will find that students will frequently look up to see if the teacher is there. At first it is important to "be there" and look back at the student as he looks at you. The student needs the security of the teacher's interest and presence in the class. By the glances of the students, the teacher can tell if they are having difficulty and need help, suggestions, or praise to keep them involved and learning. Some teachers control a class only with their eyes, becoming expert in "eye-balling" a class, making eye contact with each student. The teacher should try to see all and hear all that is happening in the class.

A variety of *signals* may be used to bring a student or the entire class back to order or to distract a student from what could lead to further deviant behavior. Flicking the lights, slamming the door, ringing a bell or sounding a buzzer, a stern facial expression, or snapping of fingers may serve as attention-getting signals to indicate disapproval. Teachers so need to develop approval signals such as a smile, winking (at a particular student), or a hand signal. Signals are not effective when the student or group is too excited or aggression is too deep seated.

Everyone has space around him that he regards as his own and personal. By stepping in close to the student or by moving around the room, the teacher can calm the student quietly. In *proximity control*, the student has to adjust to the teacher's presence rather than continue what he was previously doing. The teacher's presence interrupts the student's disruptive behavior.

In some instances, *planned ignoring* is better than a direct reaction when the behavior remains within the range of tolerance. This range should be kept constant so that students know what is expected of them. However, when the boundaries of tolerance have been overstepped, the teacher must react.

Verbal Techniques

There are many verbal approaches available to teachers in exerting leadership and bringing about classroom control. The successful teacher should be aware of these, which may be used in conjunction with the nonverbal approaches. A teacher cannot rely upon any one technique but should use different methods from time to time, each behavioral situation requiring a different approach.

The teacher must exhibit *assertive action* in a class or some student will take over the leadership role. There are various ways of being verbally assertive but it usually means verbally establishing a firm stance in your class and being where the action is. When there is laughter and merriment in a class, the teacher should be in the middle of it laughing the loudest. When things are serious, the teacher must be the most serious, always playing the role model that students follow. The teacher leads by taking a very definite course of action, thus giving a feeling of security to the class. This is especially important at the junior high level. Frequently the teacher leads by praising good-to-outstanding behavior in the art room. This, by far, is the most pleasant and positive approach to assertive action on the part of the teacher—positive reinforcement. Especially at the junior high level, make it a point to call the attention of the class to students who are performing well on each behavior appropriate and necessary for a high level of learning. Such praise should be directed toward all students who deserve it and not limited always to the same few. Because we all love to be recognized and be accepted, everyone in the class will begin to emulate the praised behavior so that they, too, may be positively recognized.

One's *voice* is the greatest personal tool of the teacher in the classroom. The teacher who speaks distinctly, firmly, and with confidence will find that students accept his leadership by recognizing the authority in the voice. The tone and pitch of the voice are just as important as the words that are spoken. Through the voice, the art teacher communicates acceptance and rejection, not only concerning socially acceptable behavior in the classroom, but also concerning the art procedures and art work. Taping your class is a good practice and will tell you much, not only about your voice but also about your classroom management and the total learning situation. You may find that you whine, are too quiet, talk too much, use sarcasm, or favor certain students.

Bringing *humor* into a situation tends to interrupt the sequence of self-stimulated and aggressive action on the part of a student. It is incompatible with anxiety and fear. Tense situations tend to dissolve when humor is introduced. Because of this, it is a face-saving device and gives the student an out. Humor is especially important at the high school level.

Task assistance is necessary for students who find tasks in the art room too difficult. These students often are frustrated and become discipline problems. However, for some students difficult tasks are energizers to learning and these students attempt to perform the task to meet the challenge or to relieve anxiety. If the

Humor is not only a means the teacher can use in classroom control but it is also a means of stimulating students for their art work. Note the humor shown in this montage/drawing by a junior high school student.

teacher finds the task for a particular student too difficult, assistance should be given. The task may be restructured, phrased in a different manner, or broken down into simpler parts. Many times demonstrations are appropriate here.

Interest-boosting and encouraging remarks tend to redirect thinking and get the student back to the task at hand. Learn to speak to those students whose attention is wavering. Usually it is not difficult to bring back those who are about to be lost through daydreaming. Always try to be positive, making students feel they can learn and are important to you.

Other means of *diversion* may be used with students who tend to be disruptive. Asking a question, displaying a reproduction that has not been seen before by the class, introducing a new material, or pointing out a particularly aesthetic aspect of a student's art work interrupts the deviant stimulus-response sequence. Creative teachers can divert behavior in many ways. Timing is important here. The teacher must sense when students are losing interest before they become disruptive.

Teachers can make a direct *appeal to reason* based upon the teacher's personal relationship with the student, such as "I thought we were friends." Some students will feel touched by such an appeal and will then seriously think about their behavior. Another appeal can involve personal safety: "You could hurt yourself (or someone else) doing that." A third appeal can be one that involves the peer group: "Would you do that to your friends?" A fourth appeal can involve values and the self: "You don't really want to be like that do you?" Another appeal can involve the parents: "What would your father or mother say?" All of these relate to the student's sensitivities to self and others and the student's ability to use common sense in relating to various deviant behaviors. Obviously, these various approaches would only be meaningful for some students.

RESTRICTING BEHAVIOR

Sometimes it is necessary to force obedience and order; however, the teacher should try to anticipate difficulties before they reach the crisis stage. It is easier to stop little things in the beginning. Many disciplinary problems that seem insignificant in the early stages may become serious later on.

At this point it should be pointed out that the creative people we hope to develop through art experiences are individual and often do not conform readily to some of the necessary school routines. Frank Barron (1961, p. 19) observes that "we are too much inclined to reward docility and niceness in our students and that the independent, off-beat, and sometimes unruly students, whom we are much inclined to undervalue and deplore, often may have the greatest potential for creative achievement." Although some restrictions are necessary, we must not inhibit students in their creativity. However, keeping this in mind, some behaviors are not appropriate or permissible in the classroom. The teacher, therefore, must restrict these deviant actions.

Although some restrictions may be necessary, *no* rules should be handed down to a class, but guidelines for class behavior should come about naturally in the classroom as you, the teacher, and the students become socially conscious and see a need for them. "We cannot all be at the sink at one time because there is not enough room. When we tried it yesterday, several students got paint on their clothes." Or, "Everyone must listen so that you will know what to do." Students will then understand that the rules that are developed are for their own well-being (Glasser, 1977). Teachers who start a class with rigid rules should realize the effect of these on students. Rigid rules create more anxiety; students become less task oriented; time is spent in worrying about not breaking the rules; students feel pressured and in conflict with the teacher. Some students perceive such rules as a challenge and want to see what will happen if the rules are broken. However, some techniques for restricting behavior at times are necessary.

Admonishment

Teachers may use their authority in verbally admonishing students for anti-social behavior. This usually works when excitement is temporary and students have gone too far; they know it and they want an out. In this situation, the teacher should never argue with students but should stop the disruptive action and *talk at length* about a student's responsibility to the group for socially acceptable behavior. In a milder form, the teacher may threaten that something unpleasant will follow if the disruptive behavior continues. For example, the teacher can threaten to terminate an art activity. However, if threats are not carried out upon occasion, the teacher will lose ground for further disciplinary measures. The teacher should be aware that some students may perceive a threat as a stimulus for a battle of wits.

Students generally respond more to the feelings they perceive in the teacher's voice and actions than to what is being said. Some teachers give the impression that they are confused, timid, and uneasy about insisting upon a particular behavior. This unsureness on the part of the teacher may be the result of a desire to be liked by students; a fear of being rejected by students; feeling sorry for students (especially poor, underprivileged, and handicapped); a fear of repercussions from the principal and parents; physical fear of students; and a lack of belief in the school rules you are trying to enforce. Students then see the teacher's confusion and uncertainty as a lack of firmness and continue the unacceptable behavior to the embarrassment and humiliation of the teacher. As a teacher you must decide what you want and upon a course of action and believe unequivocally in what you are doing. Be honest with yourself and the students.

Deprivation

Restriction of privileges may be a natural consequence of the disruptive behavior. There are many privileges the art teacher can delegate in the art room, from working with art materials and equipment to exhibiting art work. These opportunities may be taken away from students until they show the respect and responsibility needed.

Removal

If the class is likely to get out of hand or contagion is likely, send the disruptive student out of the room to maintain group control. The student may be sent on an errand to give him a chance to calm down. It also gives the student an out. The student may also be sent out of the room as a mild form of punishment by isolation. The treatment should be calm, dignified, and firm. Never leave a student outside the room for very long but use the isolation period as a time to talk with the student about the disruptive behavior, making suggestions for improvement. Always discuss the behavior and not the student per se. It is best to talk with the student in private.

Punishment

Some students respond to punishment and some do not. If it does not work, punishment can aggravate and contribute to delinquency. If used, punishment should be a natural consequence of the offense, immediate and consistent. After the punishment, the teacher should show the student that the matter is settled and drop it and that the student is accepted by the teacher. Do not publicize offenses and their treatment before the other students. If students have damaged property, let them propose a method of restitution. If practical, let them carry out their ideas but see that they do what they promise to do. Never use subject matter as a means of punishment, that is, writing sentences and computing math problems. However, assisting in cleaning the art room and the care of art materials may be appropriate for some students. Some teachers use an after-school detention as a time to become better acquainted with the student.

In the beginning, you may need to overlook many undesirable behaviors since any effort at punishment will be futile if it opposes the standards of the group. For example, you probably cannot eliminate outbursts of loud talk in the art room until group opinion is against it, or until you have been accepted as a leader/teacher and can make rules that will be accepted by the majority of students. Be careful not to draw an issue so closely that somebody has to give in. This puts tremendous pressure on both you and the student. Nor should there by any punishment of a whole class for the fault of a few.

Concerning punishment, Lee Canter (1980) argues that the teacher must be assertive and have a plan of action for discipline similar to a lesson plan, knowing what will be done on first, second, third, and fourth offenses when the rules of the classroom are broken, as well as what will be done for severe negative behavior. He goes on to say that the teacher should review the plan with the principal and get his approval before using it in the classroom. The plan, including the rules of the classroom, should also be presented to the students and their parents. However, Canter emphasizes that all acceptable behaviors of students be recognized, using positive reinforcement for desired behaviors. In this approach self-discipline comes about via the student choosing to break a rule or choosing not to break a rule.

AUTHORITARIAN VERSUS DEMOCRATIC MANAGEMENT

There are some major differences between authoritarian and democratic approaches to discipline. (See Table 10.) A teacher's approach to discipline reflects his philosophy of art and his orientation to teaching, which can also be seen in the

TABLE 10
Authoritarian Versus Democratic Classroom Management

AUTHORITARIAN (DOMINATIVE)	DEMOCRATIC (INTEGRATIVE)
Emphasis on the negative, pointing out mistakes, criticizing	Emphasis on the positive, pointing out successes, encouragement
Emphasis on repression of student interest and enthusiasm	Emphasis on developing student interest and enthusiasm
Control of students through fear	Control of students through social consciousness and their own good feelings
Teacher-centered room	Student-centered room
Strict rules and regulations handed down by the teacher	Rules evolve based upon standards of conduct developed by teacher and students
Emphasis on quiet, order, and passiveness	Emphasis on interest in class work, learning, cooperation, and helpfulness
Emphasis on achievement of teacher's objectives and penalties for not complying	Emphasis on individual achievement and social consciousness, teacher disappointment for not complying
Emphasis on dictatorial control of student by the teacher	Emphasis on student-teacher cooperation
Emphasis on talking down to students	Emphasis on talking with students
Emphasis on conforming and imitating	Emphasis on creating, personalizing, and sensitizing
Feelings and ideas of students ignored	Feelings and ideas of students respected

resulting objectives, curriculum, and methodology in the classroom. The authoritarian teacher usually perceives art as being made up of skills and concepts to be
mastered by the student; the democratic teacher usually perceives art as a means
of personal and creative communication/expression to be developed by the student.
Most teachers are not completely authoritarian or completely democratic in their
approach but tend to fluctuate somewhere between the two. However, it is important for teachers to know where they are on this continuum and the effect their
approach to discipline has upon their students.

SOME PROBLEM TYPES

It is easier for the teacher to comprehend certain motives of students and to adjust
classroom responses to more satisfactory solutions when student behaviors can be
identified and classified. Four types of problem students are considered here: the
show-off; the bully; the introvert; and the dependent. Students on drugs, another
major problem type, were discussed in chapter 3. Teachers will find that student
behavior may be a combination of these somewhat typical problem types rather
than a classic example of any one type.

The Show-Off

This student is the attention-getter, the smart aleck, who makes wisecracks
and clowns around in class, wanting to be noticed. These students need more
attention than most and do not know how to get it in a positive way but are doing
something about it. Show-offs have a lot of energy, pep, and courage. Some will
try almost anything to be noticed. There are many things the teacher can do to
help. You may focus on their strong points: what they do well. Play up the good
aspects of their art work. The teacher can help them develop specific skills and
abilities in art so that they can excel. This may be done through closure experiences
(see chapter 5 under Mechanical Orientation). Then these skills and abilities as
seen in their art work can be pointed out to the class and their art work exhibited
in the school, giving them the recognition they crave. Try to call attention to these
show-offs before they have a chance to misbehave. Perhaps come back to them
several times during a class period and praise their work. This constant positive
attention will satisfy their egos so that they will not feel a need to be disruptive.

The art teacher may play up their possessions, such as special art books and
art materials they bring to class. In this way, the spotlight is put on them. You
may even note new clothes ("What a beautiful sweater you're wearing") and
outstanding physical characteristics ("Your eyes are such a rich blue color").

Possibly during the art class, the teacher may have friendly conversations with
these students, getting to know them better. If you detain them after school, talk
with them about their hobbies, part-time jobs, trips, and other out-of-school activities. They will feel that they really have your attention and friendship. Then,
relate any of this information to their art work when appropriate in class.

With the show-off student who needs attention, do not punish so as to push
him out of the group. Do not label this student "bad." Others will pick up the
label; the student may become tagged and try to live up to it.

The Bully

Students of this orientation are unhappy, worried, frightened, and react in a rebellious manner. These students are fighting back at something bigger than themselves, that is, they didn't make the team; there's a new baby in the family; parents are divorced; a parent has died; they are not accepted by peers; or there is poverty at home. Because these students may not really know why they are acting the way they do, the teacher should not insist upon reasons for their negative behavior. Do not pile on more punishment and pressure; they already have more than they can handle. However, we cannot let them continue hitting and fighting so we must stop them, but do not be angry. Be firm but sympathetic and maybe disappointed.

You may look for causes—and there may be several; these students are simply protecting themselves in the only way they know: by fighting back at everyone. The teacher need not know the causes for their behavior to work with them in the classroom. They simply need an opportunity to release pent-up feelings, ways of getting back at the world. They need to pound and hit something, to shout back. In the art class the teacher should find media and processes that involve strong, aggressive action (hitting, punching, squeezing, shouting, and loud talking) in a socially acceptable manner. Water-base clay requiring kneading; large wood sculptures, metal forming, and large constructions involving the use of hammers and other tools; and puppets in plays (Punch and Judy) involving much bossing, hitting, and shouting are some examples. When these students hit less they may threaten more by bullying with words; then, they are improving.

Our goal is to get them to feel safe and secure with people and not have to fight back. They need love and kindness. The teacher should give lots of attention and praise every improvement. If you are kind, at first they may not trust you because so little kindness has been shown students exhibiting this type of aggressive behavior. Teachers seldom are sympathetic toward them. Their reactions to kindness may be unusual since kindness is a new experience for most of these students. The teacher must be prepared to accept any type of unusual response. If you scold or criticize, these students will simply continue in their old fighting pattern of getting back at the world.

The Introvert

These students want to socialize and participate with their peers but are so insecure and unsure of themselves that they withdraw, crawl into their shells, and are very unhappy. Teachers may have to look for these students in class because they are so quiet, seldom if ever ask questions, and never volunteer for any class activities. If asked, they may even refuse. They project this insecurity and timidity in their art work, creating stereotyped and rigid drawings and paintings which seldom have strong contrast and dynamic action. Many times they will draw only in one corner of a large page, feeling incapable and afraid of attacking the whole area.

As teachers, we need to build up the ego and confidence of these students. First, they need to feel at ease. This can be accomplished by a friendly attitude on the part of the teacher: smiling, speaking to them as they enter the room, noticing, and praising their behavior whenever possible. These students should be encouraged in the art class in any way that would be appropriate: praising their abilities (displaying their work). They may be taught something in art at which they can be outstanding so that they may feel secure in their ability. The teacher must work slowly with these students or they may withdraw even more unto themselves. Coming out of their shell is a very gradual process for most introverted students.

The Dependent

These students have a need to overseek love and acceptance. They may either feel unloved or are overprotected at home, making them dependent upon the teacher at school. They demand constant attention and acceptance and need to develop self-reliance and self-esteem. The teacher must be friendly and not push them away because the more you withhold yourself the more they will feel a need for your acceptance and attention. These students tend to monopolize the entire class time, needing approval of everything they do in the art room. The teacher should give them as much attention as possible without disrupting the learning situation of the class. There are many ways this can be accomplished. Speak to them when they first enter the room. Note new clothing, books, and so on. Choose them to help you and to be beside you whenever possible. Catch their eye in the classroom and wink or smile. Call on them to run errands. Work with them whenever possible concerning their art work, praising when appropriate. The teacher must decide just how far he can go and still carry on the class. Limits may have to be set but do this in a friendly way. Other teachers may be solicited to help give attention to these students.

You may make a game of seeing how long these students can work without showing their work to you. Try to notice them before they insist upon your attention so that they feel they can work independently. Praise them for their ability to work without your help. Try for an increasingly longer time period of individual work. We must see these students for what they are—hungry and craving for love and affection. Satisfying these needs is a long-time process for the student who is dependent.

YOUR APPROACH

All teachers decide upon the type of classroom student behavior with which they are most comfortable. This choice tends to depend upon the teacher's personality. Some teachers naturally command attention and respect by their mere presence in the classroom; others consciously have to plan for getting attention. Some can tolerate more talking, noise, and moving about in the art room than others. However, all teachers must maintain order and control to the extent that learning does take place at the highest possible level for every student.

Many aspects of managing adolescents have been presented here so that teachers may select those which seem most appropriate for each situation. Just as one should not rely upon a single teaching style, similarly, one should not rely upon a single approach to discipline. A variety of approaches will keep students attentive and alert. Art teachers should be as creative in the area of classroom management as they are in their own art work.

REFERENCES

Barron, F. Creativity: What research says about it. *N.E.A. Journal,* 1961, *50* (3), 17–19.

Canter, L., and Canter M. *Assertive Discipline.* Los Angeles: Lee Canter and Associates, 1980.

Discipline: an overview. *Practical Applications of Research,* Newsletter of Phi Delta Kappa, 1981, *4* (1), 2–3.

Fromm, E. *Escape from Freedom.* New York: Rinehart and Company, 1941.

Gallup, G. H. The 14th annual Gallup poll of the public's attitudes toward the public schools. *Phi Delta Kappan,* 1982, *64* (1), 37–50.

Glasser, W. Ten steps to good discipline. *Today's Education,* 1977, *66* (4), 61–63.

Jones, L. H. Jr., Student and teacher interactions during evaluative dialogues in art. *Art Education,* 1965, *18* (4), 13–15.

Szekely, G. Creative designs for classroom routines. *Art Education,* 1981, *34* (6), 14–17.

Tagatz, G. E. The disciplined self in a disadvantaged society. *The Junior High School Newsletter,* 1969, *7* (2) 1–3.

Webster's Third New International Dictionary. Springfield, Massachusetts: G. and C. Merriam Company, 1976.

SUPPLEMENTAL READINGS

Alschuler, Alfred S. *School Discipline: A Socially Literate Solution.* New York: McGraw-Hill, 1980. Principles of social literacy used in resolving interpersonal, classroom, and schoolwide conflicts—a primary prevention approach.

Blackham, Garth J. and Silberman, Adolph. *Modification of Child and Adolescent Behavior* (3rd ed.). Belmont, California: Wadsworth, 1980. Behavior modification principles and procedures used to alter maladaptive behavior in the classroom and other settings.

Canter, Lee, and Canter, Marlene. *Assertive Discipline: A Take-Charge Approach for Today's Educator.* Los Angeles: Lee Canter and Associates, 1980. Forceful and positive approach to classroom control based upon assertive training.

Charles, C. M. *Building Classroom Discipline: From Models to Practice.* New York: Longman, 1981. Sources and various disciplinary models related to school situations.

Curwin, Richard L., and Mendler, Allen N. *The Discipline Book: A Complete Guide to School and Classroom Management.* Reston, Virginia: Reston Publishing Company, 1980. Emphasis on preventive discipline, awareness, theories, and practical actions in the classroom-school situation.

Frey, Sherman H. (ed.). *Adolescent Behavior in School: Determinants and Outcomes.* Chicago: Rand McNally, 1970. Authorities discuss school influences and other factors—family, peer, self-concept, physical—and reaction patterns of adolescents.

Gallagher, Jack R. *Changing Behavior: How and Why.* Morristown, New Jersey: Silver Burdett Company, 1980. Behavior modification techniques used to strengthen desirable behavior, to eliminate inappropriate behavior, and to develop new desirable behavior and maintain it.

LaGrand, Louis E. *Discipline in the Secondary School.* West Nyack, New York: Parker Publishing Company, 1969. Practical approach to discipline, with special reference to essential teacher traits and principles of student-teacher relationships.

Martin, Gary, and Pear, Joseph. *Behavior Modification: What It Is and How to Do It.* Englewood Cliffs, New Jersey: Prentice-Hall, 1978. Elementary principles, procedures, and practical skills, with application to behavior modification among many different populations.

Ramsey, Robert D. *Educator's Discipline Handbook*. West Nyack, New York: Parker Publishing Company, 1981. Holistic approach by means of successful examples. Many "how to" techniques discussed.

Wolfgang, Charles E., and Glickman, Carl D. *Solving Discipline Problems: Strategies for Classroom Teachers*. Boston: Allyn and Bacon, 1980. Many discipline models, techniques, and methods for handling classroom behavior problems are presented.

CHAPTER 7

WHERE WE'VE BEEN
A Retrospect

In studying the development of any aspect of education, it is apparent that school practices have come about as a result of rather strong beliefs and values held by people outside the school in the community at large, seldom coming from those inside the school—teachers, administrators, and students. Like other school personnel, most art teachers have been nonassertive and passive, usually accepting the points of view and demands of others rather than taking a leadership role in determining the direction of the field. Some educators see this passive acceptance as the appropriate role of school personnel—to do the bidding of the community without question, schools having originally been developed to serve the interests and needs of the community. However, when the community does not understand and appreciate an area of basic human experience such as art, it is the responsibility of those in the area to set up lines of communication and relate the values of the area to the community. Until recently, this public relations aspect of art education has not been considered the responsibility of art teachers (N.A.E.A., 1973). In the past, art educators accepted the demands handed down to them and developed applicable objectives and methodology, simply adopting the point of view given to them by those outside the field.

Because of the many different emphases over the years, a knowledge of the background of art education provides the art teacher with myriad objectives, curricula, and methods for meeting the various needs of students at the secondary level. These greatly increase the teacher's awareness of many teaching possibilities and should provide richer and more meaningful learning experiences for students. It also gives a feeling of confidence in one's teaching ability.

What we are today is determined to a great extent by what we were yesterday. The better we understand the past, the better qualified we are to perceive the present and possibly to shape the future. Not knowing or understanding the past forces us to face the future naïvely—blindfolded—acting only upon our knowledge of the present. Because of the lack of literature in depth about the background

162

and history of art education (P. J. Smith, 1982), we have been handicapped in our ability to see the field for what it is and to give direction and significance to our work.[1] We must be aware of the emphases of society in the past and recognize how these have affected philosophical ideas, purposes, and practices of art educators if we are to have greater insight and to avoid pitfalls as we justify the place of art in the school and develop contemporary valid programs, curricula, and teaching methodology. Each succeeding generation should not have to start from scratch in "rediscovering the wheel" of art education objectives, theory, and practice. An understanding of the past gives us a strong base for our operations in the classroom, as well as in the community.

The following historical survey of approaches to art education in American schools reflects the various responses art teachers and school personnel have made over the years to the beliefs and resulting demands of society. No precise dates for each approach are given because, for the most part, these approaches came about gradually with one overlapping another. For each approach, art teachers developed a philosophic base plus appropriate objectives and methodologies. Aspects of most of these approaches and accompanying methodologies are still practiced in the field. The past is not dead but lives on in what we do today. The following review should make us aware of the antecedents of what we currently do in our classrooms. This review in no way pretends to be all inclusive of every personage, book, article, and event in the history of art education. On the contrary, the emphasis is upon objectives and methods that have a direct bearing upon art instruction today.

It should also be pointed out that until the twentieth century, the adolescent period, as we think of it today, did not exist. Very early in life, boys were in the market place and girls became homemakers. Before the child labor laws, it was not uncommon for boys of eleven, twelve, and thirteen to be working on the farm or in the factory alongside their fathers. It was not until 1919 that every state had some law prohibiting child labor although even at this time some laws were weak and poorly enforced. Those adolescents who remained in school were looked upon as children even though they may have been teenagers several times over. Early on, these students usually remained in the "common school"; the first high school was not founded until 1821 in Boston for boys who did not enter college. The public high school was differentiated from the Latin grammar school (which was the secondary college preparatory school of the time) and the academy (which offered more of a practical education for life in the Colonies) by being publicly supported and controlled. Soon however, preparation for college was added to the high school curriculum and girls were gradually admitted. High schools became the school for all adolescents in America. By 1890 there were 2,500 high schools in the United States with 22,000 students in attendance. Today, there are more than 25,000 junior and senior high schools with 19,000,000 in attendance. The first junior high schools were founded in 1910 as a result of finally recognizing that the needs of early adolescents were different from the needs of later adolescents.

---

[1]Three books have been published concerning the development of art education in this country: Clarke's *Industrial and High Art Education the United States* (1885); Haney's *Art Education in the Public Schools of the United States* (1908); and Logan's *Growth of Art in American Schools* (1955).

THE INDUSTRIAL ARTS APPROACH

In 1765 the steam engine was invented in England, a fact that eventually greatly affected education, especially art education in this country, since it was primarily this invention of a source of energy that brought about the Industrial Revolution. Drawing ability became an asset in getting a job in a factory. Parents wanted a better life for their children than they had had, and drawing provided a means for this better life. Drawing, it was argued by the manufacturers, would increase skill and improve physical judgment of distance and proportion. Drawing eventually became essential for the training of children/adolescents of factory workers and was gradually pressured into the school curriculum.

The Colonial Period

There were sporadic instances in isolated school situations when drawing had been included. Generally, this was the result of the efforts of a single person who had a strong interest, feeling, and/or training in art. A listing of the best known of these early pioneers in art education should include the following: Peter Pelham, the first recorded teacher of art for children in the Colonies, established his own elementary school in Boston around 1730; William Bentley Fowle, perhaps the first art educator in the public schools, taught slow learners in Boston in 1821; Amos Bronson Alcott included art in the curriculum of his private Temple School in Boston in 1834; Rembrandt Peale initiated art classes at the Philadelphia High School in 1840; William Minifie taught art classes at the Baltimore Boys' High School in 1848; and William Newton Bartholomew taught art at the Boston Girls' High and Normal School in 1853.

Geometrical Drawing

That much of the drawing taught by these early innovators was of a geometric nature (as preparation for industry) is evidenced by the titles of books on drawing by Fowle, *An Introduction to Linear Drawing* (1830), and Minifie, *A Textbook of Geometrical Drawing* (1850). Horace Mann, the first secretary of the Massachusetts State Board of Education, became concerned with industrial drawing in answer to the growing criticism that schools did little for the future mechanical and industrial worker. In his famous seventh annual report, Mann (1843) expounded at some length on the value of drawing, stating that not only was drawing an aid in writing but that it was also needed by the architect, engineer, engraver, pattern designer, draughtsman, and mechanic. After a trip to Europe where he observed the board drawing of Prussian school masters, particularly that of Peter Schmid, Mann reproduced twenty-four drawing lessons from Schmid's book, *A Guide to Drawing*, in the *Common School Journal* in 1844. The bimonthly *Journal* had been founded in 1838 as a means for Mann and the school board to communicate their thoughts to teachers and eventually to bring about improvement of instruction.

The drawing lessons of Schmid consisted of geometric blocks that were stacked in various manners. Students, probably of junior high school age, were to copy these with great precision, utilizing points and connecting them with straight lines as described in the following excerpt from his introductory passages:

Never draw a line before you have decided to your satisfaction the points are right.

Never draw a coarse line. Make all your lines hairlines. Remember this particularly. If you find that you have drawn a coarse line, rub it out and draw a fine one, because you can never draw well with coarse lines. You will be tempted to conceal a false, imperfect line under these coarse, scratched marks (Schmid, 1844, p. 255).

By the third lesson, the drawings become complicated, challenging the most astute students.

Laws and an Art Administrator

Geometrical and mechanical drawing continued to be demanded by the public for the vocational preparation of adolescents as seen in a petition included in the thirty-fourth report of the secretary of the Massachusetts Board of Education (1864):

Your petitioners respectfully represent that every branch of manufactures in which the citizens of Massachusetts are engaged requires . . . some knowledge of drawing and other arts of design on the part of the skilled workmen engaged.

The petitioners pointed out that there was no widespread provision for instruction in drawing in the public schools, and, because of this, our manufacturers compete under disadvantage with the manufacturers of Europe where provision is made for instruction of drawing in the schools. In 1852, we imported $47 million worth of textiles from France and Great Britain. Clearly, we needed craftsmen and designers who could produce textiles and other products that were attractive to people abroad, as well as at home. Finally, in 1864, drawing became a required subject in the Boston public schools and the pressure of the electorate became so great that the state legislature of Massachusetts passed the following law on May 18, 1870:

Section 1. The first section of Chapter 38 of the general statute is hereby amended so as to include drawing among the branches of learning which are by said section required to be taught in the public schools.

Section 2. Any city or town may, and every city or town having more than 10,000 inhabitants shall, annually make provision for giving free instruction in industrial or mechanical drawing to persons over fifteen years of age, either in day or evening schools, under the direction of the school committee.

Section 3. This act shall take effect upon its passage.

In order to carry out this legislation, the school committee of Boston, after much correspondence, brought Walter Smith, headmaster of the South Kensington School of Industrial Drawing and Crafts in Leeds, England, to Boston for an interview (Logan, 1955). In the fall of 1871 Smith accepted a joint position with two-fifths of his time given to the state (the first state art director) and three-fifths to the city of Boston. His duties were many:

His duties, equitably divided between his two employers, the city and the state, were as State Director to visit those cities and towns which were by law compelled to introduce drawing, and by lectures and "teachers institutes" to initiate their teachers in their new duties; to visit the state normal schools; to organize and set in motion the evening classes in industrial and mechanical drawing; subsequently, to organize and take charge of the Boston Normal Art School.[2] The director also prepared carefully arranged schedules of instruction for the public schools, through all grades; as well as courses of study for the evening drawing schools and for the Normal Art School (Clarke, 1885, p. 61).

To educate his charges concerning his approach, Smith (1874) wrote a book, *Teachers' Manual for Freehand Drawing*. His method started with dots and lines, the pupils generally following specific directions or drawing from specific examples—a copy method. Eventually, exercises were given requiring drawing from nature, but even these were stylized. In 1873, the Massachusetts Normal Art School came into being, partially as a result of the work of Smith in an effort to comply more fully with the law of 1870. With the aid of his writing, lectures, and the new training school, Smith had a profound influence in developing drawing of a precise, stylized, and mechanical nature that may be called an *industrial arts approach* to art education. By 1876, Smith had a well established reputation and was invited to display his courses of study and the art works of his students at the Philadelphia Centennial Exposition. As a result, his influence was greatly extended; by 1885 sixty-nine cities in nineteen states had made serious efforts to include drawing in the curriculum (Art Department Report of the N.E.A., 1885, p. 7). The demands of the public were beginning to be met by the school personnel, setting a precedent for us in art education that has changed little over the years.

The trend away from the rigid vocational industrial arts approach is noted in the writings of Walter Sargent and Elizabeth Miller (1912 and 1916), who saw drawing as a language and a tool with which to think. They wrote:

> Drawing an object means translating one's perceptions into terms which have been evolved by the race, and which demand careful selection. It means organizing one's sensations so as to determine what produces the impression and the modes in which that impression can be interpreted. To draw an object requires a mental activity comparable to that which occurs when a thought is translated from one language to another (1912, pp. 5–7).

Sargent and Miller believed that the student must have something to say, having some idea or image he wants to express; for the most part, however, they adhered to the methodology of using devices to work from, such as three-dimensional models and pictures to copy. J. Liberty Tadd, director of the Public Industrial Art School of Philadelphia, also questioned the rigid geometrical approach to drawing in an address at the 1894 meeting of the National Education Association (Logan, 1955, p. 119).

THE ACADEMIC ART SCHOOL APPROACH

As a result of the Industrial Revolution, many manufacturers and industrialists in the United States became wealthy. What do wealthy people do? They travel and buy things! And so the new wealthy Americans traveled, usually going to Europe. During the late 1800s and early 1900s, most people in the United States looked to

---

[2]The correct title for this institution is the Massachusetts Normal Art School, which was located in Boston.

the "old world" for leadership in art, as well as in most other areas. A widespread desire to own imported art objects developed, especially among the *nouveaux riches* who were finding and buying "culture" and bringing it home to America.

The Rise of Museums

Returning with shiploads of artifacts, the wealthy built mansions to house their collections. A few outstanding examples of these great houses, which are now museums and open to the public, are the Biltmore in Asheville, North Carolina; the Frick Museum in New York City; the Breakers in Newport, Rhode Island; Vizcaya in Miami, Florida; and San Simeon south of San Francisco. After collecting and enjoying the art work, many wealthy persons became concerned with providing art for everyone to view and enjoy, hoping to bring culture to America. It was during this period, therefore, that we find many art museums being established by gifts from collectors: New York's Metropolitan Museum in 1870; the Museum of Fine Arts in Boston, also in 1870; the Art Institute of Chicago in 1879; the Cincinnati Art Museum in 1881; and both the Fogg and Carnegie museums in 1895 to mention a few.

The ability to recognize a painting by Rembrandt, Titian, or Dürer became a coveted mark of culture and taste. Art instruction was greatly influenced by this development in society. It was during this period that colleges and universities began to add art history courses in response to the need of the heirs of wealthy collectors to become as knowledgeable about their art possessions as they were about their investments in stocks and bonds.

This movement, which may be called "art for art's sake," was not systematically developed by laws, as was the industrial arts approach, but nevertheless it had a temendous influence upon school art programs. Basically, the movement embodied the idea that the contemplation of beauty in works of art can bring about a general rise in public taste and morality (establishing principles of right and wrong in behavior). Henry Turner Baily, a graduate of the Massachusetts Normal Art School and editor of *School Arts* from 1903 to 1919, was influential in promoting this idea, believing that art was a haven for the spirit after the grime of daily work (Logan, p. 133). It was only natural, then, that lessons in picture study to develop art appreciation and improve morals came about in the school curriculum as a result of this initial interest in art by the wealthy in the late 1800s.

New Rules for Making Art: Design Principles

In addition to art appreciation lessons, the making of art was stressed as a means for developing taste, morals, and an understanding of art. At first secondary schools accepted the typical art school approach which, at the time, was characterized by naturalistic drawing from plaster casts, still-life objects, and nature, in addition to anatomy lessons, and exercises in perspective, with great concern for skillful rendering. Secondary school art classes were modeled after those of professional art schools and became places where students were expected to perform as artists. *Art Education for High Schools*, published in 1908, is a typical comprehensive text of the art school type, discussing pictorial, decorative, and constructive art, historic ornament, and art history.

The typical academic art school approach was initially characterized by naturalistic drawing of plaster casts and still life as shown in this charcoal sketch by a high school student. Emphasis was placed upon correct proportion and skillful rendering.

Into this setting came Arthur Wesley Dow, professor of fine arts at Columbia University, who wrote *Composition* (1899), a book that was popular with art teachers and exerted great influence (thirteen editions, issued between 1899 and 1929). Dow (1912, pp. 3, 6) developed what he called a synthetic method of creating art versus the traditional academic method of the art schools. (See Charts 4 and 5.) He believed that drawings, paintings, and designs were created from line, notan (dark and light), and color using five principles: opposition, transition, subordination, repetition, and symmetry instead of from nature and historic styles. Dow arrived at this new conception of art structure by studying Oriental art, first at Boston's Museum of Fine Arts with Ernest F. Fenollosa and then in Japan. His three fundamental elements and five principles represented the alphabet and subject matter to be learned and used in making art, not far removed from the content of many college design classes and design books today. Dow believed that art was not made by mere imitation of nature or by mechanical drawing but, rather, that "the power is within" (1899, p. 21). This power is expressed through the *correct* use of the elements and principles that were taught to adolescents. Dow's synthetic method became the new "academic" approach—the new rules—for making art, generally replacing the old rules that involved the copying of nature. Both approaches, however, were concerned with producing an acceptable art product from an adult viewpoint. Dow wrote, "Effective progress in composition (art) depends upon working with an organized and definite series of exercises, building one experience upon another, calling for cultivated judgment to discern and decide upon finer and finer relations" (1899, p. 21). His approach became little more than a prescription of activities (exercises, as he called them) for the making of art work.

CHART 4
Dow's Synthetic Method

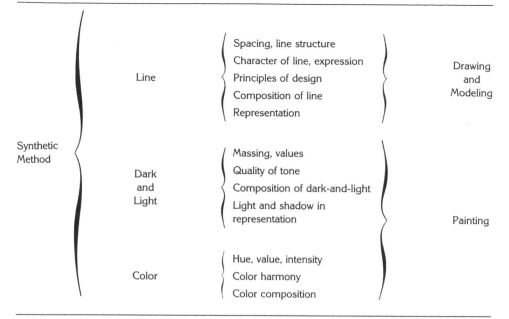

From A. W. Dow, *Theory and Practice of Teaching Art* (2nd. ed.), p. 6.

CHART 5
Traditional Academic Art School Method
(c. 1900)

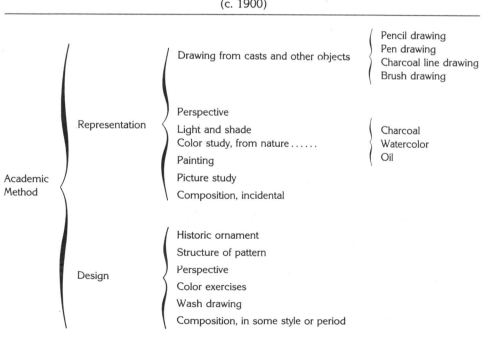

From A. W. Dow, *Theory and Practice of Teaching Art* (2nd ed.), p. 3.

In using Dow's synthetic method, students are directed to use principles of composition in producing their art work, as shown in this design of jungle animals by a junior high school student.

His method was one of following directions with some opportunity for personal choice—a glimmer of creativity was recognized in this synthetic development of composition. This then is a directed *academic art school approach* for the public schools, an academicism characterized by adherence to prescribed principles. Art teachers became primarily concerned with what we usually think of as "the fine arts": design, drawing, painting, and sculpture—appreciation and production. Dow included picture study as an important aspect of his approach, noting that artistic ability follows the exercise of the appreciative faculty—training in appreciation being the foundation of all art education.

THE NONDIRECTED CREATIVE ART APPROACH

The third demand upon the field of art education came about as a result of rather diverse developments in the fields of psychology, art, and philosophy—developments still outside public school art. Eventually all three influences became integrated into what may be called a *nondirected creative art approach*, which was to some extent characterized by the Progressive Education Association in its writings on art education during the thirties and forties. Some aspects of this force overlap the previous two approaches (industrial arts and academic art school) and were developing over a period of many years before enough potency was engendered to bring about significant changes in art education.

The Child Study Movement

The first of these aspects appeared as a result of the rise of psychology as an area of study. Wilhelm Max Wundt, German psychologist and philosopher, established the first psychological laboratory at Leipzig in 1879. One of the first Americans to study with Wundt was G. Stanley Hall, from 1878 to 1880. Hall's great interest in the new psychology centered around adolescent development and pedagogy (1904) and later resulted in his leadership of the child study movement. At the time, teenagers were thought of as children and were included in the movement. One was either a child (a juvenile) or an adult, and children were seen as being simply miniature adults. Persons in the new child study movement no longer viewed a child in this way but as a unique individual; attention was focused upon his needs, abilities, and unique qualities. The child was elevated to a new level of importance. Childhood and adolescence were discovered. Hall, Francis W. Parker, Herman T. Lukens, M. V. O'Shea, and other leaders of the movement were mainly concerned with the natural development of children and adolescents—the stages and processes involving growth and learning. Earl Barnes, editor of *Studies in Education* and professor at Stanford University and Hall, editor of *Pedagogical Seminary* and president of Clark University from 1888 to 1920, conducted many studies of the drawings of children and adolescents and founded a more scientific basis for teaching drawing. For the most part, the early studies were concerned with interests and preferences of young children. However, by 1908, findings of researchers in the child study movement in this country, along with those of Europe, suggested stages of development of interests, attitudes, and characteristics of drawing, formulating something of a theory of natural development in art by children up to adulthood. But this theory never became operational for classroom use at the time. However, Sargent and Miller (1912) did call their approach "psychological," but it relied little upon the actual developmental levels of students as we know them today.

As a result of the child study movement, the child and adolescent were discovered as unique in their own right. This discovery and ensuing research had a profound influence upon general education and eventually affected art education.

Discovery of Child/Adolescent Art

It was near the end of the past century that a young man, Franz Cizek, came to Vienna to study at the Academy of Fine Arts. Cizek stayed with a family that included several children who, upon seeing him paint, desired to do likewise, requesting paper, paints, and brushes. The paintings of the children, which were so very different from his own, enthralled Cizek and eventually motivated him to start his juvenile art class in 1897. Cizek included teenagers in these classes and continued to hold art classes throughout his lifetime (until 1938). His teaching gained so much recognition that the state offered him a room in the art school, the Kunstgewerbeschule, in 1903. It was in Cizek's classes that aesthetic quality in child/adolescent expression—child art as it became known—was discovered. Wilhelm Viola (1944), his biographer, wrote, "Thousands came to Vienna every year to see his [Cizek] work, the greatest numbers coming from Great Britain and America" (p. 13). The influence of Cizek was especially felt in this country after World War I when it became more and more commonplace to have exhibitions of child/adolescent art—the art work finally accepted as having aesthetic value by the public in both Europe and America.

It was during the first two decades of the twentieth century that much experimentation by artists took place, and the foundations of what we now call "modern art" were laid and developed. Fauvism, Cubism, Expressionism, Surrealism were but a few of the new art approaches. Primitive art, African art, and Oriental art were discovered by European artists. It is not surprising, then, that an interest in child/adolescent art would develop. It is important to point out that this interest, for the most part, came about in society and the world of art outside the public schools. Cizek, himself, was a painter and professional artist in Vienna and had many friends in the Secessionist art movement there.

Art as Experience

The third aspect is philosophical and developed gradually in the minds of art teachers, perhaps starting with the work of Sargent and Miller, and became full blown in the definitive writing of John Dewey in his book, *Art as Experience* (1934). The essence of Dewey's contextualistic approach to art lies in his insistence that art is actually the doing, the experience, the product being the residue after art has taken place. This statement by Dewey has continued to have a tremendous impact upon the field. Today, a half-century later, one finds frequent reference to Dewey's work in this area. His theory concerning the process, the doing of art, became important in the thinking of most art educators in the forties and fifties and was harmonious with the Existentialist pragmatic point of view so popular at the time.

The Integration

These three aspects (psychology, art, philosophy) became integrated when art teachers realized that the child/adolescent is a unique individual whose creative process with art media based upon his experience is really an expression that possesses aesthetic qualities and is therefore considered art. Freudian psychological theories of the time aided and abetted this emphasis on the process by purporting art expression to be an important means of emotional release, a vital aspect of life adjustment, especially for adolescents. Those holding to this therapeutic point of view saw art expression as a revelation, in a nonverbal way, of the needs and unconscious concerns of the individual (Naumberg, 1947). Art classes no longer were concerned with correct naturalistic proportions, skill, and exercises involving art elements and principles, and with picture study, but became laboratories wherein expressive activity involving materials became the goal and an end in itself. Emphasis was upon the creative capacities of students and improved personal, social, and civic life. Creative self-expression for life adjustment became the main objective. A number of art educators[3] wrote about the creative abilities of children/ adolescents, pointing out that art experiences play an important role in creative development. As this approach evolved, the art teacher became a mere dispenser of materials, judging it inappropriate to interfere with the uniqueness of each student and fearful of interrupting the mystical creative art process. The psychology of inhibition (personality defects that result from inhibitions imposed during childhood and adolescence) also contributed to this "hands off" and "free expression"

---

[3]See, for example, Belle Boas (1924); C. Valentine Kirby (1927); Leon L. Winslow (1928); Sallie Tannahill (1932); Margaret Mathias (1932); Felix Payant (1939); Natalie Robinson Cole (1940); Rosabell MacDonald (1941); Victor D'Amico (1942); and Manuel Barkan (1960).

method since, at this time, it was believed any interference with the student would bring about irreparable damage to his personality.

That art teachers responded to these demands and outside influences is exemplified by the writing of the Committee on the Function of Art in General Education, which was under the auspices of the Progressive Education Association, and whose report, *The Visual Arts in General Education*, was published in 1939. The committee, chaired by Victor D'Amico, was one of a number of committees working in various subject matter areas. In this report, oriented toward the secondary level, the art room was viewed as an artist's studio where there was great freedom; the individuality and the creativity of each student were important considerations. Process was emphasized, and laissez-faire, "hands off" became the most appropriate method for the art teacher.

THE APPLIED ART APPROACH

Whereas many art teachers were concerned with the intrinsic qualities of the individual and his adjustment, growth, and development through art experiences, others became more concerned with making art socially relevant, with applying art learnings to everyday living—to dress, the home, the church, the business world, industry, and the community (city parks, city planning). The objectives of this latter approach may appear to be somewhat similar to those of the industrial arts approach, but here the emphasis was upon creative designing and appreciation of and response to well designed objects based upon sensory aspects, media, and aesthetics. These attitudes were in sharp contrast to the emphasis on mechanical skill and neatness required for the precise geometric drawing of the industrial arts approach. However, both approaches were concerned with using the school art class as a means for raising society's level of taste concerning man-made objects in our environment.

One of the early proponents of the applied art approach was the German Bauhaus, founded by Walter Gropius (Bayer, Gropius, and Gropius, 1938) in 1919, in which a crafts and design school was merged with a fine arts academy. Emphasis in this new school was placed upon studying the inherent aesthetic qualities of many materials by all students, who were simultaneously trained to be expert technicians and first-rate artists. It was assumed that students with such an education were eminently qualified to design for industry since they had training in both art and technology. The Bauhaus was, in reality, one of the first schools of industrial design. Closed by Hitler in 1933, the influence of the Bauhaus was not felt in America until after its demise, when exhibitions of Bauhaus work were held at the Museum of Modern Art in 1933 and 1939. During the thirties instructors from the Bauhaus emigrated to the United States and began to teach and publish in this country: Walter Gropius (Harvard), Marcel Breuer (Harvard), Josef Albers (Yale), and László Moholy-Nagy (Institute of Design, Chicago).

At about the same time Bauhaus influence was being felt, the Owatonna Art Project was initiated as the result of a speech given in 1930 by Dean Melvin E. Haggerty of the School of Education, University of Minnesota, to a Western Arts Association conference, in which he pointed out the ugliness and lack of aesthetic quality in the Midwest in spite of the school art being taught. Taking up Haggerty's challenge for art education to become more meaningful in the lives of people, the Carnegie Foundation funded a project called "Art, a Way of Life." This project proposed introducing art activities in a representative drab, small city—Owatonna, Minnesota—and noting changes in community life. Of the three persons who were the resident staff of the project, Edwin Ziegfeld was chosen to teach art in the public schools, the other two persons being involved with service projects—giving advice on painting interiors and exteriors; landscaping; window displays; and providing art classes for adults. The service staff also undertook before-and-after photographic documentation of the physical environment of Owatonna. The project was a great success and resulted in many publications (for example, Ziegfeld and Smith, 1944). Unfortunately, World War II interrupted the project and, in all probability, lessened its influence, but the art teacher and the two resident staff members did have a profound influence upon the visual, the intellectual, and the social environment of this Midwestern town.

Many books emphasizing the importance of visual art in our daily lives have been, and continue to be, published.[4] In recent years Frederick Logan (1955) and June King McFee (1961) have emphasized the importance of responding to aesthetic aspects of our environment and stressing the importance of appreciating and understanding world cultures.

The method of teaching in the applied art approach is to apply art aspects creatively to the designing and appreciation of (responding to) objects and sometimes to the total environment. Teachers influenced by Bauhaus theories tend to have students work directly with various materials and technical procedures, the design often growing out of this experimentation. Others tend to approach design and interpretation more academically, applying design principles to the particular materials and situation. Regardless of the method, the objective is the same: to increase the students' sensitivity about the aesthetic quality in a given applied area, such as personal dress, the home, church, industry, business, commerce, the community, and/or all of life.

THE PSYCHOLOGICAL APPROACH

Many art teachers did not become concerned with the applied art approach because of the great emphasis upon child-centered education so popular at the time and characterized by the nondirected creative art approach in art education. However, art classes of teachers who seriously followed this latter approach tended to end in chaos. Except for supplying materials and maintaining order, art teachers had no role to play—they were either afraid of inhibiting the students or ignorant of a means of bringing about a higher level of creativity, aesthetic-perceptual sensi-

---

[4]See, for example, *Art in Everyday Life* (Goldstein and Goldstein, 1932); *Art Today* (Faulkner, Ziegfeld, and Hill, 1941); *Art Education for Daily Living* (Russell and Gwynne, 1946); and *Art, Search, and Self-Discovery* (Schinneller, 1961). Typical of the widespread influence of the applied art approach was Baltimore's *Course of Study* (1945), with lesson plans and units of study on such topics as "Art and Your School," "Art in Your Home," "Art and Your Church," "Adventures in Design," and "Art in Advertising." Leon L. Winslow was director of art education in Baltimore at the time and was a leading proponent of the applied art approach.

tivity, aesthetic problem solving, and other learnings in art. Many administrators and parents began to think of art classes as "play time." Pressure began to mount for more structured and purposeful art classes.

In response to this demand and as a result of greater understanding of child and adolescent development in art, the psychological approach based upon growth and development through art came into being. This approach was characterized by the work of Herbert Read (1943) and of Viktor Lowenfeld in his several editions of *Creative and Mental Growth* (1947, 1952, 1957), as well as other writers of the time: Daniel Mendelowitz (1953), Charles and Margaret Gaitskell (1954), Ralph L. Wickiser (1957), Italo L. DeFrancesco (1958), and John A. Michael (1964). Using the natural developmental stages in art expression as a basis, the art teacher was given a methodology for guiding art expression, with emphasis on the art process and in achieving many of the life adjustment and personality development goals of the Art Committee of the Progressive Education Association. The teacher was seen as a guide and was now given specific instructions concerning stimulation, curriculum planning, and evaluation at each level of child/adolescent development. Growth and learning through the art activities of the student at every level was

In the psychological approach, emphasis is placed upon depicting various personal experiences for achieving expressive, aesthetic/creative, and life adjustment goals. Here we see a student's interpretation of a visit to the dentist.

CHART 6
General Evaluation Chart

ATTRIBUTES OF GROWTH		LITTLE	SOME	MUCH
Emotional Growth	Free from stereotyping Lack of generalization of objects (trees are not alike, etc.) Constant deviations from generalizations Inclusion of experiences of the self Use of free lines and brush strokes			
Intellectual Growth	Inclusion of many subject-matter details Differentiation in color Other indications of active knowledge			
Physical Growth	Visual and motor coordination (how well he guides lines) Conscious projection of body movements (representation of them) Unconscious projection of body (body image) Skillful use of techniques			
Perceptual Growth	Visual experiences: light, shadows, perspective space, and color differentiation Nonvisual experiences: tactile, texture, and auditive Kinesthetic experiences (body movements)			
Social Growth	Faces his own experiences in his work Identification with the needs of others Inclusion and characterization of social environments (home, school, factory, office) Participation in group work Appreciation of other cultures Enjoyment of cooperation, directly (through work) or indirectly (through the topic)			
Aesthetic Growth	Integration of thinking, feeling, and perceiving Sensitiveness toward harmonious color, texture, lines, and shapes Preference for decorative design patterns			
Creative Growth	Independence without copying Originality without imitating style of others Creativeness and inventiveness in regard to content Can immediately be distinguished from others in mode of expression Is entirely different from others			

From Viktor Lowenfeld, *Creative and Mental Growth* (3rd ed.), pp. 70–71. Copyright © 1957 by Macmillan Publishing Co., Inc.

broken down into areas (intellectual, emotional, perceptual, physical, social, creative, and aesthetic), which were used for evaluation purposes. (See Chart 6.) The teaching method became one of guiding and facilitating, so that maximum development/learning in each area took place. The teacher was given a vital role: responsible for stimulation, making suggestions, directing learning, and evaluating. The creative process, personal development, and emotional adjustment goals of the nondirected creative art approach continued to be important aspects of this psychological approach to teaching art. Emphasis remained on the making of art as it had usually been in the past, although the process of art production was now seen as the means of achieving growth and learning in all areas—concern for the whole student—and was called self-expression. Research in art education, especially research involving child/adolescent art and creativity, became an important adjunct to this approach (Davis, 1967). In many ways the psychological approach was a continuation of the child study movement, the great difference being that now a teaching methodology was developed with great specificity. Order and purpose returned to art classes.

THE CONTENT APPROACH

Suddenly, after the Russian Sputnik I in 1957, there was much public criticism of American schools, especially of the math and science areas. It was alleged that the United States was behind in the space race because of poor school programs in these areas. In response to this criticism the National Science Foundation, in 1959, called a conference at Woods Hole, Massachusetts, to assess the situation and to consider means for improving school math and science programs. This conference was reported in 1960 by Jerome S. Bruner, psychologist at Harvard University, in what is now the famous and historical publication, *The Process of Education*. This book, concerned with the teaching of math and science, introduced the content approach to the field of education. Emphasis was placed upon developng a spiral curriculum wherein various concepts and principles of a subject (content) were presented at each grade level, one level building upon another.

This new subject-matter emphasis was seen by many in our field as putting "art" back into art education. A widely discussed survey by Elliot Eisner (1966) pointed out the lack of art knowledge among high school and college students. As a result of this new emphasis on cognitive content, art history and humanities courses—many times team-taught—were instituted as necessary adjuncts to the regular studio art offerings in many secondary schools.[5] Emphasis was taken off the whole individual and his psychological adjustment and placed on the student's learning the subject matter per se. In art classes, students were taught to be intelligent and sensitive viewers, critics, and interpreters of art.

In general education, classification of educational objectives (Bloom et al., 1956; Krathwohl et al., 1964) and specific behavioral objective methodology (Mager,

---

[5]The following are a few publications in the two areas. Art history: *The Story of Modern Art* (Cheney, 1958), *Mainstreams of Modern Art* (Canaday, 1959), *History of Art* (Janson, 1962). Humanities: *Art and Education in Contemporary Society* (Kaufman, 1966), *Art as Image and Idea* (Feldman, 1967), and *Becoming Human Through Art* (Feldman, 1970).

1962) skyrocketed in importance. In 1968 and 1969 the National Art Education Association sponsored research institutes that were training sessions conducted by Ashael Woodruff and funded by the U.S. Office of Education to introduce art educators to the behavioral method which had become so popular in academic subject matter areas. These institutes resulted in several publications; among them, and especially noteworthy, were *Behavioral Emphasis in Art Education* (Davis, 1975) and *A Matrix System for Writing Behavioral Objectives* (Brouch, 1973).

The behavioral method primarily consists of stating performance behaviors involving facts, concepts, and skills that the student will acquire in the subject being taught, giving a pretest, and a final test to determine if the student is competent in these specified behaviors. Herein, behavior "refers to any visible activity displayed by the learner [student]" (Mager, 1962, p. 2). The teacher selects the behaviors thought to be most valid in art or any other subject being taught. In writing behavioral objectives, the teacher selects words that are open to very few interpretations and that denote specific actions, such as to write, to compare, to identify, and to construct, rather than to know, to understand, to appreciate, and to believe. In the behavioral method, students are simply told what they are to do or to make with all qualifiers included in the original statement. For example: The student will list five Italian painters of the Renaissance noting one painting that is typical of the work of each painter. The student is tested at the conclusion of the behavioral method to determine if he has developed ability to perform the particular behavior.

By 1970, the cost of education to taxpayers had increased substantially because of inflation and the increased number of pupils in schools. With more and more tax dollars required to run the public schools, taxpayers became more concerned about getting their money's worth. Schools had to be accountable. Most educators, as well as the public, saw the behavioral method, wherein knowledges and skills to be learned were pinpointed, as a means of demonstrating that teachers were performing successfully in the classroom and that students were learning. Several states passed laws requiring that every curriculum, including the art curriculum, be behaviorally based. In such programs, art was generally concept- or skill-oriented and was conceived as being no different from an academic subject (Lanier, 1980) wherein the teacher's behavioral method included recognition/identification, imitation, following directions, and skill development.

In response to public concern, the National Institute of Education funded the National Assessment of Educational Progress program, which was to conduct evaluations of various school subject areas including art. The first art assessment was conducted in 1974–1975 and the second in 1978–1979. A committee, headed by Brent Wilson (1971), developed specific art objectives in five general art areas. Students were to (1) perceive and respond to the aspects of art; (2) value art as an important realization of human experience; (3) produce works of art; (4) know about art; and (5) make and justify judgments about aesthetic merit. Specific objectives were listed under these general headings for the nine-, thirteen-, and seventeen-year-old age levels that were evaluated. Only one of these areas involved the making of art; therefore, these objectives, developed by a government agency, encouraged teachers to instruct primarily in the content of art so that their students would do well on the cognitively oriented assessment tests.

THE AESTHETIC EDUCATION APPROACH

Although some art educators became much concerned with their students' reading, knowing, and talking about art, artists, and art history, with emphasis upon rather sterile behavioral methods, others, in contrast, believed that teachers should be placing emphasis upon developing students' feeling, identification with experience, and sensitivity. Merle Flannery writes of the resulting empty quality of human life devoid of the awareness of feeling when she says, "Life becomes a grey, tasteless shell" (1973, p. 13). Undoubtedly, this was a reaction to the somewhat impersonal, computerized society in which people began to see themselves as being a number—a Social Security number.

It was during this time (1965–1975) that sensitivity training, encounter groups, and T-groups (Paris, 1968) became popular as a means of allowing persons in small groups to express themselves freely—personal feelings and attitudes—in an unthreatening atmosphere of honesty and openness and to explore more constructive self-behavior. Such sensitivity training was used to a great extent in the business field and spilled over into education, promoted by prominent psychologists such as Abraham Maslow and Carl Rogers. These encounter methods became known as the Human Potential Movement and were a reaction to an impersonal and technological society in which the individual felt that he did not matter. The aesthetic education approach tended to mirror this movement by emphasizing a similar concern for sensitivity and feeling.

Flannery (1973) perceived aesthetic education as a means of salvaging the human qualities of an individual; her approach is based upon feeling and aesthetics as defined by Susan Langer and Alexander Baumgarten. Langer (1962, p. 16) posits feeling as meaning anything that may be felt, including pleasure/displeasure; sensation (as no feeling in a paralyzed limb); sensibility (as hurting someone's feelings); emotion (as to evoke tender feeling); a directed emotional attitude (as feeling strongly about something); and one's physical condition (as feeling ill). And Baumgarten (Croce, 1960) believes that aesthetics is the science of sensuous knowledge. Flannery (1973) combined Langer's concept of feeling and Baumgarten's concept of aesthetics, noting two types of aesthetic knowledge concerning feeling: sensory knowledge and sensuous knowledge. Sensory knowledge comprises all the sights, smells, sounds, body motions, and other perceptions and includes identification and comparison of feelings, making for a kind of perceptual/conceptual knowledge. On the other hand, sensuous knowledge is immediate and exists for the moment. "It occurs when one fuses with one's feeling to the exclusion of everything else" (Flannery, 1973, p. 11). No identification, comparison, or like process is involved here.

Many art educators became enamored with the aesthetic education approach, which interpreted sensory experiencing as an end in itself, the objective being for students to focus feeling and to become conscious of it, with little need for an art product. Students were made aesthetically aware in order to respond to sensuous changes, and thus their lives were enriched.

Wellington J. Madenfort (1972), another proponent of aesthetic education, includes the sensuous and the immediately sensuous, in which concepts are deemphasized, the primary purpose being to allow for the development of the student's ability to experience the world as it appears "in all the immediacy of its sensuous-ness, without the mediation of concepts" (p. 10). Both Flannery and Madenfort hold to the idea that it is the experiencing that is important, linking students meaningfully with life itself. Emphasis is placed upon all the senses in this experiencing, the process becoming very important. The method of the aesthetic education approach encourages students to attend and focus on their feeling. Students are "invited" to join in aesthetic encounters, such as experiencing the snow gently falling on tree branches and the patterns of the branches against a winter sky or the feel of sand on one's feet and the resulting pattern of footprints on the beach. Seeing, hearing, moving, touching, tasting, and feeling become the bases for the art program. The curriculum becomes one of many sensitizing experiences involving the senses. Discovery and a fusion of the self with the experience become all-important. Teachers plan for activities wherein students become aware of aesthetic/sensuous qualities. The aesthetic education program of CEMREL, Inc., a national education laboratory in St. Louis, under the direction of Stanley S. Madeja (1973), was designed specifically for developing such sensitivity and awareness. Titles of some of their learning packages are "Texture, Shape, Tone Color"; "Introduction to Light"; "Introduction to Motion"; "Making Sound Patterns"; and "Analyzing Characterization." Madeja (1976, p. 33) writes that an aesthetic education curriculum should demonstrate that all phenomena in our environment have aesthetic qualities and should heighten the student's capacity for recognizing, analyzing, and experiencing these qualities and their contribution to the condition of our environment. In the latter aspect, Madeja seems to go beyond the experiencing of Flannery and Madenfort by relating the aesthetic experience to various perceptions and art areas, becoming a bridge to the arts education approach.

THE ARTS EDUCATION APPROACH

The arts education approach evolved out of the content and aesthetic education approaches, although some consider the aesthetic education and arts education approaches to be one and the same. However, each approach appears to have different objectives and methods. Many people believe that a strong emphasis upon content, especially in the academic and technological areas, should be balanced in the school program by consideration of all the arts, not just visual art. The goal of the arts education approach is to increase the student's capabilities to experience aesthetic values in the environment through significant encounters, as described in one of the leading studies in this area, *Guidelines* (Barkan, Chapman, and Kern, 1970), in which curricular units were developed in great detail. Accompanying this concern was a belief within the various art fields that more could be accomplished for the advancement of any one of the arts if all the arts—dance, creative writing, music, theater, and visual art—were joined together and were considered as one area of the school curriculum. The arts education approach was also supported and fostered by the U.S. Office of Education, through the Arts Education Program, initiated in 1974, which offered grants to local school systems for establishing and improving arts programs as an integral part of the regular curriculum of elementary and secondary schools. The professional associations of the various art areas supported the arts education approach and many organizations were founded specifically to promote the arts in education: the Alliance for the Arts, the Arts, Education and Americans, and the Educational Arts Association.

In the arts education approach, the arts are infused with one another and with all the other subjects in the curriculum on the premise that the arts can help students make connections between disciplines. The arts are used to stimulate, interest, give greater understanding and new insights, and add new significance to any subject being studied. Seeing, hearing, touching, moving, and feeling become the basis of any method to get students to want to learn in a particular subject area. The arts are conceived as fundamental and basic ways of knowing, of relating to the world (Kohl, 1982). In learning to communicate and express themselves, students become aware and perceive. The symbolic systems of the various arts communicate information that aids in explaining human existence. The whole range of human experience is involved. The arts education approach revitalizes the teaching process, in which the teacher must be a person who encourages and leads speculation in order to help students learn about an unknown. It requires a method, a metaphor, in which the known and unknown can meet, each taking meaning from the other.

The following is an example of the arts education approach used in a science class engaged in the study of simple machines: the lever, wheel and axle, pulley, incline plane, wedge, and screw (incline plane that winds around a spiral). At first, students may be shown diagrams or models of the various machines and their functions. Each student, then, acts out his own movement relative to a particular machine and then makes the various movements with partners and finally with the whole group. The movement becomes an aspect of dance. Sounds of various machines reflecting the rhythm and patterns of the movements are then created with the body, voice, various materials, and combinations of these. The movements (dance) and sounds (music) of the various machines are incorporated into actual creative constructions (visual art) of machines that produce a product. Large cartons may be used as basic forms with which to work. Arms and legs may protrude through openings to show the movement. Materials emphasizing line, color, and texture may be added to the constructions to express the movements, sounds, and functions of the machines. A sound film or video tape (theater) of the machine will let students see their ideas and expression concerning the simple machines. Students usually will want to revise, adjust, and add to their original expression. New ideas evolve and creative learning takes place as the arts are infused with learning about simple machines in science class.

Through the method of infusion, the teacher relates the basic aspects of the arts, such as rhythm and pattern in the above example, to the subject matter and this develops motivation for learning. By understanding the symbolism of various art forms that communicate about life and by learning to express themselves via these, students develop perceptions and understandings, necessary aspects of the total educational process.

In the arts education approach, the arts become a part of everything in school—students can explore their own expressive and communicative abilities and can find an art area that is most satisfying to their needs. Appreciation for all the arts is brought about. The learning environment becomes more humanized and creative. The arts add zest, excitement, and a valuable dimension to life.

A series of curricular materials for the elementary level has been developed under the direction of Paul F. Brandwein (1974). These may be up-graded for the secondary level. Few commercial materials are available for the secondary level because the rigid scheduling of subjects in most junior and senior high schools makes the integration of subjects in the arts education approach very difficult. However, some creative secondary art teachers pursuing the arts education approach have been able to integrate the arts into the regularly scheduled visual art class.

ECLECTICISM

These approaches in art education have generally come about as a result of happenings and emphases outside the field, but from them art educators have inherited a rich background for a multifaceted art education providing varied purposes/ objectives, methods, and curricular information that can be used in meeting the needs of students in art classes at the secondary level. (See Table 11.) If we accept the premise that one's primary function as a teacher is that of getting students to develop their many abilities to the highest possible level through art activities, then

TABLE 11
Approaches to Art Education

HISTORICAL APPROACH	PRIMARY OBJECTIVE	PRIMARY TEACHING METHOD
Industrial Arts	Geometric drawing, vocational preparation for industry, skill development	Imitation, copying, rigidly following directions from simple to complex
Academic Art School	Skilled production of art work and appreciation of art, morality	Rigidly using art elements and applying art principles, following directions
Nondirected Creative Art	Free expression with art media emphasizing creativity and the individual's personality development	Laissez-faire, learning by experience as an artist, correlation with other subjects
Applied Art	Aesthetic taste in choosing objects	Relating design principles to objects and environmental aspects
Psychological	Self expression with art media emphasizing psychological adjustment (intellectual, creative, emotional, perceptual, social, aesthetic, physical development)	Guidance and facilitation (stimulation, suggestions, praise, reinforcement), integration with other subjects, concern for needs of student
Content	Knowledge of art/artists/art history, art appreciation	Exposure to art/artists/art history (reading, memorization, viewing, analysis, criticism)
Aesthetic Education	Sensitivity, sensuous knowledge, aesthetic awareness	Experiential activities involving the senses—seeing, hearing, touching, moving, tasting, feeling-assimilation
Arts Education	Comprehending relationships underlying the arts (dance, literature, music, theater, visual arts), and life	Infusion—introduction to the study of the other arts and subject matters through visual art

aspects of all approaches presented here may be appropriate and valid for particular students—each student being unique, having particular personal and aesthetic/cultural needs that require certain specific objectives and methods. It is also imperative that the problem of the artist be kept paramount in the mind of the teacher and in the minds of the students. An integration of the human qualities of thinking, feeling, perceiving, as well as creating, which are the basic attributes of art, are basic to all of living. The arts provide a discernible (visual) personal expression of these that is not possible in any other area.

At various times, then, art teachers can employ aspects of all the approaches presented here in their classes. The teacher who does this is using an eclectic approach. A knowledge and understanding of all approaches is invaluable in working with students if we are to provide a varied, individualized, exciting, and meaningful art program.

For example, when teaching procedures and skills such as throwing on the potter's wheel, using carving tools, printing procedures, and some aspects of lettering, imitation—the method of the industrial arts approach—is most appropriate. If students have difficulty getting involved with an art activity, teacher stimulation and guidance, an aspect of the psychological approach, is needed. If students need to extend their frame of reference concerning the field of art, a knowledge and use of art elements and principles, the method of the academic art school approach, is necessary. Or, if an awareness of artists and art history is needed, the method of the content approach may be appropriate or at least an option for the art teacher. If students need perceptual experiences as a basis for their art work or to develop sensitivity, activities involving the senses are needed—the method of the aesthetic education approach. If students are involved in their art work—there surely are periods when they should be left alone—the laissez-faire method of the nondirected creative art approach can be helpful. A master teacher is aware of many different curricula and methods of teaching art just as he must be aware of many art media and processes. With this knowledge, the teacher can confidently meet any educational situation in the art room and make teaching truly a profession.

REFERENCES

Art Department Report of the National Education Association. *Instruction in Drawing in Public and Normal Schools*. Boston: Prang Educational Company, 1885.

Art Education for High Schools. New York: Prang Educational Company, 1908.

Barkan, M. *Through Art to Creativity*. Boston: Allyn & Bacon, 1960.

Barkan, M., Chapman, L. H., and Kern, E. J. *Guidelines: Curriculum Development for Aesthetic Education*. St. Louis: Central Midwestern Regional Educational Laboratory, 1970.

Bayer, H., Gropius, W., and Gropius, I. *Bauhaus 1919–1928*. Boston: Charles T. Branford Company, 1938.

Bloom, B. S., et al. *Taxonomy of Educational Objectives, Handbook I: Cognitive Domain*. New York: Longman, Inc., 1956.

Boas, B. *Art in the School*. Garden City, New York: Doubleday, 1924.

Brandwein, P. F. *Self Expression and Conduct: The Humanities*. New York: Harcourt Brace Jovanovich, 1974.

Brouch, V. M. *A Matrix System for Writing Behavioral Objectives*. Phoenix: Arbo Publishing Company, 1973.

Bruner, J. S. *The Process of Education*. Cambridge: Harvard University Press, 1960.

Canaday, J. *Mainstreams of Modern Art*. New York: Simon and Schuster, 1959.

Cheney, S. *The Story of Modern Art*. New York: Viking Press, 1958.

Clarke, I. *Industrial and High Art Education in the United States*. Washington, D.C.: Bureau of Education, 1885.

Cole, N. R. *The Arts in the Classroom*. New York: John Day, 1940.

Course of Study: Art for Secondary Schools of the City of Baltimore. Baltimore: Department of Education, 1945.

Croce, B. *Aesthetics* (trans. by Douglas Ainslie). New York: Noonday Press, 1960.

D'Amico, V. (ed.), *The Visual Arts in General Education*. New York: D. Appleton-Century, 1940.

D'Amico, V. *Creative Teaching in Art*. Scranton: International Textbook, 1942.

Davis, D. J. (ed.). *Behavioral Emphasis in Art Education*. Reston, Virginia: National Art Education Association, 1975.

Davis, D. J. Research trends in art education. *Art Education*, 1967, *20* (7), 12–16.

DeFrancesco, I. L. *Art Education: Its Means and Ends*. New York: Harper and Brothers, 1958.

Dewey, J. *Art as Experience*. New York: Minton, Balch & Company, 1934.

Dow, A. W. *Composition*. Garden City: Doubleday, Page and Company, 1899.

Dow, A. W. *Theory and Practice of Teaching Art* (2nd ed.). New York: Teachers College, Columbia University, 1912.

Eisner, E. W. The development of information and attitude toward art at the secondary and college levels. *Studies in Art Education*, 1966, *8* (1), 43–58.

Faulkner, R., Ziegfeld, E., and Hill, G. *Art Today*. New York: Holt, 1941.

Feldman, E. B. *Art as Image and Idea*. Englewood Cliffs, New Jersey: Prentice-Hall, 1967.

Feldman, E. B. *Becoming Human Through Art*. Englewood Cliffs, New Jersey: Prentice-Hall, 1970.

Flannery, M. Aesthetic education. *Art Education*, 1973, *26* (5), 10–14.

Fowle, W. B. *An Introduction to Linear Drawing*. Boston: Hilliard, Gray, Little, and Wilkins, 1830.

Gaitskell, C. D., and Gaitskell, M. R. *Art Education During Adolescence*. New York: Harcourt Brace, 1954.

Goldstein, H. I., and Goldstein, V. *Art in Everyday Life*. New York: Macmillan, 1932.

Hall, G. S. *Adolescence*. New York: D. Appleton, 1904.

Haney, J. P. (ed.) *Art Education in the Public Schools of the United States*. New York: American Art Annual, 1908.

Janson, H. W. *History of Art*. Englewood Cliffs, New Jersey: Prentice-Hall, 1962.

Kaufman, I. *Art and Education in Contemporary Society*. New York: Macmillan, 1966.

Kirby, C. V. *The Business of Teaching and Supervising the Arts*. Chicago: Abbott Educational Company, 1927.

Kohl, H. *Basic skills: A Plan for Your Child; A Plan for All Children*. Boston: Little, Brown, 1982.

Krathwohl, D. R., Bloom, B. S., and Masia, B. B. *Taxonomy of Educational Objectives, Handbook II: Affective Domain*. New York: Longman Inc., 1964.

Langer, S. *Philosophical Sketches*. New York: Mentor, 1962.

Lanier, V. Six items on the agenda for the eighties. *Art Education*, 1980, *33* (2), 16–23.

Logan, F. M. *Growth of Art in American Schools*. New York: Harper and Brothers, 1955.

Lowenfeld, V. *Creative and Mental Growth*. New York: Macmillan, first edition 1947, second edition 1952, third edition 1957.

MacDonald, R. *Art as Education*. New York: Holt, 1941.

Madeja, S. S. The arts in the curriculum. *The National Elementary Principal*, 1976, *55* (3), 30–35.

Madeja, S. S. *The Five Sense Store: The Aesthetic Education Program*. New York: Viking Press, 1973.

Madenfort, W. J. Aesthetic education: An education for the immediacy of the sensuous experience. *Art Education*, 1972, *25* (5), 10–14.

Mager, R. F. *Preparing Instructional Objectives*. Palo Alto, California: Fearon Publishers, 1962.

Mann, H. Report of the secretary of the state board of education, Boston, 1843, in *National Education in Europe*. New York: Charles B. Norton, 1854.

Mathias, M. E. *The Teaching of Art*. New York: Scribner, 1932.

McFee, J. K. *Preparation for Art*. San Francisco: Wadsworth Publishing Company, 1961.

Mendelowitz, D. M. *Children Are Artists*. Stanford: Stanford University Press, 1953.

Michael, J. A. (ed.) *Art Education in the Junior High School*. Washington, D.C.: National Art Education Association, 1964.

Minifie, W. *A Textbook of Geometrical Drawing*. Baltimore: The author, 1850.

National Art Education Association. *Public Relations for Art Education*. Washington, D.C.: National Art Education Association, 1973.

Naumberg, M. *Studies of the "Free" Art Expression of Behavior Problem Adolescents as a Means of Diagnosis and Therapy*. New York: Coolidge Foundation, 1947.

Paris, N. M. T-grouping: A helping movement. *Phi Delta Kappan*, 1968, *59* (8), 460–463.

Payant, F. *Create Something*. Columbus, Ohio: Design Publishing, 1939.

Read, H. *Education Through Art*. London: Faber and Faber, 1943.

Russell, M. and Gwynne, E. W. *Art Education for Daily Living*. Peoria: The Manual Arts Press, 1946.

Sargent, W., and Miller, E. *Fine and Industrial Arts in Elementary Schools*. Boston: Ginn, 1912.

Sargent, W., and Miller, E. *How Children Learn to Draw*. Boston: Ginn, 1916.

Schinneller, J. A. *Art, Search and Self-Discovery*. Scranton: International Textbook Company, 1961.

Schmid, P. A guide to drawing. *Common School Journal*, 1844, *6*, 14–24.

Smith, P. J. Germanic foundations: A look at what we're standing on. *Studies in Art Education*, 1982, *23* (3), 23–30.

Smith, W. *Teachers' Manual for Freehand Drawing*. Boston: James R. Osgood, 1874.

Tannahill, S. B. *Fine Arts for Public School Administrators*. New York: Teachers College, Columbia University, 1932.

Viola, W. *Child Art* (2nd ed.). Peoria: Chas. A. Bennett Company, 1944.

Whitford, W. G. *An Introduction to Art Education*. New York: D. Appleton, 1929.

Wickiser, R. L. *An Introduction to Art Education*. Yonkers-on-Hudson, New York: World Book, 1957.

Wilson, B. *Art Objectives*. Denver: National Assessment Office, 1971.

Winslow, L. L. *The Organization and Teaching of Art*. Baltimore: Warwick and York, 1928.

Ziegfeld, E., and Smith, M. E. *Art for Daily Living: The Story of the Owatonna Art Education Project*. Minneapolis: University of Minnesota Press, 1944.

SUPPLEMENTAL READINGS

Belshe, Francis. A history of art education in the public schools of the U.S. Unpublished doctoral dissertation, Yale University, 1945. In-depth study of the background and development of art education.

DeFrancesco, Italo L. *Art Education, Its Means and Ends*. New York: Harper and Brothers, 1958. The evolution of concepts in art education is discussed in chapter 2.

Efland, Arthur D. Conceptions of teaching in art education. *Art Education*, 1979, *32* (4), 21–33. Orientations and historic traditions in art education.

Eisner, Elliot W. *Educating Artistic Vision*. New York: Macmillan, 1972. The historical view is presented in chapter 3.

Eisner, Elliot W. and Ecker, David W. (eds.). *Readings in Art Education*. Waltham, Massachusetts: Blaisdell Publishing Company, 1966. Historical development is presented in Part I.

Keel, John S. "Art Education, 1940–64." In W. R. Hastie (ed.), *Art Education: Sixty-fourth Yearbook of the National Society for the Study of Education*, Part II. Chicago: University of Chicago Press, 1965.

Logan, Frederick M. *Growth of Art in American Schools*. New York: Harper and Brothers, 1955. The most complete study of the development of art education in the United States, to 1955.

Logan, Frederick M. Up date '75: Growth in American art education. *Studies in Art Education*, 1975, *17* (1), 7–16.

Macdonald, Stuart. *The History and Philosophy of Art Education*. New York: American Elsevier Publishing Company, 1970. Historical developments in art education in Britain, France, Germany, and the United States.

Wygant, Foster, *Art in American Schools in the Nineteenth Century*. Reston, Virginia: National Art Education Association, 1983. A comprehensive look at art education in the 1800s.

APPENDICES

BIBLIOGRAPHY

INDEX

WILSON-STUCKHARDT ART ATTITUDE SCALE

This scale[1] is made up of statistically significant items that differentiate between students who value art (i.e., have a good attitude) and students who do not. Each item is scored on a five-point basis by giving the correct response five points and the least correct response one point. For example, when Strongly Agree is the correct response, Strongly Agree = 5, Agree = 4, Uncertain = 3, Disagree = 2, and Strongly Disagree = 1. The reverse applies when Strongly Disagree = 5. The underlined responses indicate the correct answers and reflect the most positive attitudes toward art.

This scale should be typed without the underlines, duplicated, and distributed to the students before art instruction is begun, and repeated afterward—preferably with a semester time lapse. A change in score indicates a change in attitude toward art.

ART ATTITUDE SCALE

Directions for students: The following pages contain statements concerning attitudes toward art for which there is no general agreement. People differ widely in the way they feel about each of these items. The purpose of this scale is to see how people feel about each item, and, therefore, what is needed is your own honest feeling toward each of these statements. This is not a test.

Read each statement carefully and quickly underline the phrase that best expresses your feelings about the statement. Work rapidly. Be sure to respond to every item.

---

[1]Reprinted by permission of Christine W. Sanders and Michael H. Stuckhardt.

1. Art can be examined from many points of view.
   <u>Strongly Agree</u>   Agree   Uncertain   Disagree   Strongly Disagree

2. Art is a universal language.
   <u>Strongly Agree</u>   Agree   Uncertain   Disagree   Strongly Disagree

3. Art awakens emotional responses.
   <u>Strongly Agree</u>   Agree   Uncertain   Disagree   Strongly Disagree

4. Art permits man to express that which is otherwise unutterable.
   <u>Strongly Agree</u>   Agree   Uncertain   Disagree   Strongly Disagree

5. Art is the fruit of experience.
   <u>Strongly Agree</u>   Agree   Uncertain   Disagree   Strongly Disagree

6. Art is in a hopeless condition.
   Strongly Agree   Agree   Uncertain   Disagree   <u>Strongly Disagree</u>

7. Art is not necessary.
   Strongly Agree   Agree   Uncertain   Disagree   <u>Strongly Disagree</u>

8. Art provides opportunities for achieving personal fulfillment.
   <u>Strongly Agree</u>   Agree   Uncertain   Disagree   Strongly Disagree

9. Art can be experienced from many points of view.
   <u>Strongly Agree</u>   Agree   Uncertain   Disagree   Strongly Disagree

10. Art provides for the stimulation for independent thinking.
    <u>Strongly Agree</u>   Agree   Uncertain   Disagree   Strongly Disagree

11. Art is directed toward touching into life's specific experiences.
    <u>Strongly Agree</u>   Agree   Uncertain   Disagree   Strongly Disagree

12. Art on all levels is an expression of the human spirit.
    <u>Strongly Agree</u>   Agree   Uncertain   Disagree   Strongly Disagree

13. Art is the symbolic expression of otherwise inexpressible ideas.
    <u>Strongly Agree</u>   Agree   Uncertain   Disagree   Strongly Disagree

14. Art has a potentially vital role in the education of our children.
    Strongly Agree   Agree   Uncertain   Disagree   <u>Strongly Disagree</u>

15. Art really isn't very important.
    Strongly Agree   Agree   Uncertain   Disagree   <u>Strongly Disagree</u>

16. Art does not give opportunity for self-expression.
    Strongly Agree   Agree   Uncertain   Disagree   <u>Strongly Disagree</u>

17. Art enriches the intangible life.
    <u>Strongly Agree</u>   Agree   Uncertain   Disagree   Strongly Disagree

18. Art is the creation of forms symbolic of human feeling.
    <u>Strongly Agree</u>   Agree   Uncertain   Disagree   Strongly Disagree

19. Art can contribute to general education.
    <u>Strongly Agree</u>   Agree   Uncertain   Disagree   Strongly Disagree

20. Art Education is nonsense.
    Strongly Agree   Agree   Uncertain   Disagree   <u>Strongly Disagree</u>

21. Art springs from the personal consciousness of the individual.
    <u>Strongly Agree</u>   Agree   Uncertain   Disagree   Strongly Disagree

22. Art creation gives the creator a new sense.
    <u>Strongly Agree</u>   Agree   Uncertain   Disagree   Strongly Disagree

23. Art is not a good thing.
    Strongly Agree   Agree   Uncertain   Disagree   <u>Strongly Disagree</u>
24. Art is a mode of expression that is understood universally.
    <u>Strongly Agree</u>   Agree   Uncertain   Disagree   Strongly Disagree
25. There are many meanings in a work of art.
    <u>Strongly Agree</u>   Agree   Uncertain   Disagree   Strongly Disagree
26. Art is a reflection of man's mind.
    <u>Strongly Agree</u>   Agree   Uncertain   Disagree   Strongly Disagree
27. An art museum visit is a worthwhile venture.
    <u>Strongly Agree</u>   Agree   Uncertain   Disagree   Strongly Disagree
28. Art exposes you to genuine emotional experience.
    <u>Strongly Agree</u>   Agree   Uncertain   Disagree   Strongly Disagree
29. Art is not a universal necessity.
    Strongly Agree   Agree   Uncertain   Disagree   <u>Strongly Disagree</u>
30. Art is unlimited in its modes of expression.
    <u>Strongly Agree</u>   Agree   Uncertain   Disagree   Strongly Disagree
31. Art is a means of response to ever-changing relationships.
    <u>Strongly Agree</u>   Agree   Uncertain   Disagree   Strongly Disagree
32. Art is not an individualistic expression of emotion.
    Strongly Agree   Agree   Uncertain   Disagree   <u>Strongly Disagree</u>
33. Art is the ultimate form that will communicate what one person has experienced to another.
    <u>Strongly Agree</u>   Agree   Uncertain   Disagree   Strongly Disagree
34. Art aims at producing delight in the mind through the intuition of the senses.
    <u>Strongly Agree</u>   Agree   Uncertain   Disagree   Strongly Disagree
35. Art gives expression to the human soul.
    <u>Strongly Agree</u>   Agree   Uncertain   Disagree   Strongly Disagree
36. Art is the structuring of a uniquely significant universe of expression.
    <u>Strongly Agree</u>   Agree   Uncertain   Disagree   Strongly Disagree

OUTCOMES OF A SECONDARY ART PROGRAM

1. Has his ability to express himself creatively with many materials been developed in the art class?
   a. Does he find satisfaction in art activities?
   b. Is he confident in expressing himself with many different materials?
   c. Does he experiment and explore to find out the possibilities of a material?
   d. Does he work in a free and spontaneous manner using a trial-and-error approach in preference to a preconceived approach?
   e. Does he do the original and unusual with his art materials?
   f. Do ideas come quickly, one after the other concerning his expression?
   g. Does he continue to express himself with art materials when he is outside the art class?
   h. Does he discover new materials in his environment with which to express himself?
   i. Is he resourceful in his leisure time activities?
   j. If his art work does not develop to his liking, is he flexible and does he continue by trying other solutions?
   k. Is he familiar with procedures and processes by which he may express himself, and is he developing skill commensurate with his needs?
   l. Does he understand the creative art process and recognize its importance?
2. Has the pupil learned to understand himself and others better as a result of his experiences in the art room?
   a. Does he feel he is a more adequate (confident) person because of the successful solution of art problems which he has helped select?
   b. Does he recognize his strengths and make the most of them?
   c. Does he recognize his weaknesses and want to do something about them?

From John A. Michael (ed.), *Art Education in the Junior High School*, pp. 147–149.

    d. Does he see himself in relation to others in a more adult and realistic way?

    e. Does he see himself more objectively?

    f. Does he relate aesthetic values to his whole life?

    g. Has he considered the role of the arts in his adult life?

    h. Is his expression more sincere, and does it truly represent him?

    i. Does he have greater social sensitivity as a result of group art projects and identification with the needs of others as experienced in his art work?

    j. Has he developed an awareness of the uniqueness of himself and others?

3. In what specific areas of growth have his creative art experiences helped the pupil to grow?

    a. *Creative growth*

      To what degree has the pupil shown independent, inventive, original and uncommon responses?

      Does the pupil interpret his idea in as creative and individual a way as possible?

      Has the student selected problems which are meaningful to him?

      Has he shown growth in his ability to visualize, develop, and carry through his projects to successful completion?

      Has he used materials in ways which are new and personal to himself?

      Does he manifest an exploratory and experimental attitude?

      Does he investigate diversified solutions in his attempt to solve a problem?

      Has he demonstrated resourcefulness and initiative in planning for his leisure time activities?

    b. *Physical growth*

      Has the student developed skill in handling materials, tools, and processes?

      Has he developed better body coordination as seen in his art activity?

      Has his desire to master processes and techniques intensified his growth in control?

      Has he shown progress in his ability to move freely in the classroom with agility of movement in such a task as distributing the art supplies?

    c. *Intellectual growth*

      Has the student progressed in his ability to solve more complex problems?

      Does he see and understand relationships concerning ideas and materials?

      Does an awareness and knowledge of himself and his environment show in the work he produces?

      Has he developed in his ability to comprehend abstract art concepts?

      Has he accumulated greater understanding of art and information about the visual arts?

      Has he developed in his ability to transfer learning from one area to another?

      Is he increasing his art vocabulary and his ability to discuss his own experiences in relationship to the experiences of others and to the development of art historically, as well as in our contemporary culture?

d. *Emotional growth*

Is he confident in his ability to express himself with art media?

Is he flexible in his ideas and in his ways of expressing them?

Does he express his feelings and emotions freely in his art work?

Is the pupil receptive to changes in plans in the classroom and in his own work?

Does he find release and increasing satisfaction in his art expression?

Is he developing initiative in working toward self-directed goals?

e. *Social growth*

Does the pupil participate in group activities in the art class?

Is he considerate of the rights and ideas of others and appreciative of their contributions?

Does he cooperate in group evaluation?

Does he include others in his pictures?

Is he aware of the way in which art enriches his life and the life of his community?

Does he show a growing interest in community art projects and in cultural recreation activities?

Does he show an increasing ability for leadership?

f. *Perceptual growth*

Is the pupil more aware of visual qualities in his environment, such as light, form, color, texture, space, and volume?

Does the pupil observe, watch for visual relationships, and look for more detail?

Has the student made progress in responding to what he sees visually so as to note similarities as well as differences?

Has the pupil developed sensitivity and skill in expressing auditory and tactile perceptions?

Does the pupil experiment with texture and pattern in his art work?

g. *Aesthetic growth*

Does he organize his art experience and express this organization in his art work?

Are the parts of his expression consistent and related to the whole?

Is there a harmonious use of line, form, color, and texture?

Does he relate his own experiences in art to recognition of the aesthetic qualities in the art of others and the art of other cultures?

Does he have a growing understanding of the function and qualities of art in daily living?

Is he sensitive to the need for beauty?

Is he developing a greater appreciation of art?

Does he select materials which are suited to his purpose?

Has his ability to communicate with a variety of art media increased through his own involvement with art?

4. Have the tensions of growing up been released in and through his art experiences?

a. Does he integrate and relate his experiences, making them his own, and does he see relationships?

  b. Is he able to express his feelings in his art expression?
  c. Have the art experiences been a stabilizing factor in his life?
  d. Does he show certain elements in his work to be more important by an increase of detail or by exaggeration?
  e. Does he express himself with free strokes?
  f. Does he enjoy the doing of art?
  g. Is he able to work well in a difficult situation?
5. Has his taste, his aesthetic sensitivity and awareness been developed?
  a. Is he concerned about color schemes?
  b. Is he sensitive to small differences in shape, color, line, value, and texture?
  c. Is he aware of the aesthetic quality of elements in his everyday life?
  d. Is he concerned with the organization of his visual environment, as well as his experiences?
  e. Is he concerned with the quality of his experience?
  f. Does he use good taste in his dress and appearance?
  g. Does he perceive pattern and texture in his environment?
  h. Does the pupil want to continue art in high school?
6. Has a consciousness of good design been instilled through his creative art work and other experiences in the art curriculum?
  a. Does he intuitively notice well designed objects?
  b. Is he sensitive to the arrangement of bulletin boards and displays at school?
  c. Does he envisage ways to rearrange the art room, his own room at home, or the areas of his environment?
  d. Does he critically evaluate the package designs of objects he uses?
  e. Is he aware of the design quality in the plan of his local community, which may encompass the civic area, residential area, industrial area, and commercial area?
  f. Has he related his consciousness for good design to other areas of his own life?
  g. Does he consider good design qualities when purchasing objects?
7. Has intercultural understanding been developed?
  a. Is he interested in other cultures as a result of his art experiences?
  b. Does he compare other cultures with our own as a result of his art experience?
  c. Is he interested enough in the art of other cultures to read about it?
  d. Does he ever express his feelings concerning other cultures in his own art work?
8. Has his appreciation of the art of other people of the past, as well as of the present, been developed as a result of the art program?
  a. Is he aware of the art expression of the past?
  b. Does he enjoy seeing films concerning art?
  c. Does he enjoy the value of trips to the art museum or the art gallery?
  d. Does he collect reproductions of art work?
  e. Does he collect art work of his peers or adults?
  f. Does he seek out artists and designers to talk to them?
  g. Does he read articles in current periodicals concerning art?

    h. Is he concerned with the work of contemporary artists?

    i. Does he enjoy visiting an important building just to see the building itself?

    j. Does he read books about art and artists?

    k. Is he aware of the possibilities of art vocations in our society?

    l. Does he subscribe to any art periodical?

9. Has he acquired a greater awareness of high quality art in his community?

    a. Is he aware of original art work in the school building?

    b. Is he aware of the "design" of the school structure?

    c. Is he aware of monuments of note in his community?

    d. Has he attended the art gallery or museum in his community lately?

    e. Is he conscious of aesthetic factors in community planning?

    f. Is he aware of special showings of art work in the community?

    g. Does he read any art news in his local newspaper?

SELF/PEER/TEACHER EVALUATION RATING SCALES

These rating scales can be used by both the students and the teacher in a class. Students may rate their own work, as well as that of their peers. These evaluation forms are suggestive. Art teachers can create their own scales (or in cooperation with students) to emphasize specific objectives in a class. By students evaluating their own work and that of their peers, greater sensitivity and understanding is developed, thus raising consciousness and eventually the quality of art work and the art experience. When using these scales, carefully consider each item for evaluation, and insert a rating in the blank at the right of the item, using poor = 1 and excellent = 10 as guidelines.

DRAWING, PAINTING, SCULPTURE[1]

POOR◄————►EXCELLENT
1 2 3 4 5 6 7 8 9 10

1. Communication/Expression (ideas and feelings obviously portrayed) _____
2. Confidence/Self-Esteem (a strong visual statement, conviction) _____
3. Perceptual Development (sensitivity to visual and nonvisual qualities) _____
4. Aesthetic Organization (balanced, rhythmical, flowing, all parts belong, consistent) _____
5. Knowledge of the Field of Art (style, design, abstraction) _____
6. Creativity (unique, personal, uncommon) _____
7. Skill/Craftsmanship (control of tools and processes) _____
8. Enjoyment/Satisfaction (obvious involvement with ideas, processes, media) _____

[1]For a development of subtopics for each of these eight items, see Table 3, pages 39–41.

CREATIVE LETTERING

POOR←——————→EXCELLENT
1 2 3 4 5 6 7 8 9 10

1. Creative Qualities

     Original, unique, imaginative   _____

     Empathy, expression (design of the work suggests what it means
        through color, shape, organization)   _____

2. Skill and Craftsmanship

     Consistent width of strokes and lines   _____

     Appropriate and consistent color   _____

     Skillful application of paint and ink   _____

     Straight lines are precise; curved lines, graceful   _____

     Neatness   _____

3. Aesthetic Qualities

     Appropriate placement on the page   _____

     Harmonious colors, lines, and shapes   _____

     Attractive and interesting   _____

POSTER DESIGN

POOR←——————→EXCELLENT
1 2 3 4 5 6 7 8 9 10

1. Carrying Quality (message can easily be seen at a distance)   _____

2. Message (confined to a few words; words organized into groups)   _____

3. Design Integration (illustration and words fit together)   _____

4. Simplicity (elimination of all that is not necessary to the message; lettering is not difficult to read)   _____

5. Originality (imaginative and unusual)   _____

6. Harmonious Composition (positive and negative spaces related; eye is carried to all parts, interesting and attractive)   _____

7. Value Arrangement (well planned and balanced)   _____

8. Color (appropriate for the subject)   _____

9. Character (convincing and sincere)   _____

10. Selling Quality (you remember what is advertised)   _____

11. Skill and Craftsmanship (control of media and processes)   _____

12. Overall Presentation (integration of all parts)   _____

ADOLESCENT SENTENCE-COMPLETION RESPONSES

1. When I'm 30 I expect to be
2. Fellows at school like a girl who
3. Girls at school like a boy who
4. A good teacher is one who
5. It's human nature to
6. My father
7. If something is called school policy here at school, it means
8. When I need help, I can usually turn to
9. The rules around here are really made by
10. Kids who get out of line
11. I guess I'm
12. I feel proud when
13. When you get into trouble here
14. The nicest thing about school is
15. What seems to me really unfair is
16. When I feel very happy, I
17. I feel very happy when
18. At home, we
19. My mother and I
20. When I think what the future will be like
21. Politics
22. The most embarrassing thing to me is
23. Kids need
24. Kids should
25. When people criticize me, I
26. It's no use to
27. Most people think of me as

From Edgar Z. Friedenberg, *The Vanishing Adolescent*, pp. 150–155. © Dell Publishing Co., 1959.

28. I'm usually punished
29. Love is
30. When something gets me real mad, I
31. My best friend
32. Nobody but a fool would
33. The people who don't love me don't
34. The kids here would hang together if
35. Brothers and sisters
36. In picking my life work, the most important thing is
37. Our student government
38. I'm not really very much like
39. The worst thing that could happen to me is
40. The worst thing about me is
41. People are wrong if
42. What I hate most around here is
43. Working-class people are

Note: According to Friedenberg, the sentence-completion technique is one of the oldest and most useful procedures for studying adolescents' perceptions of themselves and their situations. It is a semiprojective approach of great value suggesting the character of an individual's involvement in the situation around him/her, a form that facilitates comparison and contrast to other individuals. These beginning parts of sentences or stubs will suggest others that may be even more appropriate for particular teaching situations.

FREEHAND DRAWING

The following steps help the student observe and plan/design perceived lines and shapes on the picture plane. While these seven steps primarily involve *seeing* and *composing,* drawing becomes art only when one expresses his thoughts and feelings concerning what he has perceived and then harmoniously and consistently organizes these on the page.

Steps in Drawing

1. Sit so that you can see what you are drawing and your paper simultaneously without turning your head.
2. Decide if the composition will be horizontal or vertical and arrange your paper accordingly.
3. Plan the picture with your hands on the paper so that all that you observe fits on the page.
4. Hold your pencil by the side so as to make long swooping strokes. This results in rough, suggestive sketch lines—approximations. Keep the wrist stiff but the arm loose at the shoulder and elbow.
5. Swing one to three strokes (angles and directions) on each object so as to suggest its place in the composition.
6. Observe carefully, correcting and adding more angles and directions so as to give the character of each object but still work on all the objects—one object or part should *not* be finished before another. The drawing develops as a whole, growing all over at once.
7. Put in the smaller angles, observe very carefully, and draw very little at this time.

Subsidiary Approaches

CONTOUR DRAWING.   This exercise develops sensitivity in the observation of objects or people. Look at the subject. Select one place on the contour/edge of the object or person and put the pencil point at a comparable place on the paper.

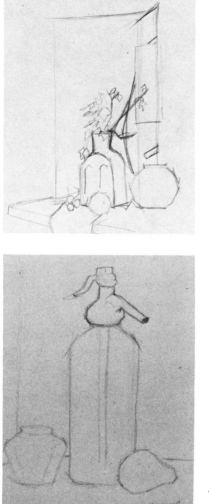

These examples were drawn by high school students who were taught by the seven-step method.

As the eye *slowly* moves around the edge of the subject, move the pencil simultaneously on the paper. You may look at the paper as often as you like to find a place to put the pencil but do *not* look at the paper when you move the pencil. Keep the pressure on the pencil constant so as to produce a consistent line quality. The purpose here is to develop visual sensitivity and perception, not to produce works of art.

GESTURE DRAWING.   This exercise develops a feeling for the action/movement primarily of a figure. Do not look at the drawing paper but look at the figure. Draw lines continuously, indicating the action of the torso, head, arms, and legs. In drawing these actions, do not lift the pencil from the paper. Draw what the

These figure studies were drawn by high school students who were taught by the seven-step method

whole body is doing, not what it looks like. Try to feel what the model feels. Repeat drawing the directions several times. This should be done very rapidly, taking no longer than ten to twenty seconds per figure. The teacher may indicate body parts, directing the procedure. For example, "Put the pencil on the paper where the left hand is seen. Now, without looking at the paper, draw the action/direction of the head, the right hand, back to the head, the left leg, the body, the right leg, the right arm, and so on." This will force the student to feel the movement.

LETTER TO AN EDUCATOR

Judith Ott Belle

Dear Teacher:

As the year ends and I receive my grade from you, I feel the need to share my evaluation of our experience together.

You call yourself a teacher.
I place a lot of value on that term.
But it occurs to me that you and I
see this role in a different light.
I see a teacher as one who inspires
And believes in his students.
Who encourages and supports their
    efforts
to grow in their chosen direction.
My year with you has been one of
discouragement and misunderstanding.
I have learned from your expertise
but have been stifled by your
    assumptions
which underestimate my creative zeal.
You have assumed that I am naïvely
    searching
in my chosen medium of clay
without direction.
Without a feel for its essence.
You have no awareness of how it
    speaks to me.
How deep is my bond to
Mother Earth.

You assume that my personal dignity
and feelings
are not equally as intense
or valid
as yours.
That you can talk down to me
without thinking first.
(Because I am "the student"
You—"the teacher")

Years of disappointment with student
    performance
have clouded your vision.
Instead of seeing in each of us
    unlimited potential
and hope,
you see our inadequacies, our vain
    searchings,
the lack of discipline in some of us,
and overlook the powerful creative
    force
working in others of us
who want to believe in our power
and who care

about what we have to say
in our chosen media.
Your expectations are different now
than they once were.
Now you look
for failure and weakness
And that is what you find.

But even as I write these words
I feel pangs of guilt
at pointing out your weaknesses.
I sound self-righteous,
as if I didn't own any myself.
Of course that could not be true
for we all fall short of our
own expectations,
and constantly seek growth . . .

I see the good in you.
I see the spot where you care.
But your efforts not to let it show,
keep me separated from you.
Do you keep your distance in fear of
being on equal terms with us?
Are we the enemy?
I can't believe it's true.

Today I screamed my hurt at you in
    rage.
I am sorry for my uncontrollable
    emotions
For hurling blame at you
to soothe my own hurt.
I owe you more respect than that.
But I can't seem to give it
unless I feel you respect me
on equal terms.
You speak of my work as if
it were not a part of me.
As if it were somehow invulnerable
to abuse, misunderstanding, pain.
I am my work.
My work is pure emotion.
When you tell me it is going nowhere
you are making a statement about me.
You are revealing how little
you know about me.

How little you have perceived in our
    year together
Of my direction
Of the integration of my thoughts,
    emotions, and ideals
into my creative acts.

The point is, that I do know where
    I'm going.
And I do respect your opinion
More than you realize.
My hurt is not from your criticism.
That I can take
in due respect
for your artistic judgment and
    experience.
My pain is a direct reaction
to your methods of delivery
of your truth.
The medium is the message, dear
    Teacher.
Your body language, your words,
your consistent attitude
of disbelief
in us
have become your medium.
You bestow your judgments
As one who knows what is right for
    another.
The pain is further intensified
by your assumptions
That I am "burning myself out"
in nonlinear explorations
when what's burning
is the fires of my love affair with clay.
You assume that I do not have a
    direction
That I'm just pushing the material
    around
in a meaningless way
because my work is experimental and
    "naïve,"
because clay is a new acquaintance of
    mine
and I lack the sophistication
of pursuing a well defined series
of intentional statements

about purposeful forms . . .
When all the while I am going wild
with anticipation of my next piece
I'm intrinsically motivated, self-
        propelled,
highly philosophical,
dedicated and inspired . . .

My question/plea to you is this:
Why don't you *ask me* where I'm
        going
instead of concentrating your
        judgment
on unsuccessful fragments
of my total aesthetic experience,
as if they were ends in themselves?
Instead of assuming that I have no end
        in sight,
why don't you ask
what it is?
Or if that is not possible,
perhaps you could try listening
when I talk to you,
instead of thinking of what you
will say next?
When I tell you, for instance,
what I am trying to do with the human
        face
With the contorted, distorted anguish
I feel living in a nuclear world,
surrounded by greed and hate
and the possibility of total
        destruction . . .
Don't look at my determined attempts at
expression of this fear
and coldly dissect them
on the basis of pure, intellectual
design elements,
saying "Oh, you pushed the clay
        around a little
but it doesn't amount to much. . . ."
dismissing the works I found most
        meaningful,
and pointing out your favorites,
        saying:
"Do ten more of these."
As you talk in this manner
you do not hear my protests

which become more silent
with each meeting.
Internalized.
And I retreat from you once again
and vow to prove to you that I *do*
        have a goal.
I silently assemble my self-respect
and leave the presence of
my Teacher.

I have every intention of following
        your advice
In addition to my own inner guidance.
The uncanny thing is—
I have already realized what you
thought you were teaching me.

One who looks for the positive
would have noticed and supported
my independence
in pursuing my own idea.
One looking for the negative
would see all of the other directions,
unrelated, diffused
not perceiving the rapid evolution of
        my idea
toward the direction
you also chose for me.
One looking for chaos and
        disintegration
will see a haphazard collection
of primitive statements
and predict burn-out.
And what you are looking for,
my dear Teacher,
is what you will find.
But I have learned to look
at myself
and my work
with both compassion and detachment.
I can see where I have fumbled
and failed.
I can feel the power of
my successful works
and know that they speak to me
And to you.
And I can see the recognition
in your eyes as you

briefly enter my world
and share my awareness
and feel for me, cautioning me
not to allow myself to feel too much.
At times like this
I know we are one.

And now our time together has come
    to an end.
We have loved/hated each other
and somehow have survived
the experience.
Your medium was resistance;
Mine was belief in myself.
I just wish somehow
we could have spared each other
the pain.
I envision how my spirit could have
    soared
in a positive atmosphere
of belief and support . . .
As it was, I flew somewhat shakily,
propelled by my own emotion,
nurtured on by the love of the clay
for my hands . . .
the inner peace and harmony
it shared with me.
I stimulated myself with
the salt slip
of my tears falling
on mounds of Mother Earth
as she squeezed through my fingers

and I moaned
her possible death
and all life's dreams of Unity . . .

Hours of timeless meditations
and endless thoughts
have entered into
my aesthetic experience
of contact with clay.
And the clay saved me
From total desperation.
It gave me a purpose
A driving goal to express.
The clay, then, was my teacher.
And I have learned my lessons well
    from it.
It taught me not to fear its power.
Unlike your dire predictions,
It did not let me burn myself out
And made sure that your words
did not ring true . . .
(that, "in the end, I would have
    learned nothing")
In the end, I have learned everything I
    needed
to learn
at this point in time.
And perhaps most important of all
I have learned to accept you, dear
    Teacher,
And feel your pain.

SECONDARY ASSIGNED-TOPIC STIMULATIONS

1. Swaying: trees; fields of grain in a gentle breeze, the wind, a storm, the rain; dancers; buildings in an earthquake
2. Going fast: a roller coaster; racing cars, boats; running
3. In a narrow place: between tall buildings; a gorge; narrow streets; in a crowded room
4. Tired: a child; a farmer; people huddled together
5. Traffic jam: a wreck; police, excitement; the expressway
6. A scary place: spooky cemetery; graveyard at night; a lonely road
7. Night: in the rain, in winter, in summer; moonlight
8. The intruder or invader: shadows, strange noises; a stranger in our midst
9. Mountain climbing: stretching, pulling, hanging, falling; ropes
10. Backyards: olde towne; gardens; wash on the line; a picnic; children
11. A prison: riots; gloom; depression; loneliness; bars; isolation
12. Circus: clowns; conductor; trainer; excitement; banners; animals; parade; trapeze; music
13. Assembly line: factory walls; monotony, rhythm, noise; factory moods; three o'clock whistle; making things; automation, robots
14. Water: various moods; under the sea; moonlight; waves; mists; beach; driftwood; storms
15. Highway patterns: roads; trucks; signs; bridges; overpasses
16. A building in progress: workers; cranes; tools, building materials, machinery
17. In a high place: crossing a high bridge; looking down; shaking; flying over
18. City of the future: skyline; riverfront; space
19. Feeling sick: dizzy; pain, fever
20. A crowded room: closeness; busy; noise; people
21. Barren land: Openness; space; nothingness
22. Sunday morning: church; Sunday paper; prayer
23. Conflict: an argument; war; fighting
24. In a drizzle: wetness; umbrellas, raincoats; reflections

RESOURCE MATERIALS

Catalogues are generally available from the following art materials/equipment suppliers and from producers and distributors of audio-visual materials.

ART SUPPLIERS

Chaselle Arts and Crafts, Inc.
9645 Gerwig Lane
Columbia, Maryland 21046

Colborn School Supply Co.
999 South Jason Street
Denver, Colorado 80223

Dick Blick
P.O. Box 1267
Galesburg, Illinois 61401

Educational Materials Division
Binney & Smith Inc.
1100 Church Lane
P.O. Box 431
Easton, Pennsylvania 18042

Interstate School Supply
P.O. Box 1059
Jackson, Mississippi 39205

John R. Green Company
411 West Sixth Street
Covington, Kentucky 41012

J. L. Hammett Company
100 Hammett Place
Braintree, Massachusetts 02184

J. S. Latta Company
2218 Main Street
Cedar Falls, Iowa 50613

John Bodley Enterprises Ltd.
972 Bexhill Road
Mississauga, Ontario, Canada

McKilligan Supply Company
Johnson City, New York 13790

Nasco
901 Janesville Ave.
Fort Atkinson, Wisconsin 53538

Pyramid Artists' Materials
P.O. Box 27
Urbana, Illinois 61801

Pyramid Paper Company
6510 North 54th Street
Tampa, Florida 33616

Sax Arts and Crafts
P.O. Box 2002
Milwaukee, Wisconsin 53201

S&S Arts and Crafts
Dept. 1084
Colchester, Connecticut 06415

Texas Art Supply Company
2001 Montrose Blvd.
Houston, Texas 77006

The American Crayon Company
1706 Hayes Ave.
Sandusky, Ohio 44870

Utrecht Linens, Inc.
33 35th Street
Brooklyn, New York 11232

Western School Supply Company
Hassalo Street
Portland, Oregon 97213

ART FILM DISTRIBUTORS

American Handicrafts Company
6837 W. 159th Street
Henley Park, Illinois 60477

BFA Educational Films
2211 Michigan Avenue
P.O. Box 1795
Santa Monica, California 90406

British Information Services
845 Third Avenue
New York, New York 10022

Canyon Cinema
2325 Third Street, Suite 338
San Francisco, California 94107

Centre Productions
1327 Spruce Street, Suite #3
Boulder, Colorado 80302

Centron Films
1621 West 9th Street
Lawrence, Kansas 66044

Churchill Films
662 North Robertson Blvd.
Los Angeles, California 90069

Coronet Instructional Media
65 E. South Water Street
Chicago, Illinois 60601

Educational Audio Visual, Inc.
Pleasantville, New York 10570

Encyclopaedia Britannica Films
425 North Michigan Avenue
Chicago, Illinois 60611

Film Classics Exchange
1914 South Vermont Avenue
Los Angeles, California 90007

Films Incorporated
733 Green Bay Road
Wilmette, Illinois 60081

Girl Scouts of America Film Library
830 Third Avenue
New York, New York 10022

Handel Film Corporation
8730 Sunset Blvd.
W. Hollywood, California 90069

International Film Bureau
332 South Michigan Avenue
Chicago, Illinois 60604

Learning Corporation of America
1350 Avenue of the Americas
New York, New York 10019

Manson Kennedy Films
519 Southwest Park Avenue #604
Portland, Oregon 97205

McGraw-Hill
110 Fifteenth Street
Del Mar, California 92014

National Film Board of Canada
111 Wacker Drive, Suite 313
Chicago, Illinois 60601

Phoenix Films
468 Park Avenue
New York, New York 10016

Pyramid Films
Box 1048
Santa Monica, California 90406

Sulani Films
215 West 91st Street, No. 136
New York, New York 10024

University of Southern California
Audio-Visual Services
Dept. of Cinema
3518 University Avenue
Los Angeles, California 90007

Walt Disney Education Materials Co.
500 South Buena Vista Street
Burbank, California 91521

Weston Woods Studio
Weston, Connecticut 06880

ART SLIDE, FILMSTRIP, CASSETTE DISTRIBUTORS

American Council on Education
1 Dupont Circle
Washington, D.C. 20036

American Library Color Slide Co.
P.O. Box 5810
Grand Central Station
New York, New York 10017

Barron's
113 Crossways Park Drive
Woodbury, New York 11797

Boston Museum of Fine Arts
Dept. of Photographic Services/
Slide Library
465 Huntington Avenue
Boston, Massachusetts 02115

Center for Humanities
Two Holland Avenue
White Plains, New York 10603

Educational Dimensions Corporation
Stamford, Connecticut 06904

Encore Visual Education, Inc.
1235 South Victory Boulevard
Burbank, California 91502

Grolier Educational Corporation
Sherman Turnpike
Danbury, Connecticut 06810

Kai Dib Films International
P.O. Box 261
Glendale, California 91209

Konrad Prothmann
2378 Soper Avenue
Baldwin, New York 11510

Life Filmstrips
Time-Life Building
Rockefeller Center
New York, New York 10020

McGraw-Hill
1221 Avenue of the Americas
New York, New York 10020

McIntyre Visual Publications, Inc.
716 Center Street
Lewiston, New York 14092

Metropolitan Museum of Art
255 Gracie Station
New York, New York 10028

Museum of Modern Art Library
11 West 53rd Street
New York, New York 10019

Philadelphia Museum of Art
Division of Education
25th Street and Benjamin Franklin Pkwy.
Philadelphia, Pennsylvania 19130

Phoenix Films
468 Park Avenue
New York, New York 10016

Sandak, Inc.
180 Harvard Avenue
Stamford, Connecticut 06902

School of the Art Institute of Chicago
280 South Columbus Drive
Chicago, Illinois 60603

Society for Visual Education
1345 Diversey Parkway
Chicago, Illinois 60614

Son-A-Vision, Inc.
110 Washington Avenue
Pleasantville, New York 10570

Spoken Arts
Dept. R
P.O. Box 289
New Rochelle, New York 10802

University Prints
21 East Street
Winchester, Massachusetts 01890

Warner Educational Productions
P.O. Box 8791
Fountain Valley, California 92708

Wilton Art Appreciation Programs
P.O. Box 302
Wilton, Connecticut 06897

COLOR REPRODUCTION SUPPLIERS

Art Education, Inc.
28 E. Erie Street
Blauvelt, New York 10913

Art Extension Press
Box 389
Westport, Connecticut 06881

Associated American Artists
663 Fifth Avenue
New York, New York 10022

Catalda Fine Arts
12 W. 27th Street
New York, New York 10001

Harry N. Abrams
110 East 59th Street
New York, New York 10022

Imaginus, Inc.
RR 1, Box 552
Lee, Massachusetts 01238

Konrad Prothmann
2378 Soper Avenue
Baldwin, New York 11510

Metropolitan Museum of Art
Book and Art Shop
Fifth Avenue and 82nd Street
New York, New York 10028

Museum of Modern Art
11 West 53rd Street
New York, New York 10019

National Gallery of Art
Department of Extension Programs
Washington, D.C. 20565

New York Graphic Society
140 Greenwich Avenue
Greenwich, Connecticut 06830

Oestreicher's Prints
43 West 46th Street
New York, New York 10036

Penn Prints
31 West 46th Street
New York, New York 10036

Raymond and Raymond, Inc.
1071 Madison Avenue
New York, New York 10028

Reinhold Publishing Company
600 Summer Street
P.O. Box 1361
Stamford, Connecticut 06904

Shorewood Reproductions
Department S,
475 10th Avenue
New York, New York 10018

UNESCO Catalogues
Columbia University Press
562 West 113th Street
New York, New York 10025

University Prints
21 East Street
Winchester, Massachusetts 01890

BIBLIOGRAPHY

BOOKS/MONOGRAPHS

The following are in addition to the "Supplemental Readings" at the end of each chapter.

Aiken, Henry D. *Learning and Teaching in the Arts*. Washington, D.C.: National Art Education Association, 1970.

Anderson, Harold H. *Creativity and Its Cultivation*. New York: Harpers, 1959.

Andrews, Michael F. (ed.). *Aesthetic Form and Education*. Syracuse: Syracuse University Press, 1958.

Andrews, Michael F. (ed.). *Creativity and Psychological Health*. Syracuse: Syracuse University Press, 1961.

Arnheim, Rudolf. *Art and Visual Perception* (rev. ed.). Los Angeles: University of California Press, 1974.

Arts and Humanities Staff, Office of Education. *Try a New Face: A Report on HEW-Supported Arts Projects in American Schools*. Washington, D.C.: U.S. Government Printing Office, 1979.

Barkan, Manuel. *A Foundation for Art Education*. New York: Ronald Press, 1955.

Blakeslee, Thomas R. *The Right Brain: A New Understanding of the Unconscious Mind and Its Creative Powers*. Garden City, New York: Anchor Press, 1980.

Brittain, W. Lambert. *Creativity and Art Education*. Washington, D.C.: National Art Education Association, 1965.

Bruner, Jerome S. *The Process of Education*. Cambridge: Harvard University Press, 1960.

Clark, Gilbert, and Zimmerman, Enid. *Art/Design: Communicating Visually*. New York: Art Education, 1978.

Collins, Mary R., and Riley, Olive L. *Art Appreciation for Junior and Senior High Schools*. New York: Harcourt Brace, 1932.

Conant, Howard, and Randall, Arne. *Art in Education*. Peoria: Chas. A. Bennett, 1958.

D'Amico, Victor (ed.). *The Visual Arts in General Education*. New York: D. Appleton-Century, 1940.

D'Amico, Victor. *Creative Teaching in Art*. Scranton: International Textbook, 1942.

Davis, Beverley J. *Chant of the Centuries: The Visual Arts and Their Parallel in Music and Literature*. Austin: W. S. Benson, 1969.

Dewey, John. *Art as Experience*. New York: Minton, Balch, 1934.

Dorn, Charles M. *Report of the NAEA Commission on Art Education*. Reston, Virginia: National Art Education Association, 1977.

Dow, Arthur W. *Theory and Practice of Teaching Art* (2nd ed.). New York: Teachers College, Columbia University, 1912.

Edman, Irwin. *Arts and Man*. New York: New American Library, 1949.

Faulkner, Ray, and Ziegfeld, Edwin. *Art Today* (5th ed.). New York: Holt, Rinehart and Winston, 1974.

Feldman, Edmund B. *Art as Image and Idea* (2nd ed.). Englewood Cliffs, New Jersey: Prentice-Hall, 1972.

Field, Dick, and Newick, John. *The Study of Education and Art*. London: Routledge and Kegan Paul, 1973.

Fleming, William. *Art, Music and Ideas*. New York: Holt, Rinehart and Winston, 1970.

Gaitskell, Charles D., and Gaitskell, Margaret R. *Art Education During Adolescence*. New York: Harcourt Brace, 1954.

Getzels, Jacob W., and Csikszentmihalyi, M. *The Creative Vision*. New York: John Wiley, 1976.

Getzels, Jacob W., and Jackson, Phillip W. *Creativity and Intelligence*. New York: John Wiley, 1962.

Gowan, John C., Demos, George D., and Torrance, E. Paul. *Creativity: Its Educational Implications*. New York: John Wiley, 1974.

Guilford, J. Paul. *Creative Thinking in Children of Junior High Level*. Los Angeles: University of Southern California Psychological Laboratory Reports, 1961.

Guilford, J. Paul. *Intelligence, Creativity and Their Educational Implications*. San Diego, California: Robert R. Knapp, 1968.

Haney, James P. (ed.). *Art Education in the Public Schools of the United States*. New York: American Art Annual, 1908.

Hardiman, George W., and Zernich, Theodore (eds.). *Curricular Considerations for Visual Arts Education*. Champaign, Illinois: Stipes, 1974.

Hastie, Reid W. (ed.). *Art Education: Sixty-Fourth Yearbook of the National Society for the Study of Education*, Part II. Chicago: University of Chicago Press, 1965.

Hastie, Reid W. *Encounter with Art*. New York: McGraw-Hill, 1969.

Hatfield, Thomas A., and Dunn, Phillip C. *Finding a Job in Art Education*. Columbia, South Carolina: Southern Art Education Associates, 1982.

Hathaway, Walter (ed.). *Art Education: Middle/Junior High School*. Washington, D.C.: National Art Education Association, 1972.

Horn, George F. *Art for Today's Schools*. Worcester, Massachusetts: Davis Publications, 1971.

Hurwitz, Albert. *The Gifted and Talented*. Worcester, Massachusetts: Davis Publications, 1983.

Hurwitz, Albert. *Programs of Promise*. New York: Harcourt Brace Jovanovich, 1972.

Karel, Leon C. *Avenues to the Arts: A General Arts Textbook for the Secondary Schools*. Kirksville, Missouri: Simpson Publishing Company, 1966.

Keiler, Manfred L. *The Art in Teaching Art*. Lincoln, Nebraska: University of Nebraska Press, 1961.

Kepes, Gyorgy. *Language of Vision*. Chicago: Paul Theobald, 1944.

Kuh, Katherine. *Art Has Many Faces*. New York: Harper, 1951.

Lally, Ann (ed.). *Art Education in the Secondary School*. Washington, D.C.: National Art Education Association, 1961.

Lanier, Vincent. *Essays in Art Education: The Development of One Point of View* (2nd ed.). New York: MSS Educational Publishing, 1976.

Lanier, Vincent. *The Arts We See: A Simplified Introduction to the Visual Arts*. New York: Teachers College Press, 1982.

Lowenfeld, Viktor. *The Nature of Creative Activity* (rev. ed.). New York: Harcourt Brace, 1952.

Lowenfeld, Viktor, and Brittain, W. Lambert. *Creative and Mental Growth* (7th ed.). New York: Macmillan, 1982.

Luca, Mark. *Art Education: Strategies of Teaching*. Englewood Cliffs, New Jersey: Prentice-Hall, 1968.

MacDonald, Rosabell. *Art as Education*. New York: Holt, 1941.

Madeja, Stanley (ed.). *Exemplary Programs in Art Education*. Washington, D.C.: National Art Education Association, 1969.

Michael, John A. (ed.). *Art Education in the Junior High School*. Washington, D.C.: National Art Education Association, 1964.

Miel, Alice (ed.). *Creativity in Teaching*. Belmont, California: Wadsworth, 1962.

Morman, Jean M. *Art: Of Wonder and a World*. Blauvelt, New York: Art Education, 1967.

Morman, Jean M. *Tempo of Today*. Blauvelt, New York: Art Education, 1969.

Munro, Thomas. *Art Education: Its Philosophy and Psychology*. Indianapolis: Bobbs-Merrill, 1956.

Munro, Thomas. *The Creative Arts in American Education*. Cambridge: Harvard University Press, 1960.

Murphy, Judith, and Jones, Lonna. *Research in Arts Education: A Federal Chapter*. Washington, D.C.: Office of Education, U.S. Department of Health, Education, and Welfare, 1978.

National Assessment of Educational Progress. *Art and Young Americans, 1974–79: Results from the Second National Art Assessment*. Denver: NAEP, 1981.

National Assessment of Educational Progress. *Attitudes Toward Art: Selected Results from the First National Assessment of Art*. Denver: NAEP, 1978.

Nicholas, Florence W., et al. *Art for Young America* (3rd ed.). Peoria: Chas. A. Bennett, 1960.

Nichols, George W. *Art Education Applied to Industry*. New York: Harper and Brothers, 1877.

Palmer, Frederick. *Art and the Young Adolescent*. Oxford: Pergamon Press, 1970.

Paston, Herbert S. *Learning to Teach Art*. Lincoln, Nebraska: Professional Educators, 1973.

Paterakis, Angela G. (ed.). *Art Education: Senior High School*. Washington, D.C.: National Art Education Association, 1972.

Pearson, Ralph. *The New Art Education*. New York: Harper and Brothers, 1941.

Piaget, Jean. *The Grasp of Consciousness* (trans. by S. Wedgewood). Cambridge: Harvard University Press, 1976.

Prang Educational Company. *Art Education for High Schools*. New York: Prang Educational Company, 1908.

Pullias, Earl V., and Young, James D. *A Teacher Is Many Things*. Bloomington, Indiana: Indiana University Press, 1968.

Rannells, Edward W. *Art Education in the Junior High School*. Lexington, Kentucky: University of Kentucky, 1946.

Read, Herbert. *Education Through Art* (1st ed.). London: Faber and Faber, 1943.

Reed, Carl. *Early Adolescent Art Education*. Peoria: Chas. A. Bennett, 1957.

Rich, Alan. *Music: Mirror of the Arts*. New York: Frederick A. Praeger, 1969.

Rosenthal, Robert, and Jacobson, Lenore. *Pygmalion in the Classroom*. New York: Holt, Rinehart and Winston, 1968.

Samples, Bob. *The Metaphoric Mind: A Celebration of Creative Consciousness*. Reading, Massachusetts: Addison-Wesley, 1976.

Schaefer-Simmern, Henry. *The Unfolding of Artistic Activity*. Berkeley: University of California Press, 1950.

Schwartz, Fred. *Structure and Potential in Art Education.* Waltham, Massachusetts: Ginn-Blaisdell, 1970.

Smith, Ralph (ed.). *Aesthetics and Criticism in Art Education.* Chicago: Rand McNally, 1966.

Steveni, Michael. *Art and Education.* London: Batsford, 1968.

Strickler, Frederick. *An Art Approach to Education.* New York: A.G. Seiler, 1943.

Taylor, Calvin W. *Creativity: Progress and Potential.* New York: McGraw-Hill, 1964.

Thomson, Beatrice. *Drawings by High School Students.* New York: Reinhold, 1966.

Toffler, Alvin. *The Culture Consumers.* New York: Random House, 1973.

Torrance, E. Paul. *Guiding Creative Talent.* Englewood Cliffs, New Jersey: Prentice-Hall, 1962.

Vernon, Magdalen D. *Perception Through Experience.* London: Methuen, 1970.

Wachowiak, Frank, and Hodge, David. *Art in Depth: A Qualitative Program for the Young Adolescent.* Scranton: International Textbook, 1970.

Walter, W. Grey. *The Living Brain.* New York: Norton, 1953.

Wertz, Morris. *Problems in Aesthetics: An Introductory Book of Readings* (2nd ed.). New York: Macmillan, 1970.

Whitford, William G. *An Introduction to Art Education.* New York: D. Appleton and Company, 1929.

Wickiser, Ralph, *An Introduction to Art Education.* Yonkers-on-Hudson, New York: World Book, 1957.

Winslow, Leon L. *Art in Secondary Education.* New York: McGraw-Hill, 1941.

Ziegfeld, Edwin (ed.). *Art for the Academically Talented Student in the Secondary School.* Washington, D.C.: National Art Education Association, 1961.

Ziegfeld, Edwin, and Smith, M. E. *Art for Daily Living: The Story of the Owatonna Art Education Project.* Minneapolis: University of Minnesota Press, 1944.

PERIODICALS

Art Education. National Art Education Association, 1916 Association Drive, Reston, Virginia 22091. Bimonthly.

Arts and Activities. Publishers' Development Corporation, 591 Camino de la Reina, Suite 200, San Diego, California 92108. Monthly except July and August.

School Arts. Davis Publications, Inc., 50 Portland Street, Worcester, Massachusetts 01608. Monthly, nine times a year.

Studies in Art Education. National Art Education Association, 1916 Association Drive, Reston, Virginia 22091. Three issues a year: Fall, Winter, and Spring.

Visual Arts Research. University of Illinois Press, 54E. Gregory Drive, Box 5081, Station A, Champaign, Illinois 61820. Twice yearly.

INDEX